RAF Bomber Command Squadron Profiles

617 Squadron

by Chris Ward

RAF Bomber Command Squadron Profiles

617 Squadron

by Chris Ward

Bomber Command Books
from

MENTION
THE WAR
PUBLICATIONS

This edition first published 2015 by Mention the War Ltd., 32 Croft Street, Farsley, Pudsey, LS28 5IIA.

Copyright 2015 © Chris Ward.

Cover design: Topics - The Creative Partnership www.topicsdesign.co.uk

A CIP catalogue reference for this book is available from the British Library.

ISBN 978-0-9933360-9-6

To read a full wartime history of 617 Squadron, including the loss of the Tirpitz from the German side, and an insight into life as a member of ground crew, read *Dambusters: Forging of a Legend*, by Chris Ward with Andy Lee and Andreas Wachtel, published 2003 by Pen and Sword Aviation, available from Amazon.

Also by Chris Ward:

Dambusters- The Definitive History of 617 Squadron at War 1943-1945
by Chris Ward, Andy Lee and Andreas Wachtel, published 2003 by Red Kite.

Dambuster Crash Sites
by Chris Ward and Andreas Wachtel, published 2007 by Pen and Sword Aviation.

Images of War: 617 Dambuster Squadron at War
by Chris Ward and Andy Lee, published 2009 by Pen and Sword Aviation.

1 Group Bomber Command. An Operational History
by Chris Ward with Greg Harrison and Grzegorz Korcz, published 2014 by Pen and Sword Aviation.

3 Group Bomber Command. An Operational History
by Chris Ward and Steve Smith, published 2008 by Pen and Sword Aviation.

4 Group Bomber Command. An Operational History
by Chris Ward, published 2012 by Pen and Sword Aviation.

5 Group Bomber Command. An Operational History
by Chris Ward, published 2007 by Pen and Sword Aviation.

6 Group Bomber Command. An Operational History
by Chris Ward, published 2009 by Pen and Sword Aviation.

Series Introduction

RAF Bomber Command Squadron Profiles first appeared in the late nineties, and proved to be very popular with enthusiasts of RAF Bomber Command during the Second World War. They became a useful research tool, particularly for those whose family members had served and were no longer around. The original purpose was to provide a point of reference for all of the gallant men and women who had fought the war, either in the air, or on the ground in a support capacity, and for whom no written history of their unit or station existed. I wanted to provide them with something they could hold up, point to and say, "This was my unit, this is what I did in the war". Many veterans were reticent to talk about their time on bombers, partly because of modesty, but perhaps mostly because the majority of those with whom they came into contact had no notion of what it was to be a "Bomber Boy", to face the prospect of death every time they took to the air, whether during training or on operations. Only those who shared the experience really understood what it was to go to war in bombers, which is why reunions were so important. As they approached the end of their lives, many veterans began to speak openly for the first time about their life in wartime Bomber Command, and most were hurt by the callous treatment they received at the hands of successive governments with regard to the lack of recognition of their contribution to victory. It is sad that this recognition in the form of a national memorial and the granting of a campaign medal came too late for the majority. Now this inspirational, noble generation, the like of which will probably never grace this earth again, has all but departed from us, and the world will be a poorer place as a result.

RAF Bomber Command Squadron Profiles are back. The basic format remains, but, where needed, additional information has been provided. Squadron Profiles do not claim to be comprehensive histories, but rather detailed overviews of the activities of the squadron. There is insufficient space to mention as many names as one would like, but all aircraft losses are accompanied by the name of the pilot. Fundamentally, the narrative section is an account of Bomber Command's war from the perspective of the bomber group under which the individual squadron served, and the deeds of the squadron are interwoven into this story. Information has been drawn from official records, such as group, squadron and station ORBs, and from the many, like myself, amateur enthusiasts, who dedicate much of their time to researching individual units, and become unrivalled authorities on them. I am grateful for their generous contributions, and their names will appear in the appropriate Profiles. The statistics quoted in this series are taken from *The Bomber Command War Diaries*, that indispensable tome written by Martin Middlebrook and Chris Everitt, and I am indebted to Martin for his kind permission to use them.

Finally, let me apologise in advance for the inevitable errors, for no matter how hard I and other authors try to write "nothing but the truth", there is no such thing as a definitive account of history, and there will always be room for disagreement and debate. Official records are notoriously unreliable tools, and yet we have little choice but to put our faith in them. It is not my intention to misrepresent any person or RAF unit, and I ask my readers to understand the enormity of the task I have undertaken. It is relatively easy to become an authority on single units or even a bomber group, but I chose to write about them all, idiot that I am, which means 128 squadrons serving operationally in Bomber Command at some time between the 3rd of September 1939 and the 8th of May 1945. I am dealing with eight bomber groups, in which some 120,000 airmen served, and I am juggling around 28,000 aircraft serial numbers, code letters and details of provenance and fate. I ask not for your sympathy, it was, after all, my choice, but rather your understanding if you should find something with which you disagree. My thanks to you, my readers, for making the original series of RAF Bomber Command Squadron Profiles so popular, and I hope you receive this new incarnation equally enthusiastically.

This Profile is largely an abridged version of *Dambusters, Forging of a Legend*, published by Pen & Sword in 2009. I have added a little material to the account of Astell's loss during Operation Chastise, in an attempt to put an end to the false belief that flak played a part. I have also revisited the "Denekamp incident" during the attack on the Dortmund-Ems Canal in September 1943, adding a short eyewitness account and an appraisal of the available evidence. Finally, more than 120,000 men served as aircrew with Bomber Command during WWII, and to most of us the vast majority are nothing more than a name, often in a casualty report. Some, a very few in the overall picture, became known to the general public, but most were known only to their friends and family. I have written a little about F/S Phillip Moore, who served as a flight engineer with S/L Ralph Allsebrook, and died with him during the Dortmund-Ems Canal operation just mentioned. I have also included photographs to give him a face and to demonstrate that he had a life and loved ones to mourn his loss. I am indebted to Sandra Murphy, Phillip's great niece, and to other members of his family for providing the information and photos. Andreas Wachtel and I have already approached the owner of the restaurant on the quayside at Bergeshövede, just yards from where Phillip and his crew mates died, with a view to erecting a simple memorial on his forecourt to honour the dead, and he was open to the idea.

Finally I am indebted to Simon Hepworth, founder of Mention the War Publications, for recognizing the potential of RAF Bomber Command Squadron Profiles, and taking the opportunity to bring them back. I am also indebted, as always, to my very good friends, the gang of three, Andreas Wachtel in Germany, Steve Smith in deepest, darkest Kent, and Greg Korcz in Poland. They are amazing and meticulous researchers in their own right, who share generously the fruits of their labour.

Chris Ward. Lutterworth. October 2015.

Contents

Section One: Narrative WWII History

617 SQUADRON

Motto: **APRES MOI LE DELUGE (**After me the flood)

Codes **AJ KC YZ**.

Wing Commander Guy Penrose Gibson VC, DSO and bar, DFC and bar (Crown).

March to May 1943

Formed from scratch on the 21st of March 1943, 617 Squadron was destined to become the most famous squadron, not only in the history of the RAF, but perhaps in the history of world aviation. When Wing Commander Guy Penrose Gibson arrived at Scampton that day, he was returning to familiar ground, having already completed a tour of operations from there with 83 Squadron, beginning on the day war broke out. After completing his first tour a year later with thirty-eight operations to his credit, he escaped screening from operations by wangling for himself a night fighter tour with 29 Squadron. He had also elicited from the then A-O-C of 5 Group, Air Vice-Marshall Sir Arthur T Harris, the promise of a return to bombers in the future, which he redeemed in March 1942, when he was given command of 106 Squadron. His success at bringing 106 Squadron to a peak of efficiency, and to the top of the Command bombing ladder, made him the obvious choice from among 5 Group contenders, to be given the task of forming 617 Squadron, specifically, though not exclusively, to breach the Ruhr dams.

Much has been written about the formation of 617 Squadron, not all of it accurately. Many accounts suggest that Gibson handpicked the entire squadron aircrew personnel, which is untrue and apparent from the relative inexperience of some of those posted in. He did, however, avail himself of the best amongst those whom he knew, as in the case of his former 106 Squadron colleagues, F/Ls Hopgood and Shannon and P/O Burpee, the last-mentioned one of a large number of Canadians to join the squadron as founder members. Shannon, an Australian, had joined 106 Squadron in June 1942, and having completed his first tour had volunteered to join the Pathfinders, which since the 8th of January had been designated 8 Group. He had just arrived at Warboys to begin Pathfinder training, when the offer came through from Gibson to join the new unit. Shannon was one of those who had flourished under Gibson at 106 Squadron, his tough Australian character shielding him from the intimidation that many experienced under Gibson's command style, and a strong bond developed between the two men. With the exception of his Canadian navigator, Danny Walker, his crew declined to accompany him to Scampton, and like some other pilots he would fill the vacancies once there.

Hopgood had begun his operational career with 50 Squadron in July 1941, and had completed ten sorties by the time he was posted to 25 O.T.U at the end of October. Here he converted to the twin-engine Avro Manchester, and in February 1942 was signed off and posted to 106 Squadron, where he too would become one of Gibson's inner circle. The nucleus of the squadron was, in fact, provided by 57 Squadron, fellow Scampton residents, whose entire C Flight under S/L Young, was posted en-masse across the tarmac. This was not a move which was appreciated by all of those involved. Henry Melvin "Dinghy" Young was, at the age of twenty-seven, a little older than many of the pilots to join the squadron. Born in Belgravia in London in May 1915, he had spent his life from the age of thirteen in America, where he met his future wife Priscilla Rawson. Eventually, he followed in his father's footsteps by going up to Oxford, where he became a rowing Blue, and was a member of the university's winning crew in the 1938 Boat Race. He joined the RAF Volunteer Reserve in August 1939, and after training he arrived at 4 Group's 102 Squadron as a Whitley pilot in June 1940. As was standard practice in the early days of WWII he learned his trade as second pilot, and did not become crew captain until his squadron was loaned to Coastal Command in September. During a patrol in early October his aircraft ran out of fuel, and having ditched in the Atlantic, he and his crew took to their dinghy, and spent an uncomfortable twenty-two hours in it before rescue came. In late November, after returning to bombing duties, his Whitley ran out of fuel on the way home from Turin, and this necessitated another ditching, this time off the coast of Devon, from where they paddled ashore. As a result of his fondness for floating home, he gained the nickname Dinghy,

13

which he would carry through to his untimely death. He was screened in early 1941 to take on instructor duties, and returned to operations in September with 104 Squadron, a unit operating the Merlin-powered Mk.II Wellington. The squadron was posted to the Middle East in October, and Young continued to operate until June 1942, at which point with fifty-one sorties to his credit, he was promoted to squadron leader and assigned to administrative duties with 205 Group. Following a period in America, where he married Priscilla, he rejoined Bomber Command and arrived at 57 Squadron in March 1943.

Other pilots came from all over 5 Group, most bringing a Lancaster with them still bearing the codes of their parent units. These would soon be replaced with the new 617 Squadron code of AJ. Some pilots came with complete crews, while others formed new ones at Scampton from the pool of aircrew trades gathering there. 50 Squadron provided S/L Maudslay as the other flight commander, a man of great character, sporting prowess and experience as a pilot and leader of men. He was born in Leamington Spa in Warwickshire to a wealthy family who owned the Maudslay Motor Company and had connections to the Standard Motor Company. Educated at Eaton, where he excelled as a miler and oarsman, he joined the RAF in June 1940. After training in Canada he was posted to 44 Squadron in May 1941, where he completed a tour of operations. Thereafter he was attached to various organisations, including Rolls Royce, becoming acquainted with many types of aircraft, and it was during this period that he learned to fly the Lancaster. He became an instructor with 44 Squadron Conversion Flight in January 1942, and took part in all three one thousand bomber raids during May and June, although the first two found him in Manchesters of the conversion flight, each with a reputation as a "hack". July saw him posted as an instructor to a Lancaster conversion unit at Wigsley, where he came into contact with future colleagues at 617 Squadron. He asked to return to operations, and in January 1943 he joined 50 Squadron at Skellingthorpe, where he completed a further thirteen operations before his posting to Scampton.

50 Squadron also contributed the Australian P/O Les Knight and his crew, along with a number of others who would team up with a pilot once they arrived at Scampton. Among these was Canadian bomb-aimer John Fraser, who would join Hopgood's crew. He was engaged to an English girl, and would be granted a forty-eight hour pass to marry her shortly before the operation took place. Low flying expert F/L Martin from Australia, a former 50 Squadron pilot, was languishing at an HCU when he received the call, and he brought his old Australian crew mates with him. From 97 Squadron came the experienced trio of New Zealander F/L Les Munro, Englishman F/L David Maltby and American F/L Joe McCarthy, while 49 Squadron supplied the services of Sgts Anderson and Townsend. Townsend was approaching the end of his tour, but Anderson had only recently begun his, and remained at 49 Squadron for a while to get a few more operations under his belt. F/L Barlow, another Australian, arrived from 61 Squadron and was very close to the end of his tour. There was a suggestion that he and his crew were sold the posting on the basis of carrying out just one more operation, rather than the two necessary if they stayed at Skellingthorpe. Barlow, at thirty-two, was older than the majority of those posted in, and among his crew was wireless operator and fellow Australian Charlie Williams, who, at the age of thirty-five, was the oldest man on the squadron. Williams was another who was engaged to an English girl, but unlike John Fraser and his fiancée, their union would never take place.

F/L Harold Wilson arrived from 44 Squadron, along with F/S Ken Brown, yet another Canadian, and his countryman, P/O Vernon Byers, was posted in from 467 Squadron RAAF. Byers was thirty-two years of age, and had only four operations to his credit. P/O Warner Ottley was born in Battersea, London, and according to the story, while serving with 207 Squadron he had applied for a posting to the Pathfinders. Unaccountably, it seems, he was informed that no vacancy existed. This is inconceivable in view of the fact that 8 Group employed G/C "Hamish" Gilbert Mahaddie to visit the bomber stations and actively recruit fresh blood, for which he acquired the title of "Pathfinder Horse Thief". Rebuffed by 8 Group,

ED817 was the second prototype of the Type 464 (provisioning) Lancaster and is seen here bearing the original 617 Squadron code.

Ottley approached Gibson personally, or so the story continues, and he and his crew were among the later arrivals.

Gibson made as one of his first tasks the removal of the existing adjutant, F/L Pain, who was posted to 18 OTU on the 1st of April. In his place Gibson brought in acting F/L Humphries, whom he knew well from his time at 106 Squadron. Two further crews, those of Lovell and Lanchester, who had been among the 57 Squadron C Flight recruits, were also dismissed during the early stages, for failing to attain the required standard. A replacement was found in the form of P/O Divall and crew, also from 57 Squadron, and they arrived on the 10th of April, almost two weeks into the training schedule. Training over lakes and reservoirs prepared the crews for the forthcoming operation, and the problems of a suitable bombsight, and establishing a correct bomb release height were solved through simple expedients. A wooden hand-held triangular device, boasting two nails and a peephole, would provide the bomb aimers with a precise point of release, and a calibrated spotlight altimeter, as used on occasions in the past by Coastal Command, could guarantee an exact release height. In the event, some bomb aimers elected to use an alternative and more stable system of sighting, using chinagraph marks on their clear vision panels instead of the nails, and a triangulation of string, attached to nuts either side of the Perspex nose.

More problematic was the weapon itself, which came to be known as the "bouncing bomb", but was, in fact, a revolving depth charge. Testing had been in progress since the nod was given for the operation to take place, and even the shape of the casing was in doubt until very late on. Originally encased in a wooden spherical skin, it proved unable to withstand the impact, even when the release height was reduced from 150 to a dangerously low sixty feet, and it failed to perform as intended. Wallis noticed, however, that on occasions, the oil drum shaped steel casing of the actual bomb, did have a limited capacity to travel horizontally across the surface of the water, and he decided ultimately, that the weapon, code named Upkeep, should be produced in this form. A number of squadron crews conducted trial drops just short of the beach at Reculver in North Kent, aiming at dummy towers erected on the dunes. When backspin was imparted to the weapon, it performed sufficiently well for the operation to be considered feasible. To say that Upkeep "bounced", was overstating the case somewhat. In no way did its performance mirror that of the smaller Highball version, which was being developed alongside for use against capital ships, and which traversed the surface in giant skips as if weightless. It, in fact, reluctantly parted company with the surface of the water, in a way which can only be described as laboured, but it worked. It was just days before the operation was scheduled to take place that the one and only live drop was successfully carried out, and the device was declared ready.

Because of the nature of 617 Squadron's wartime career, in which it acted almost exclusively as an independent unit, and in view of the outstanding success it achieved, it is all too easy to lose sight of what was going on around it. Its reputation for excellence was legitimately earned, but it was never part of the nightly grind, which was the lot of the other heavy squadrons. It was only because of the existence of these, hammering away at area targets, that 617 Squadron could retain its independence, and be guaranteed the very best in crews, most of whom had been tempered in the heat of battle with these squadrons of the line. It is right, therefore, to put 617 Squadron within the context of the Command as a whole, and to see the wider picture of contemporary events, while also tracing the development of the bomber offensive under Harris.

While the formation and progress towards operational readiness of 617 Squadron had been taking place, the other heavy squadrons of Bomber Command had been embroiled in the Ruhr offensive. A number of 617 Squadron's crews had actually participated in the first two rounds of this, on the 5/6th and 12/13th of March, both of which were directed with great success at Essen. This was the first offensive for which the Command was genuinely equipped and prepared, and it would signal the end for the hitherto elusive towns and cities of the region, which had always managed to hide beneath an ever present cloak of industrial haze. Harris had been trying to deliver a decisive blow against Essen in particular, ever since taking over the reins of Bomber Command over twelve months earlier. Thus far, however, almost every attempt had resulted in bombs being sprayed liberally around the region, and never once had he achieved anything like the concentration necessary to destroy an urban target. He had arrived at the helm with firm ideas already in place about how to win the war by bombing alone, and gradually, over the remainder of 1942, he had overseen the development of tactics and technology, which would lead him to the Ruhr and beyond. This had culminated in an unprecedented series of highly effective operations during a two week period in September 1942, and if any period in the Command's evolution to effectiveness could be identified as the turning point, then, perhaps, this had been it.

Harris had realized from the start, that to deal effectively with an urban target, it was necessary to overwhelm the defences. From the outset, he had dispensed with his predecessor's system of small scale raids on multiple targets, and introduced the bomber stream, which pushed the maximum number of aircraft across an aiming point in the shortest possible time. He also knew, that built-up areas are most efficiently destroyed by fire rather than blast, and the bomb loads carried by his aircraft soon reflected this thinking. Major successes against Lübeck at the end of March 1942, and Rostock a month later, were outstanding examples of city-busting, and were a foretaste of the devastation inflicted on Cologne by Operation Millennium at the end of May. Although the two subsequent "Thousand" raids were disappointing in comparison, Harris had made his point, and the basis of all future operations had been established. The advent of the Pathfinder Force in August had added a new dimension, and the pioneering work with the Mosquito-borne Oboe blind bombing device carried out by one of its founder units, 109 Squadron, during the remainder of the year, was to prove absolutely critical in the current campaign. It was this technological breakthrough, which allowed navigators and bomb aimers to see though the industrial haze, and for the first time to pinpoint Essen and Duisburg, and all the other towns in Germany's

Gibson beating up the beach at Reculver in ED932, to impress the audience watching the Upkeep dropping trials a matter of days before the operation took place.

An Upkeep mine falls away from its Lancaster during training for Operation Chastise (Crown).

This dramatic shot shows a dummy Upkeep mine about to hit the beach during testing at Reculver.

A rare view of Guy Gibson at the controls of a Lancaster, taken during testing at Reculver.

heartland, which were so vitally important to its capacity to wage war. With Oboe up his sleeve, and a predominantly four engined, genuinely heavy bomber force at his disposal, Harris could now embark with abandon on his quest to dismantle Germany, and win the war by bombing alone.

As already mentioned, the Ruhr campaign began on the night of the 5/6th of March, and participating in this operation, but now with 617 Squadron, were the crews of the then F/O Wilson, Sgt Townsend, F/L Knight, F/L Astell, F/L Barlow and F/S Burpee. Also on the order of battle were other future 617 Squadron stalwarts, F/L Allsebrook, Sgt Gumbley, P/O Cockshott, F/L Youseman and F/L Suggitt. The raid destroyed over three thousand houses, and damaged fifty three buildings within the giant Krupps complex, and when the operation was repeated a week later, a 30% greater degree of damage was inflicted on this munitions producing concern. On the 26/27th, equipment failure among a large proportion of the Oboe Mosquito element led to a disappointing raid on Duisburg, and this city would continue to lead a comparatively charmed life until shortly before 617 Squadron went to war for the first time.

April proved to be the least rewarding month of the Ruhr period, largely because of the number of operations directed at targets outside of the region, and beyond the range of Oboe. It began promisingly, however, with another successful tilt at Essen on the 3/4th, when over six hundred buildings were destroyed. Duisburg again escaped serious damage on the 8/9th and 9/10th, before operations to other regions of Germany resulted in a failure at Frankfurt on the 10/11th, and only modest success at Stuttgart on the 14/15th. An attempt to bomb the Skoda armaments works at Pilsen in Czechoslovakia on the 16/17th was a dismal failure for the loss of thirty-six Lancasters and Halifaxes, and a diversionary operation against Mannheim on the same night cost a further eighteen. This brought the night's total to a new record casualty figure of fifty four aircraft. A massive area in the centre of Stettin was devastated on the 20/21st, and then a moderately effective attack was delivered on Duisburg on the 26/27th. The month closed at Essen on the night of the 30th, and although this was a useful raid, it fell short of the success of the earlier efforts.

A record non-1,000 force of 596 aircraft took off for Dortmund to open May's account on the 4/5th, and those reaching the target destroyed over twelve hundred buildings. Duisburg finally succumbed to an outstandingly accurate and concentrated attack on the 12/13th, when almost sixteen hundred buildings were reduced to rubble, and sixty thousand tons of shipping was sunk or seriously damaged in the inland port. Bochum suffered a moderately damaging assault on the following night, before a nine day lull in main force operations allowed the crews a welcome rest. It was during this period, that 617 Squadron was to earn itself a place in aviation history, with its famous feat of arms against Germany's dams.

Volumes have already been written about Operation Chastise, and this account will be restricted to a basic outline of events, with particular attention to timings. It is easy to overlook the fact, that this was a complex three phase operation, spanning eight hours and forty-seven minutes, with action occurring simultaneously at widely dispersed locations, and it is interesting to see it as a whole, rather than in isolation.

At 21.28 on the evening of Sunday the 16th of May, the first specially modified Lancaster of the second wave, ED927 AJ-E, took off. At the controls was F/L Barlow, who was bound by the northern route via the Frisian island of Vlieland for the Sorpe Dam, and timed to arrive at the enemy coast simultaneously with the south-routed first wave. It was still broad daylight, for which double summertime was responsible, and darkness would not be complete until after 23.00. Barlow was followed at 21.29 by Munro in ED921 AJ-W, Byers in ED934 AJ-K at 21.30 and Rice in ED936 AJ-H at 21.31. At 21.39, Gibson in ED932 AJ-G, with Hopgood and Martin alongside in ED925 AJ-M and ED909 AJ-P respectively, began their take-off, followed

Two views of the Upkeep mine installed on Gibson's Lancaster ED932, AJ-G.

at 21.47 by Young in ED887 AJ-A, Maltby in ED906 AJ-J and Shannon in ED929 AJ-L. Last away of the Möhne/Eder contingent were Maudslay in ED937 AJ-Z, Astell in ED864 AJ-B and Knight in ED912 AJ-N at 21.59. McCarthy, whose departure should have preceded that of Barlow, finally got away at 22.01 in the spare aircraft AJ-T, his own ED915 AJ-Q having sprung a glycol leak during start up. The spare aircraft, ED825, had been flown over from Boscombe Down only that afternoon, and there had not been time to fit the VHF equipment or the altimeter spot lamps. Fortunately, neither would be of critical importance at the Sorpe. The final five crews remained at Scampton until a clearer picture of unfolding events determined where they were needed. The crews of Wilson and Divall would not take part, ostensibly because of illness, although, in the event, only nineteen serviceable Lancasters were available.

As the second wave approached the Dutch Frisians shortly before 23.00, Byers was seen to climb over the northern tip of Texel, clearly south of the planned track, which should have taken him over Vlieland. Hit by ground fire at about 450 feet, observers watched AJ-K catch fire and crash into the Waddenzee, just beyond the island at 22.57. There were no survivors. At almost the same moment, Munro's aircraft was fired on over Vlieland, sustaining damage to the intercom and master compass, without which, an accurate attack could not be conducted. Bitterly disappointed, Munro abandoned the sortie and turned for home. Rice, having crossed Vlieland, and approaching the Afsluitdijk just after 23.00, was misled by the merging of sea and sky in the twilight conditions, and struck the sea, tearing off the Upkeep weapon, which impacted the tail wheel in passing, forcing it into the Elsan toilet. The bomb bay fabrication buckled and scooped up vast quantities of water, which found its way into the rear turret as the aircraft climbed, much to the discomfort of Sgt Sandy Burns, the occupant. At 23.06 Rice was also forced to abandon his sortie and turn for home.

The status of the operation at this point is as follows.

Wave 2. Barlow is past the Afsluitdijk and over the Ijsselmeer, with McCarthy over the North Sea making up time, and Rice and Munro are clear of the Frisians on their way home.

Wave 1. Gibson, Hopgood and Martin have made landfall over the heavily defended island of Walcheren at the mouth of the Scheldt, rather than between it and Schouwen, the stronger than forecast wind having pushed them south of track. Fortunately they get away with it, and are heading inland towards Roosendal in south-west Holland. Young, Maltby and Shannon are approaching landfall, while Maudslay, Astell and Knight are over the North Sea ten minutes behind. The reserve force remains on the ground at Scampton. The operation is already behind schedule, and accurate navigation is proving difficult at such low level.

At 23.50 Barlow had just crossed the Rhine and entered Germany at the point at which the northern and southern routes converged. He turned to the east and almost immediately collided with an electricity pylon and high tension cables east of Rees. The Lancaster plunged into a field used for grazing cattle, and there were no survivors. The Upkeep weapon remained intact, and fell into enemy hands. There is a famous photograph of a local dignitary standing triumphantly on top of the cylinder, believing it to be a fuel tank. Within ten days, drawings were produced, accurately describing the device and its functions, along with accurate descriptions of the mechanisms and release, and modifications to the Lancaster. Charlie Williams had written his final letter to his fiancée earlier in the day, but as they were not yet man and wife, she would receive no official notification of his failure to return.

Meanwhile, Gibson's trio had encountered unanticipated flak concentrations in the Buchholt-Borken area, north-west of Dorsten, and again near Dülmen, the last of which inflicted damage to Hopgood's certainly sustained a severe leg wound, and P/O Burcher in the rear turret took some flak splinters, while

F/L Bill Astell. The movie depiction of Astell's loss was inaccurate, as was that of Maudslay. (Astell family photo).

Hopgood himself had possible facial injury. At 00.09 Ottley, in ED910 AJ-C, took off from Scampton as the first of the final wave. As Burpee followed in ED865 AJ-S at 0011, Gibson was transmitting a flak warning to base. Burpee was followed by Brown in ED918 AJ-F at 00.12, and by Townsend in ED886 AJ-O at 00.14. At 00.15, a number of incidents took place. Anderson completed the final take-off of the operation in ED924 AJ-Y, Gibson, Hopgood and Martin arrived at the Möhne Lake, McCarthy reached his target area around the Sorpe, and Astell and crew perished.

Most written accounts and the feature film released in 1955 describe Astell's Lancaster AJ-B falling victim to flak before crashing in flames onto farm land. This is not what happened. The sole cause of Astell's demise was a collision with an electricity pylon, and it is worth exploring the evidence in support of each viewpoint. The supporting testimony for being shot down by flak comes from a single source, Harry O'Brien, the rear gunner in Knight's aircraft. He reported that AJ-B passed between two streams of tracer from light flak batteries, and caught fire before crashing. What we need to establish is how clearly O'Brien saw the events; what was his position in relation to Astell's at the time of the incident? What is known is that Astell delayed a course change shortly after crossing into Germany, and fell behind Maudslay and Knight. What is less certain is the actual distance that developed between them before he adopted the correct course. They were travelling at a ground speed of approximately 180 miles per hour, or three miles a minute, and this is important in view of the testimony of eye witnesses on the ground. According to local farmer, Herr Tücking, as reported by German author Helmuth Euler in his book, *Als Deutschlands Dämme Brachen*, he was awoken by the noise of a low-flying aircraft, which almost removed his roof. He ran downstairs and, on going outside, observed a second aircraft strike an electricity pylon and crash in flames. A maid servant in the neighbouring farm belonging to Herr Thesing corroborated his statement. She and the old man were outside at the time, and facing the oncoming Lancasters, she watched the first one pass over the Tücking residence away to her left. A minute later a second aircraft came over, still to her left but a little closer. She confirms that the third aircraft, Astell's, followed a minute or more behind, heading straight for where she was standing, and, therefore to the right of the tracks of the first two. We all know that a minute in such circumstances could mean anything from twenty-seconds to five minutes or more, so this does not help us a great deal. What we have to consider is the time it took for Herr Tücking to wake up, gather his senses, put on some footwear and make his way downstairs and into the yard.

At three miles a minute, the gap between Knight and Astell would have stretched significantly while they were heading in different directions, and it seems reasonable to assume that Astell fell at least a minute behind Knight. It also seems reasonable to estimate that it took Herr Tücking a minute to wake up and get downstairs. This would put Astell three miles behind Knight at the moment of the crash, and one must consider how much detail O'Brien could actually have seen. At the moment of impact Knight was already around three miles beyond it, and was travelling away from it at the continuing rate of three miles per minute. He was at treetop height, probably no higher than fifty feet over perfectly flat terrain, and this would mean that the crash site was already lost behind trees and maybe even the curvature of the earth. O'Brien could, at best, have witnessed an impression of bright flashes and sparks, which, in view of the warnings at briefing that light flak was the greatest danger to the low-flying Lancasters, would lead to a perfectly reasonable interpretation. It is unlikely that a collision with a pylon even entered O'Brien's head. Why would it? Even if Astell were only half a minute behind Knight, or a mile and a half, O'Brien's impression of what happened would have been little clearer at such low level.

What actually happened to AJ-B is that it collided with the top section of an electricity pylon, instantly catching fire, before ballooning over the Thesing's roof and crashing into a field beyond the Lammers farm house next door. The Lancaster exploded in a kaleidoscope of igniting tracer ammunition. Herr Tücking then describes from his vantage point behind a wall, how a fire-red ball rolled another 150 metres, before a further violent and deafening detonation took place that shattered windows and lifted roof tiles throughout the community. It was half an hour before onlookers could approach the scene, where close to the aircraft wreckage they found the charred remains of one of the crew in "a stooping position, propped up on his hands". The bodies of Astell and his crew were laid out on the edge of the single track road joining the farms, and the area was cordoned off by the military. Never the less, in strict contravention of regulations, Ignatz Böckenhoff from nearby Raesfeld recorded the scene of the crash in three photographs taken later in the morning. Local historian Richard Sühling, who himself lives in Raesfeld, and is the curator of the town's museum, witnessed these events from his bedroom window in the family farm some two or three miles away. Later in the day he and his brother Bernard, with the curiosity of young boys, cycled over to have a look. Herr Sühling has researched Astell's crash exhaustively over the years, and is adamant that no flak batteries were situated in the area at the time. There was nothing to defend, and the single searchlight in Raesfeld was not activated until after the aircraft had passed.

By the time that Gibson was ready to begin his attack, the second trio had arrived on the scene, and gathered at the eastern end of the reservoir, awaiting their turn in the proceedings. At 00.28, Gibson carried out the first attack of Operation Chastise, in the face of a spirited defence, principally from gun emplacements in the sluice towers. Once past the dam, the Lancaster also came under fire from a flak position in the village of Günne, situated on the edge of the compensating basin. Some commentators, and the epic film of 1954, suggest that Gibson's mine scored a direct hit in the centre of the dam wall before exploding, and the squadron's Operations Record Book describes an accurate attack. In fact, as Gibson's transmission to base, GONER 68A shows, the weapon fell short by 5-50 yards, and eye-witness testimony from those on the dam, claim that it veered to the left, and detonated close to the southern sluice tower.

At 00.33, Maudslay and Knight arrived at the lake, and Hopgood carried out his attack. His aircraft was hit several times by fire from the dam, and flames erupted from one of AJ-M's engines and a wing. P/O Fraser, the bomb aimer, became aware of the commotion behind him, and released the weapon, knowing that he had done so too late. As Hopgood struggled for height, probably with only two good engines, Fraser fed his parachute into the slip-stream through the bottom hatch, was dragged clear, and found himself on the ground almost immediately. The severely wounded Minchin was crawling towards the rear exit when rear gunner Burcher found him. He clipped on his chute and pushed him through the door, pulling the rip-chord as he went, and then unpacked his own chute as he prepared for his own departure. As he stood on the threshold the aircraft exploded, throwing him clear, and he sustained a back injury after striking the tailplane. AJ-M crashed six kilometres beyond the dam near the village of Ostönnen, with Fraser and Burcher falling into enemy hands as the only survivors. The mine skipped over the crest of the dam, demolishing the generating station when it detonated on impact. [1]

At 00.38, Martin made his attack, with Gibson making a pass at right angles above the dam, to draw off the fire. Martin's bomb veered dramatically off course, suggesting that its entry into the water had been at an angle, and exploded in the mud flats on the left-hand bank. As he flew out beyond the dam, two shells punctured his starboard wing tank, but failed to explode, and the damage was not critical.

The status of the operation at this point is as follows.

The reserve wave is still over England on its way to the coast. McCarthy is having problems with his approach to the Sorpe, and is making repeated runs across the dam until his bomb aimer is satisfied. Rice and Munro are on final approach to Scampton, each unaware of the other's presence. Four Lancasters have been lost.

Rice, minus tail wheel and hydraulics, and having circled for about twenty minutes, while some unfortunate crew members pumped the wheels down, was about to land, when Munro, minus the means to communicate, cut in front and lobbed down. As Rice was completing another circuit, Young was making his attack at the Möhne, with Gibson and Martin flying above on either side to attract the defences. At about the same time, McCarthy's bomb aimer, Sgt George (Johnny) Johnson, was finally preparing to release his weapon at the Sorpe, on what would be the tenth run. The Sorpe required a different form of attack, because its construction differed markedly from that of the Möhne and Eder. Rather than being a vertical wall, its cross-section was triangular, with a gently sloping face either side of a concrete core. It provided nothing for the mine to slam into to arrest its forward progress, as in the case of a traditional gravity dam, and the water level would have ensured the mine's passage straight over the top. The attacks on the Sorpe had to be carried out along the length of the dam, rather than at right-angles to it, from as low a height and speed as possible, and without revolving the mine, which was to be released as close to the centre point as could be determined. At 00.46, McCarthy and crew did precisely this, and could report

---

[1] According to letters held by Shere McCarthy, John Fraser's daughter, who is now married to Joe McCarthy's son Joe Junior, her father evaded capture, and remained at large for a week, before being picked up by the Germans near Wesel on the Rhine, some one hundred miles from the Möhne Dam. German sources, however, suggest he was captured within hours of the raid.

crumbling of the crest, but no breach. At 00.47, Rice finally put down at Scampton, and in the absence of a tail wheel, the Lancaster sustained further damage, this time to the bottom of the fins. Despite a copy-book delivery, the first so far, Young's mine had apparently created no breach at the Möhne, and Maltby was called in to make his attack at 00.49. As he approached the dam, he was aware of debris on the top, and then identified that a breach had in fact occurred. He was about to abandon his run, when the bomb aimer, P/O Fort, released the Upkeep, which bounced four times, and impacted the dam in precisely the prescribed manner, before sinking and exploding. The enormous weight of water pushed the fractured masonry over the edge, and released a torrent of floodwater, which cascaded down the valley, engulfing villages in its path and the small town of Neheim-Hüsten. It also swept away wooden barrack buildings containing hundreds of eastern European forced women workers, many of whom died, and these contributed to the highest death toll to date from a Bomber Command operation. At 00.56, Gibson was able to transmit the long-awaited signal 'NIGGER' to base, confirming the destruction of the Möhne Dam. Martin and Maltby turned for home, while Gibson, with Young as deputy, Shannon, Maudslay and Knight headed eastwards for the fifteen minute flight to the Eder.

Despite being undefended, the Eder presented a more challenging proposition, because of the hilly terrain which surrounded it. Whereas, at the Möhne, the crews had about fourteen seconds in which to adjust track, height and speed before the point of release, the approach at the Eder allowed only half that time. On arrival at the Eder reservoir, difficulty in locating the position of the dam threw the operation further behind schedule, and it was necessary for Gibson to fire off a verey cartridge to attract Shannon from a defunct dam in another area of the lake. With the clock ticking towards 01.30, Gibson called in Shannon to make his attack. The approach took him along a valley to a cutting in the ring of hills surrounding the lake on its northern side. The Germans had thoughtfully provided a navigation point in the imposing form of Waldeck Castle, perched right on the edge of the shoulder of cliff that formed the left side of the gap from Shannon's perspective. The ground then fell away in a sheer drop of many hundreds of feet to the surface of the reservoir. This was the challenge facing Shannon and the others who still had an Upkeep to deliver. To attain the required bombing height of sixty feet it was necessary to shed altitude at a stomach-churning rate, while aiming for a spit of land reaching out into the lake directly opposite and running parallel with the dam wall. The descent had to be accomplished through the skilful use of throttles and flaps, and be under sufficient control to allow an immediate forty-five degree turn to port over the spit to find the line, height and speed ready for the bomb release. After a number of unsuccessful attempts to establish an accurate approach, Maudslay was invited to try, but experienced similar problems. It was now 01.30, and the third wave crews were just crossing the Dutch coast.

After two more dummy runs, during which Shannon angled his approach to bypass the spit of land which had been planned as the starting point for the straight and level run, and which had been responsible for the difficulties, F/S Len Sumpter, in the nose of AJ-L, released the mine at 01.39. The drop was accurate, but because of the angle of approach, the mine struck the dam wall at its right hand extremity.

Although no damage was apparent, Shannon was convinced that a small breach had occurred, and signalled 5 Group HQ accordingly. Maudslay attacked at about 01.45, with AJ-Z, according to eyewitnesses, displaying signs of damage to the underside. In Enemy Coast Ahead, Gibson comments on a curious incident as Maudslay approached Waldeck Castle in preparation for his bombing run. He describes the Lancaster pulling away suddenly as if something was wrong, but quickly resuming its course and carrying out its attack. A possible explanation for the sudden deviation and apparent damage is that AJ-Z was confronted by treetops, and pulled away to avoid them. Perhaps the Lancaster actually made

Avro Lancaster BIII Special adapted to carry the Upkeep mine. The aircraft is apparently not marked with a serial number or squadron code in this photo, suggesting it is prior to delivery (Crown).

A side view of ED925/G which carried the code AJ-M on her sole operational sortie, when she was flown by F/L Hopgood. The G suffix indicated that the aircraft carried secret equipment and was to be guarded whilst on the ground (Crown).

Joe McCarthy and crew. They had to fly the spare aircraft AJ-T rather than their allocated AJ-Q

Guy Gibson and crew are shown as they embark on Operation Chastise in ED932, AJ-G in this very famous photograph. Not one of those in the photograph would survive the war. (Crown).

The end of the road for ED925, AJ-M and five members of the crew of Flight Lieutenant Hopgood. Photo courtesy of Helmut Euler.

German personnel examine the intact Upkeep mine from Barlow's Lancaster. It is possible that at this early stage they still thought that it was a fuel tank rather than an explosive device.

A Möhne Dam Flak crew including Karl Schütte (photo courtesy Helmut Euler)

contact with trees or some other object on the ground, and either the bomb release mechanism was damaged in some way, or the bomb was knocked out of alignment between the retaining arms, thus altering the profile of the underside as seen by those watching. Alternatively, a piece of branch may have become jammed in some way around the bomb with the same result. It is also possible, that none of this happened, and that AJ-Z was simply travelling too fast at the moment of release. The mine struck the parapet of the dam and detonated on impact, with AJ-Z above but beyond the point of explosion. Maudslay responded faintly to a second R/T enquiry from Gibson, and then nothing more was heard, although a coded message was received from Maudslay by Group confirming the attack. Knight, in AJ-N, carried the first wave's last hope, and following one dummy run, delivered a perfect attack at 01.52, on a heading fifteen degrees to the left of Shannon's. A hole was punched through the wall at the point of detonation below the waterline, releasing a horizontal jet of water. The masonry above the hole collapsed, and the breach spread into that created by Shannon. At 01.53, as the onlookers watched in awe the torrent of water crashing down the valley, Maltby cleared the Dutch coast via the Helder peninsular, and gained the safety of the North Sea, with Martin only minutes behind.

As these events were unfolding, the third wave aircraft were picking their way across Holland, and were approaching the narrow gap between the enemy night fighter airfields at Eindhoven and Gilze-Rijen. Burpee, having climbed, probably to establish his position, was fired upon from Gilze-Rijen while off course, and his Lancaster was set on fire. A searchlight on a tower on the airfield blinded Burpee, and as he tried to avoid it AJ-S sank onto a wooded section and lost flying speed. It crashed in flames onto the airfield at 02.00, whereupon the bomb exploded, lighting up the scene like day, and the cost of the extensive damage to buildings was estimated by the German authorities to be one and a half million Dutch Gilders. Inevitably, there were no survivors. At 02.35, while Gibson, Young, Shannon and Knight were making their way westwards across Germany, Gibson noted an aircraft to port falling in flames over Hamm. Ottley, through an error in navigation, had turned south too early, and had come within range of the defences at Hamm, a major railway centre, and a town which had already been stirred up by McCarthy, who had darted backwards and forwards over the marshalling yards at fifty feet, while trying to find his way home over an hour earlier. McCarthy survived, Ottley did not. Hit by ground fire, the Lancaster struggled on eastwards across the village of Bockum-Hövel, before the tanks exploded in the air, and it crashed on the edge of a wood. The Upkeep detonated on the ground, and blasted the rear turret away from the rest of the wreckage. Miraculously, Sgt Tees, the rear gunner, was found alive in his turret, and was picked up by Hitler Youth members and taken to a nearby farm house to await the military. Tees proved to be the final one of only three survivors from downed aircraft during the operation.

One minute after Ottley's crew met its end, Maudslay's did likewise. At 02.36, having limped westwards from the Eder, AJ-Z was brought down by the flak defences at the frontier town of Emmerich, nestling on the eastern bank of the Rhine right on the border with Holland. It is inconceivable that Maudslay had intended to cross the Rhine at Emmerich, a town with oil storage facilities, and, therefore, a town well defended. It is likely that navigational problems had brought AJ-Z to this point, and that at such low level it was upon the blacked out town before the crew had time to react. Almost immediately the flak found AJ-Z, and it crashed northeast of the town into a meadow bounded now on its northern side by a motorway, and just two kilometres from the border with Holland. This time there were no survivors. There were four flak batteries with a total of twelve guns within range of AJ-Z as it approached Emmerich from the direction of the Ruhr. Members of two different batteries, Herr Doerwald and Herr Feldmann, later recorded their impressions of the final moments of AJ-Z. The following is a translation of their testimony.

"I belonged to Home Flak. Our position, equipped with three 2cm anti-aircraft guns, was situated near the industrial harbour in front of the River Rhine lock. Earlier in the evening aircraft had flown in the direction of the Möhne Dam and returned without load (bomb). At about 3 o'clock in the morning one single Lancaster came in flying very low. The aircraft was fired upon, and fire broke out. It came down near Klein Netterden. The crash took place in a meadow east of the Industria Brickworks along the Osterholt Road. I was a gun layer, and I received a medal for shooting down the plane. Afterwards, we heard that officers of high rank were on board the plane. The whole crew, about seven or eight men, were killed."

Reported by Johannes Doerwald.

"The aircraft returned from the Ruhr in the early morning. It was fired upon first by the anti-aircraft battery in the keep. Along the Nierenbergerstrasse and near the harbour there were 2cm anti-aircraft positions of the Home Flak. Each battery had three guns. The plane turned away, and the rear gunner fired at the battery near the lock. Then all twelve guns were shooting at the plane, and the engines caught fire. Then it crashed and exploded. People said there were seven crewmembers on board. Our battery was situated on the harbour breakwater. With our fire we shaved the poplars standing on the harbour. The aircraft was flying at such low level, that we had to aim the guns at a very low angle."

Reported by Feldmann.

Brown and Anderson continued towards their objectives, the Sorpe, while Townsend headed for the Ennepe, the progress of all three made increasingly difficult by ground mist forming in the valleys. The defences had been stirred up by the earlier waves, and all three of these late-comers had been subjected to ground fire, Townsend, particularly, having experienced a torrid time, during which he was forced to demonstrate his not inconsiderable skills as a pilot. As the time drew towards 03.00, Gibson and the others were crossing the Dutch coast, although not in sight of each other, and at different points. The plan allowed for the first wave aircraft to exit Fortress Europe via the known gap in the defences between

A contemporary German photograph shows the peaceful surroundings of the Möhne Dam prior to 617 Squadron's visit.

The devastation resulting from the breach is evident in this photograph shown shortly after the raid. Note the barrage balloons installed after the raid by the Germans in an attempt to prevent further low-level air attacks.

The Eder Dam earlier in the war.

The massive breach caused by Knight's mine is clear in this iconic photograph of the Eder Dam.

Never previously published, this photograph shows the line of flight of Burpee's Lancaster as it descended, then a clear path as it cut a swathe through the trees before crashing at the apex of the white triangle. Photo courtesy of Andreas Wachtel.

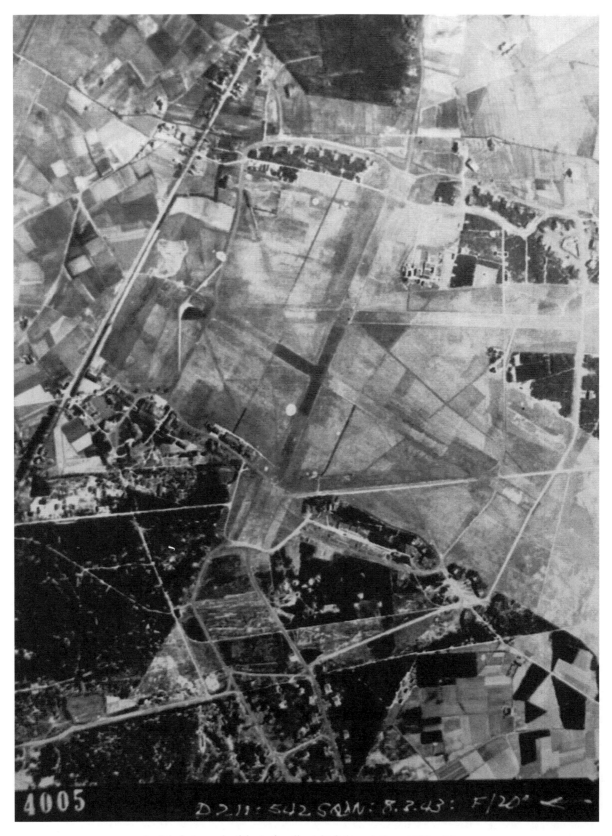

4005   D.2.11: 542 SQN: 8.3.43: F/20°

Aerial photograph of the Luftwaffe night fighter station at Gilze-Rijen.

Egmond and the Elefant radar antenna system a little to the south. This array consisted of three towers, the northernmost of which was a receiver standing thirty to forty metres high and called Kleine Heidelberg, or Little Heidelberg. A kilometre to the south stood the Grosse Elefant, or Big Elephant, a massive wooden construction of one hundred metres in height, with the fifty metre-high Kleine Elefant, or Little Elephant, a further kilometre along the headland. Stout wooden posts or Paals mark the beach at 250 metre intervals, the kilometre posts bearing consecutive identification numbers. The ideal route took the Lancasters between Paals 41 and 42, two hundred yards to the right of Kleine Heidelberg. Gibson climbed briefly to three hundred feet to establish a fix on the towers, and then stuck the nose down to gather speed for the final dash to the Atlantic Wall and freedom. The Lancaster was travelling faster than at any time that night, around 260 m.p.h., as it screamed over the shoreline within feet of the dunes. Shannon had already passed this way just a few minutes earlier, and Knight followed in Gibson's wake so low, that his tail wheel almost impacted a concrete structure nestling in the sand and coarse grass, and invisible to all on board but the rear gunner. He alone knew how close they had come to losing the wheel, if nothing else.

Gibson, Shannon and Knight had almost literally scraped the sand dunes, but Young's dislike of low flying made him an easier target. He was in fact, about ten kilometres south of his intended track, and heading directly for the small resort town of Wijk aan Zee, nestling below the dunes. The town was at the northern extremity of the Ijmuiden defence zone, and its flak batteries were the very last with a chance of bringing down a Lancaster on this night. As Young climbed to pass over the town AJ-A was hit by ground fire. Within seconds a battery on the high point of the dunes also scored hits which proved to be fatal. As AJ-A crossed the shoreline, Young pointed the nose to the north, running parallel to the beach in an attempt to carry out a controlled ditching, but at 02.59 the Lancaster crashed on a sand bar with sufficient impact to kill all on board. The wreckage lay close to Paal 47, midway between Wijk and Castricum, and over the ensuing days the bodies drifted ashore.

Meanwhile, Anderson, forced off track by searchlights, unable to establish his position, behind schedule, and with an unserviceable rear turret, was considering his options. As Maltby touched down at Scampton at 03.11, the first back from Operation Chastise, Anderson was abandoning his sortie, and returning on a reciprocal course, while Brown was following in McCarthy's footsteps at the Sorpe, trying to find his line in the mist. Finally, at 03.14, on his fourth attempt, and having dropped flares to mark his path, Brown's bomb aimer, Sgt Oancia, released his Upkeep two thirds of the way along the length of the dam. It was an accurate drop, and further crumbling of the crest resulted, but again there was no breach.

Five minutes later, at 03.19, Martin landed at Scampton, followed at 03.23 by McCarthy with a burst tyre, courtesy of the flak gunners at Hamm. Gibson, Shannon and Knight were now well into their crossing of the North Sea, Brown and Anderson were still deep in Germany, and Townsend had arrived in the vicinity of the Ennepe. He was experiencing difficulty, first in identification of the target, and then in establishing a line of approach, and he was also aware of a marked vibration when the weapon was rotated. At 03.37, the bomb aimer in AJ-O, Sgt Franklin, released the final Upkeep of the operation, and the pattern of rings in the water following the explosion, showed that it had fallen short, and the dam remained intact. In recent years, it has been suggested that Townsend attacked the Bever dam rather than the Ennepe, and evidence has been produced to support that view. However, German author Helmut Euler, whose fascination with Operation Chastise has led to exhaustive research and two books on the subject, is convinced that Townsend did indeed attack the Ennepe, and can also provide supporting evidence. Whichever is the case, Townsend's flight was an epic, which did not end with the release of his mine. He

Two of the three radar masts, part of Radar Station 'Max', on the Dutch coast that crews were looking out for in order to pinpoint the gap in German defences on the periphery of 'Fortress Europe'. Staying a few hundred yards to the right (north) of these masts was the correct position to cross the coast. 'Dinghy' Young was some six or seven miles to the south of the masts when he crashed in the sea (Provinciaal Waterleidingbedrijf' Noord-Holland / Provincial Water Company North Holland).

The wreckage of 'Dinghy' Young's Lancaster ED887, AJ-A, lies on the shore where he had attempted a controlled ditching.

F/L (later S/L) Ralph Allsebrook prior to leaving 49 Sqn in 1943.

was now alone over Germany, a good thirty minutes behind Brown, with the sky to his rear lightening perceptibly.

At 04.06, Shannon landed at Scampton, followed by Gibson at 04.15, five minutes before Knight, and at about the same time that Anderson and Brown were crossing the Dutch coast, having picked their way across Holland in daylight. Anderson landed at 05.30 with his bomb still aboard, and Brown touched down three minutes later. At 06.15, Townsend also landed, bringing Operation Chastise to a close. At a cost of eight Lancasters, fifty three men dead, and three in captivity, two dams had been breached, and one had been damaged superficially. From that moment, 617 Squadron was famous, and Operation Chastise became the most celebrated feat of arms since aviation began.

The first replacement crew, that of F/L Allsebrook, arrived on the 20th from 49 Squadron. Allsebrook came to the squadron as something of a veteran, having begun his operational career with 49 Squadron at Scampton back in the Hampden days. On the night of the 14/15th of February 1942, his crew had been one of ninety-eight dispatched to Mannheim for an area attack on the city, the first such indiscriminate raid to be officially sanctioned since the issuing of the controversial area bombing directive by the Air Ministry earlier that very day. At least part of the return journey was undertaken on one engine, and this failed as the south coast of England hove into sight. A successful ditching was carried out, and the crew took to their dinghy, which was spotted by a Beaufighter crew returning from a patrol. They were soon picked up by a coastguard launch, but three of them had by then suffered frostbite in the freezing conditions. As a Flying Officer, Allsebrook was awarded a DFC in April 1942, just as the trusty Hampden

37

was being replaced by the unpopular Manchester. He returned to 49 Squadron for a second tour at the end of January 1943 as a flight lieutenant, and operated against Hamburg on the 3/4th of February, when he experienced an engine fire over the target. Two trips to Lorient in mid-month sandwiched one to Milan, and the month ended with operations against Cologne and St Nazaire. By the end of the first week of March Allsebrook and his crew had added to their tally with sorties to Berlin, Hamburg and Essen, and then they operated against Nuremberg, Munich and Stuttgart during the course of the following six nights. The pace slackened somewhat for them in April and May before their posting to 617 Squadron, where Allsebrook would be promoted to squadron leader rank and be appointed a flight commander. Operation Chastise had taken the lives of both of the original flight commanders, and David Maltby stepped up to fill the other vacancy.

To the general public during the war a bomber crew was an anonymous collection of young men. Occasionally, an airman might gain recognition in the press for an act or acts of outstanding courage or resourcefulness, but, in many cases, awards of the Victoria Cross took place after the war, once PoWs had returned home to tell their stories of heroism by a member of their crew, and by this time the public had lost its taste for war stories. Mostly, it was senior pilots anyway, like Nettleton, Gibson, Pickard and Cheshire who became household names, and officers attracted more attention than enlisted men. That said, they needed the support of a full crew to do their job, a crew that often did not receive the recognition it deserved, despite facing the same dangers and short life expectancy. Usually, it was through the casualty reports that these names became known to the public, and each of the lost was a son, a brother, a husband or some other relative of families left behind. Allsebrook's flight engineer was twenty-three-year-old F/S Phillip Moore, who, more than seventy years after his death, is still dear to his family. Phillip Moore was born on the 4th of August 1920 in Edgehill, a terraced, working class district of Liverpool

Gibson (left) and Hutchinson in an apparently posed photograph.

west of the city centre, and within sniffing distance of the dockland occupying the east bank of the Mersey. It was dominated by large marshalling yards that connected the busy docks with the wider railway network. Phillip was the fifth of ten children borne to Michael Moore, a postman, and his wife Agnes. Michael had been born in the most deprived area of Liverpool, off Scotland Road, and he and his brother had spent time in a workhouse. At nineteen he joined the army, and fought in the Boer War, before marrying Agnes in 1909, and serving in France during the Great War. Before the war he had been a postman, and he returned to his old job after being demobbed. Michael was a great believer in education, and worked hard to provide a good education for his eight sons. Phillip joined the RAF straight from school in 1936, and was sent to Halton in Buckinghamshire as an engineering apprentice. These young men proudly bore the name Halton Brats, an appellation bestowed upon them by the father of the RAF, Lord Trenchard. Just two weeks before the outbreak of WWII Phillip was posted as a fitter 2nd class to 98 Squadron at Hucknall in Nottinghamshire, a training unit operating the Fairey Battle. Following service at a maintenance unit and an operational training unit, Phillip was posted to No 4 School of Technical Training, where courses were provided for flight engineers, flight mechanics and flight riggers.

During the early months of the war, bomber aircraft were small and carried crews of appropriate size. The advent of the genuine heavy bomber from late 1940 onwards, brought a requirement for additional crew members. Initially the seven man crew of a Manchester, Stirling and Halifax, and later the Lancaster, included a second pilot, but this position became redundant in favour of a flight engineer, a technically trained man who acted as the pilot's assistant, monitoring instruments and handling controls under supervision. Halton Brats became the main source of supply for flight engineers, as many of them volunteered for flying duties, and until quite late into the war, the role of flight engineer was filled by men from the RAF, even in otherwise Dominion nationality squadrons and crews. Phillip was posted to 1654 Conversion Unit at Swinderby in Lincolnshire in October 1942, and it was here that he first met Ralph Allsebrook and learned the ways of the Lancaster. Allsebrook was a pilot on the unit, where he was passing on his skills and experience of operational flying to trainees. Phillip logged numerous flights in Manchesters and Lancasters alongside Allsebrook, and it seems clear that his performance as a flight engineer impressed Allsebrook to the extent, that he offered him a place in his new crew when he returned to operations for a second tour with 49 Squadron in December 1942. Just five feet three inches tall, slim and wiry, Phillip possessed the ideal build to cope with the cramped confines of a Lancaster. He would have been immensely proud to be the right-hand man of such an experienced pilot as Allsebrook, and took part in sixteen operations with 49 Squadron as his flight engineer, before moving with him to 617 Squadron on the 20th of May 1943, just three days after the attack on the Dams. At 617 Squadron, Phillip, as flight engineer to a flight commander, would have had a particular status amongst his peers. For two days between the posting from 49 to 617 Squadrons, Phillip was on attachment to the USAAF 8th Air Force at Hardwick in Norfolk. He flew as a passenger on a number of occasions, but his role at the station is unclear.

As Allsebrook and his crew settled in at Scampton, the mood on 617 Squadron was still high. It was not long before the list of decorations was made known, and it was headed by Gibson, who was to receive the Victoria Cross. Thirty-two other participants in the operation also received decorations, including Townsend, who was awarded a much prized CGM. The King and Queen visited Scampton on the 27th of May, where they were guided through the events of the operation by W/C Gibson, and they were also introduced to the crews. to where Anderson and his crew returned on the 3rd of June. They did so under a cloud, their position at 617 Squadron having been made untenable in the light of the performances of Brown and Townsend under similar circumstances. Gibson's self-confessed inability to relate to other ranks, made him less sympathetic to Anderson as a NCO than to Rice as an officer, even in the face of what might be considered carelessness on the part of Rice in losing his Upkeep. Any implied suggestion

Ralph Allsebrook (seventh from right) in 1943 with air and ground crew, including Phillip Moore, standing to Allsebrook's immediate right.

that Anderson acted in a cowardly manner is misplaced and unjust. It was not the action of a coward to return with his weapon and admit failure, when he could have jettisoned it over a body of water, and concocted an irrefutable excuse to explain it, or claim to have attacked his assigned objective but without success. We will never know precisely what was said, and Anderson and his crew took their side of the story to the grave, after losing their lives on the 23/24th of September, during an operation to Mannheim, the twenty-seventh trip of their tour. They now rest side by side in the peaceful surroundings of the Rheinberg Cemetery, a few yards from where Hopgood and four of his crew lie.

While the congratulations and celebrations had been going on at Scampton, and the world was devouring the press and radio coverage, the unsung element of the Command was continuing the assault on Hitler's war materials producing Ruhr. Having sent a record force to Dortmund early in the month of May, Harris despatched a new record non-1,000 force of 826 aircraft to the same destination on the 23/24th, and completely destroyed almost two thousand buildings. A number of important war industry factories were also hit, resulting in loss of output, but the defenders fought back to bring down thirty eight bombers, the highest casualty figure at a Ruhr target during the campaign to date. Over seven hundred aircraft raided Düsseldorf on the 25/26th, but this operation failed in the face of complete cloud cover, which hampered the Pathfinders' attempts to provide concentrated marking. Almost five hundred buildings were destroyed at Essen on the 27/28th, and this was followed by one of the most awesomely destructive raids of the entire offensive. The town of Barmen was one half of the twin towns known jointly as Wuppertal, which nestles in a valley at the eastern end of the Ruhr. It was attacked by almost seven hundred aircraft on the 29/30th, and was left with over 80% of its built-up area destroyed. A little short of four thousand houses were reduced to ruins, and five of the town's six largest factories were gutted, along with over two hundred other industrial premises. The death toll exceeded three thousand people, and this was a new record for the war. The defenders again had their say, however, and thirty three bombers failed to return home.

A military tradition. Phillip Moore and other members of his family, including his grandfather (Sandra Murphy).

Phillip Moore at an early stage of his RAF career. It is not known if an astute NCO questioned the missing breast pocket button (Sandra Murphy).

F/S Phillip Moore, Allsebrook's flight engineer, with friends while on leave (Sandra Murphy).

HM King George VI enjoys a conversation with W/Cdr Guy Gibson as he is briefed on the successful raid (Crown)

HM King George VI and his entourage inspect surviving members of 617 Squadron on 27th May 1943(Crown).

June 1943

There were no major operations during the first ten nights of June, and it was not until the 11/12th that the heavy squadrons returned to the fray. Düsseldorf was the target on this night for over seven hundred aircraft, and despite an errant Oboe marker, which attracted a proportion of the bombs, massive damage was inflicted on the city. Almost nine thousand fires were recorded in an area measuring 8km by 5km, and nearly thirteen hundred people lost their lives. Another night of heavy losses cost the Command thirty eight aircraft, and a further twenty four were missing from an operation to Bochum on the 12/13th, which also inflicted severe damage on its central districts. Oberhausen wilted under an all Lancaster assault on the 14/15th, before a moderately effective raid fell on Cologne two nights later. 5 Group had always believed itself to be the elite Group, and had an independent air about it, which would become almost a reality in 1944, as a result of events within 617 Squadron. It, or one or more of its squadrons, had operated famously and independently of the main force on a number of occasions in the past, most notably against the M.A.N. factory at Augsburg in April 1942, Danzig in July, the Schneider armaments works at Le Creusot in October, and, of course, the recent Dams raid. Now, on the 20/21st of June, sixty of its Lancasters were sent to attack the old Zeppelin factory at Friedrichshafen, deep in southern Germany, close to the Swiss frontier, wherein lay the manufacturing base of the Würzburg radar sets, which were being used by the enemy night fighter force to intercept Bomber Command aircraft.

The two phase operation was led by W/C Slee of 49 Squadron, who was forced to hand over to W/C Gomm of 467 Squadron, when his Lancaster lost an engine while outbound. The second phase crews adopted a 5 Group inspired "time and distance" method of bombing, which was designed to negate the effects of smoke concealing the aiming point. The flak and searchlight defences proved to be extremely fierce, and Gomm ordered the attack to take place from five thousand feet above the planned level. The operational was not entirely successful, but 10% of the bombs hit the relatively small target, causing extensive damage. Other nearby factories were also afflicted, and the force then flew on to airfields in North Africa, in what was the first shuttle raid of the war.

A hectic round of four major operations in the space of five nights began at Krefeld on the 21/22nd. This was an outstandingly concentrated raid, which created a massive area of fire, and destroyed over 5,500 houses, while killing a thousand people. A massive forty four aircraft failed to return, however, and this was a new record for the Ruhr campaign. The investiture was held at Buckingham Palace on the 22nd of June, and in a departure from normal practice at such occasions, Gibson was honoured by being first in line, and accepted the ultimate award from the hand of Her Majesty the Queen, in the absence of the King. That night it was the turn of Mülheim to reel under a devastating blow, which accounted for over eleven hundred houses, and damaged scores of public buildings. Thirty five aircraft was another high price to pay, and "Happy Valley's" reputation was set for all time. After a night's rest, the Elberfeld half of Wuppertal went the way of its twin Barmen a month earlier, and suffered the destruction of over 90% of its built-up area, amounting to three thousand houses destroyed, with a further 2,500 and fifty three industrial premises seriously damaged. This operation cost the Command thirty four aircraft, and a further thirty were missing following a failed attempt to visit similar damage on the important oil town of Gelsenkirchen on the 25/26th. In an echo of the past, bombs were sprayed all over the Ruhr, and few fell on the intended target. The month ended with the first of three cataclysmic raids on Cologne, which spanned the turn of the month. Mounted on the 28/29th, the almost six hundred strong force, destroyed over 6,300 buildings, and killed 4,300 people. The final act of the month for 617 Squadron was the arrival of F/L Kellaway and his crew from 3 Group's 149 Squadron on the 30th.

July 1943

Two pilots were posted in from 4 Group on the 2nd, acting W/C Holden, who, in April, had completed a six month tour as commanding officer of 102 Squadron, and P/O "Bunny" Clayton from 51 Squadron. W/C George Holden was 617 Squadron's new commanding officer elect. Why was Holden, a 4 Group man to the core, selected to replace the charismatic Gibson, now the most celebrated squadron commander in the entire service? His selection actually began a trend of appointing 4 Group men to the position, Cheshire, Tait and Fauquier, men who would carry the squadron through to the end of the bombing war in late April 1945. If Harris, and one might reasonably assume some involvement on his part, was prepared to look outside of 5 Group for Gibson's successor, why did he sanction the appointment of Holden from among the wealth of qualified existing squadron commanders available? It has to be said, that there was something of the Gibson character in Holden. His career to this point had been distinguished, and he had been involved in some unusual and spectacular operations. He had also rubbed shoulders with some of the Command's finest young bloods, many of whom were gathered within the squadrons of 4 Group, and were themselves seen as shining lights. Not all had survived to the summer of 1943, and of those who had, whose operational careers had begun in 1940, Holden was unquestionably among the brightest prospects. If Dinghy Young had survived, he a 4 Group contemporary of Holden and Cheshire, or perhaps even Henry Maudslay from the "class of 41", then they would also undoubtedly have been in the frame, but they were gone, and Cheshire had progressed to the rank of Group Captain, which generally speaking at that time, precluded him from the command of a squadron. This latter restriction was in the process of being revised, however, as Pathfinder squadrons were now being led by Group Captains, with Wing Commanders filling the roll of flight commander.

Holden began basic training, presumably part time as a reservist, in May 1937. On the 1st of September 1939, the day German forces began their assault on Poland, he joined 9 FTS at Hullavington, moved on to Benson between January and early May 1940, and thence to 10 O.T.U. at Abingdon, where he learned to fly Whitleys. This was the type operated by 4 Group until the advent of the Halifax, and it would be the spring of 1942 before it was finally withdrawn from operational service with the Command. He passed out as a first pilot, day only, with an average rating on the 18th of September, and immediately joined 78 Squadron at Dishforth. Here he began working up to operational status, and undertook his first sortie as second pilot to a F/L Pattison in a raid on Antwerp on the night of the 26/27th of September. His second sortie was flown to Amsterdam with his flight commander, S/L Wildey, who would eventually take command of 10 Squadron, and lose his life in action in October 1942, the same month in which Holden would gain his first command. Finally, on the 11th of November, Holden was signed out as a fully qualified Whitley captain by the newly appointed commanding officer, W/C "Charles" Whitworth, now base commander of Scampton. Two nights later he undertook his first operation as crew captain, his eighth sortie in all, but like many others operating in poor weather conditions that night, he was forced to abandon his sortie and return home. He put matters right on the 15/16th, however, when participating in an unusually effective raid on Hamburg.

Late in 1940 Churchill pressed for the formation of a paratroop unit, as the forerunner of an airborne force for use in a future invasion of Europe. Plans were put in hand to carry out a special operation under the codename Colossus, with the purpose of ascertaining the viability of such an undertaking. Volunteers were brought together as X-Troop No 11 SAS Battalion for an attack on an aqueduct over the River Tragino in Italy to be launched from Malta. Two aircraft were to carry out a diversionary bombing attack on marshalling yards at nearby Foggia, while six others delivered the parachutists into position. 51 and 78 Squadrons were each selected to provide four aircraft and crews under the command of W/C James Tait,

Acting Wing Commander George Holden, who was to succeed Gibson, only to be lost in action within a few weeks.

who had recently begun a short spell as commanding officer of the former. Among the pilots from 78 Squadron was P/O Holden, who flew with Tait on a container-dropping test as part of the run-up on the 2nd of February. On completion of their task the surviving commandos were to gather at a point on the coast for evacuation by submarine. The force departed for Malta on the night of the 7/8th of February, and carried out the operation on the 10/11th. In the event, not all of the commandos were dropped within range of their target, and if this were not unfortunate enough, one of the diversionary Whitleys had to be abandoned in the area selected for the ground force's withdrawal, thus alerting the local defenders. Some damage was inflicted upon the aqueduct, but all of the soldiers were captured on their way to the rendezvous, and they were joined soon afterwards by the Whitley crew.

This operation was Holden's twentieth, and his last with 78 Squadron, which he left with an above average rating to join 35 Squadron at Linton-on-Ouse. 35 Squadron had been reformed at Boscombe Down in November 1940 to introduce the Halifax into operational service, and was attracting the leading bomber pilots in 4 Group. Holden arrived on the 25th of February 1941, and met up again with Tait, who had now reverted to Squadron Leader rank and was a flight commander under the portly personage of the squadron commander, W/C R.W.P.Collings, another of the Command's great characters. The Halifax suffered many teething problems, and the demand for modifications ensured only a trickle of new aircraft from the factories. As a result, following its operational baptism in March, the type operated only intermittently and in very small numbers for some time. Holden flew his first Halifax sortie against Duisburg on the 11/12th of June, and over the ensuing five weeks managed ten more. A major assault on the German cruisers Scharnhorst, Gneisenau and Prinz Eugen at Brest, the first two-named having been in residence there since the end of March, was planned for the 24th of July. The operation was to be undertaken in daylight by Halifaxes accompanied by 1 and 3 Group Wellingtons, and under extensive diversionary activity and a heavy fighter escort. It was discovered at the eleventh hour, however, that the Scharnhorst had slipped away to La Pallice, some two hundred miles further south, and it was decided to send the Halifax element after her, while the remainder of the original plan went ahead at Brest. Fifteen Halifaxes from 35 and 76 Squadrons duly attacked the Scharnhorst, causing extensive damage, but lost five of their number in the process, and all of the surviving aircraft sustained damage to some degree. Holden was forced to bring his bombs home after flak shot away the electrical release gear. One of his crew was killed, while two others were wounded, one seriously. Holden's flight commander at the time was S/L Jimmy Marks, one of the brightest stars in Bomber Command, and an officer who would gain command of 35 Squadron in 1942, only to then lose his life in action shortly after taking it into the Pathfinder Force as one of the founder units.

Holden concluded his tour on a total of thirty-two operations, and was posted to the Heavy Conversion Flight at Linton-on-Ouse on the 18th of August. Here he remained until December, when he was detached to Upavon, before progressing to Marston Moor, Leeming and Pocklington progressively in the role of instructor. At Pocklington, and now in the rank of Squadron Leader, he was put in charge of the Conversion Flight of 405 Squadron, a Canadian unit commanded by W/C Johnny Fauquier. While there, Holden flew on the second thousand bomber raid against Essen on the 1/2nd of June 1942, and the third and final one on Bremen on the 25/26th, his thirty-third and thirty-fourth sorties. In July he was posted to 158 Squadron's Conversion Flight at East Moor, where he remained until the 25th of October. In the early hours of the previous day, 102 Squadron's commanding officer, W/C Bintley, had been killed in a freak accident on the runway at Holme-on-Spalding-Moor on return from Genoa, when another Halifax had crushed his cockpit on landing. Holden was posted in as his replacement on the 25th, and began a successful period of command, during which he operated a further eleven times, bringing his tally to forty-five. He was rested again on the 20th of April 1943, and thereafter seemed to kick his heels somewhat until the call came through from 617 Squadron.

Although on the face of it straight out of the Gibson mould, Holden did not have his predecessor's leadership qualities and presence. He cut an unimposing figure, was given to acts of arrogance, and was not at all popular. On the 4th of July, two days after his arrival at Scampton, he was taken up by Martin in EE148 for a local familiarization trip, and the two paired up again on the following two days. On the 7th Holden flew with Gibson's Dams crew, and although he names the individual officers in his logbook, there is a Gibsonesque omission of Pulford's name, and for that matter, any other NCO flight engineer.

The second of the current series of heavy attacks on Cologne took place on the night of the 3/4th, when a further 2,200 houses were reduced to rubble. An all Lancaster force completed the carnage on the 8/9th, when almost 2,400 houses and apartment blocks were levelled. When the smoke had cleared and the dust settled, the city authorities were able to establish that these three raids had destroyed eleven thousand buildings, killed 5,500 people, and rendered a further 350,000 homeless. The combined cost to the Command had been sixty-two aircraft, which, at an average of twenty-one per operation, compared more than favourably with recent experiences. Another failure took place at Gelsenkirchen on the 9/10th, and although two more operations to the region would be undertaken at the end of the month, the Ruhr offensive had now effectively run its course. Harris could look back over the past five months with genuine satisfaction at the performance of his squadrons, but would derive his greatest pleasure from the success of Oboe, which had proved to be crucial to the outcome.

617 Squadron, meanwhile, had conducted no operations since the Dams. This period of inactivity came to an end on the 15th, when twelve crews were briefed for targets in Italy, which was now teetering on the brink of capitulation. The 617 Squadron elements were to be accompanied by twelve other aircraft from the Group. Two targets were to be attacked, at Aquata Scrivia and San Polo d'Enza, both of them electrical transformer stations. Assigned to the former were S/L Holden in EE931, F/L Allsebrook in ED999, still carrying 49 Squadron codes, F/L Wilson in EE197, P/O Brown in EE185, P/O Townsend in DV178, and P/O Clayton in JA703, which was still bearing 44 Squadron markings. S/L Maltby headed the second element in EE130, along with F/L Martin in EE144, F/L McCarthy in EE148, F/L Munro in EE150, P/O Divall in EE146, and P/O Rice in W5008, which was wearing a 57 Squadron code. The crews were all airborne shortly before 22.30 hours, and it was more than five hours later that the attacks were carried out, before flying on to land at Blida in North Africa. A number of crews reported fires and blue flashes at the targets, but visibility had been a problem, and the results of the raid were inconclusive. The crews remained at Blida until the evening of the 24th, when they all took off to return home, bombing the docks at Leghorn on the way.

It was on this night that Harris launched the first round of Operation Gomorrah, a short, sharp series of operations against Hamburg, designed to send shock waves resounding around the Reich. A force of almost eight hundred aircraft took off, carrying for the first time thousands of bundles of Window, the tinfoil-backed strips of paper designed to blind the enemy night fighter, searchlight and gun-laying radar, by swamping it with false returns. The device had actually been available for twelve months, but its use had been vetoed by the War Cabinet, lest the enemy copy it. The enemy, as it happened, already had its own version known as Düppel, and this had also been withheld for the same reason. The effects of Window were made apparent by the few combats taking place during the outward flight, and although a number of aircraft were shot down at this stage, they were invariably off course, and outside of the protection of the bomber stream. Once in the target area, it was noted that the usually efficient co-ordination between the searchlight and flak batteries was absent, and defence from the ground was, at best, random. The Pathfinder marking was slightly misplaced, and a pronounced creep-back developed, which cut a swathe of destruction from the city centre, north-westwards along the line of approach, and out into open country, where a proportion of the bombing was wasted. Fifteen hundred people died under the bombs, and the destruction inflicted represented an encouraging start to the campaign. Perhaps of greater significance, was the loss of just twelve aircraft, a clear sign of the efficacy of Window. On the following night, Harris switched his force to Essen, to take advantage of the body blow dealt to the enemy's defensive system by Window. This was another outstandingly accurate attack, which destroyed almost three thousand houses, and inflicted the greatest damage of the war on the Krupps complex.

F/L Youseman was posted to 617 Squadron from 214 Squadron, a Stirling unit, on the 26th, and a number of his former colleagues followed to make up his crew. Gibson went to London on temporary duty on the following day, and Holden assumed command in his absence. That night, almost eight hundred aircraft took off to return to Hamburg, and what followed their arrival over Germany's Second City was both unprecedented and unforeseeable, and the result of a conspiracy of circumstances. A period of unusually hot and dry weather had left tinderbox conditions within the city, and the initial spark to ignite it came with the Pathfinder markers. These fell two miles to the east of the intended city centre aiming point, but with great concentration into the densely populated working class residential districts of Hamm, Hammerbrook and Borgfeld. The main force followed up with unaccustomed accuracy and scarcely any creep-back, and deposited much of its 2,300 tons of bombs into this relatively compact area. The individual fires joined together to form one giant conflagration, which sucked in oxygen at hurricane speed from surrounding areas to feed its voracious appetite. Such was the force of this meteorological event that trees were uprooted and flung bodily into the flames, along with debris and people, and temperatures at its seat exceeded one thousand degrees Celsius. The inferno only subsided when all the combustible material had been consumed, by which time there was no one within the firestorm area to rescue. Forty thousand people perished on this one night alone, and on the following morning, the first of an eventual 1.2 million people began to file out of the city.

On the 29th, nine crews were briefed for a special leaflet drop over four cities in northern Italy. Assigned to Milan were S/L Maltby in EE146, F/L Kellaway in JA894, P/O Divall in W4822 and F/L McCarthy in EE148. Bologna was the destination for F/L Shannon in ED763, Turin for P/O Rice in ED305 and F/O Knight in JA703, and Genoa for A/W/C Holden in EE150, and F/L Munro in W4358. McCarthy was unable to locate Bologna, and dropped his nickels over Milan instead, after which he and the others flew on to Blida without incident. While this was in progress, over seven hundred aircraft were returning to Hamburg to deliver the third raid of the series on this tortured city. The marking was again misplaced, and this time a creep-back developed, which fell partly across the already devastated firestorm area, before hitting other residential districts to the north. Further massive damage was inflicted, and in a sign that the Luftwaffe was beginning to recover from the chaos caused by Window, the losses on this night amounted to twenty eight aircraft. On the following night, Remscheid was decimated by a force of only moderate proportions, and this operation brought down the final curtain on the Ruhr campaign.

August 1943

The end of the Gibson era came on 3rd August 1943 when he received a posting to join the Prime Minister's party on a tour of Canada. Although his time as squadron commander had been less than five months, he would always be associated with the unit he had moulded.

Seven of the shuttle crews returned from North Africa on the 1st of August, but McCarthy and Munro remained while repairs were carried out on their aircraft, the former arriving home on the 5th, and the latter on the 8th. The end of the Gibson era had come a few days earlier on the 3rd, when he was officially posted from the squadron to join the Prime Minister's party on a trip to Canada, where he would conduct a lecture tour, and W/C Holden was confirmed as his replacement. Two days later ED765 crashed at Ashley Walk bombing range while practicing at low level, and F/L Kellaway and one other sustained serious injuries, which required a lengthy stay in hospital. Having completed the series against Hamburg on the 2/3rd, an operation which was ruined by adverse weather during the outward flight, it was now the turn of the rest of the heavy brigade to traverse the Alps to Italy. This was to be the final fling against its major cities to consolidate its imminent capitulation. 1, 5 and 8 Groups opened proceedings on the 7/8th at Genoa, Milan and Turin, and the same two cities jointly or individually hosted further raids on the 12/13th, 14/15th, 15/16th and 16/17th. Earlier, Mannheim and Nuremberg had been targeted to good effect on consecutive nights on the 9th and 10th. Since the start of hostilities, intelligence had filtered through concerning German research into rocket technology. Gradually, through interception and decoding of signals, and then through photographic reconnaissance, it became clear that this activity was centred on Peenemünde, a highly secret establishment on the island of Usedom off the Baltic coast. Churchill's chief scientific adviser, Professor Lindemann, or Lord Cherwell, as he became, steadfastly refused to give credence to the feasibility of such weapons, and even remained unmoved when confronted with a photograph of a V-2 at Peenemünde taken by a PRU Mosquito as recently as June. It took the combined urgings of Duncan Sandys and the brilliant scientist, Dr R V Jones, to convince Churchill of the threat, and at last, an operation was ordered for the first available opportunity. This arose on the night of the 17/18th of August, for which a complex plan was prepared.

The overall operation was to be controlled by a Master of Ceremonies in the manner of Gibson at the Dams, and the officer selected was G/C Searby of 83 Squadron, who had posted to the Pathfinders only a few months after stepping into Gibson's shoes at 106 Squadron. Three aiming points were to be attacked, the workers' housing estate, the factory and the experimental site, each assigned to a specific wave of bombers, respectively 3 and 4 Groups, 1 Group and 5 and 6 Groups, with the Pathfinders responsible for shifting the point of aim accordingly. 597 aircraft were made available, the numbers somewhat depleted by the late arrival at their stations of a proportion of the Stirling force, which had been diverted on return from Italy the night before, and could not be made ready in time. A spoof operation by Mosquitos of 139 Squadron was laid on at Berlin to draw off the night fighters, and this was led by the former 49 Squadron commanding officer, G/C Slee. The operation began inauspiciously, when the initial markers intended for the housing estate fell more than a mile beyond, and onto the forced workers camp at Trassenheide. These inevitably attracted a proportion of the bombs, and heavy casualties were sustained by the friendly foreign nationals who were trapped inside their wooden barracks. Once rectified, the operation proceeded more or less according to plan, but when the night fighters belatedly arrived from Berlin, they took a heavy toll of bombers, both in the skies over Peenemünde, and on the route home towards Denmark. It was predominantly 5 and 6 Group aircraft in the target area at the time, and twenty nine of the forty missing aircraft belonged to them. While not totally successful, the operation caused sufficient damage to set the development programme of the V-2 back by a number of weeks, and to send the production of secret weapons underground.

Harris had long believed that Berlin, as the seat and the symbol of Nazi power, held the key to ultimate victory. Having personally witnessed the carnage of trench warfare twenty five years earlier, he believed that he could avoid a repeat, and win the war by bombing alone. The destruction of Berlin, in his opinion, would bring this about by destroying the morale of the civilian population, who would, according to the theory, lobby their leaders to sue for peace. Harris embarked on the opening phase of his campaign against the Capital on the night of the 23/24th, for which over seven hundred aircraft were despatched. Despite the markers falling onto the southern outskirts of the city, the raid developed into the most damaging yet on Berlin, with over 2,600 buildings destroyed or seriously damaged. Residential districts were those hardest hit, but industry also sustained damage, and more than eight hundred people lost their lives. The flak and night fighter defences were extremely spirited, however, and a new record of fifty-six aircraft failed to return home. F/L D J Wilson was posted to 617 Squadron on the 27th, not to be confused with F/L H S Wilson, who had trained for Operation Chastise, but missed out. A raid on Nuremberg that night resulted in most of the bombing finding open country, and this demonstrated, that operations beyond the range of Oboe were still something of a lottery.

Later, on the 28th, 57 Squadron moved out of Scampton, and took up residence at East Kirkby. On the 30th, 617 Squadron also departed the station with which it will always be synonymous, and moved to Coningsby, after which, Scampton became non-operational, while concrete runways were laid. When it was returned to active duties it was as a 1 Group station. That night, the twin towns of Mönchengladbach and Rheydt were subjected to a ferocious attack by over six hundred aircraft, which destroyed a total of 2,300 buildings. Twenty four hours later, six hundred aircraft returned to Berlin, and the Pathfinders again failed to mark the centre of the city. The markers fell well to the south, and most of the bombing undershot by up to thirty miles, a disappointment which was compounded by the loss of forty seven aircraft.

September 1943

It was an all Lancaster heavy force which conducted the final raid against the 'Big City' in the current phase on the 3/4th of September. The attack again suffered from undershooting, but a number of residential districts were hit, and some war industry factories in the Siemensstadt area suffered loss of production. It had been a costly and only partially effective series, but some compensation was gained on the 5/6th, when the twin cities of Mannheim and Ludwigshafen were the objectives. The marking was accurately placed in the eastern half of Mannheim, so that the creep-back along the line of approach would spread westwards across the city and over the Rhine into Ludwigshafen. Catastrophic damage was caused at the former, while almost two thousand fires in the latter contributed to the destruction of over a thousand houses. Later that day, six Mosquitos arrived at Coningsby, three each from 418 and 605 Squadrons of Fighter Command, to begin training in co-operation with elements of 617 Squadron, in preparation for an operation later in the month. Almost four hundred aircraft carried out an inconclusive attack on Munich that night, and this was followed by a period of minor operations and stand-down.

Finally, on the 14th, eight crews were briefed for an attack that night on the Dortmund-Ems Canal, a target with a strong 5 Group association since 1940. The first attempts to disrupt this very important component of the German communications system took place in June of that year, just before the fall of France. The point chosen for these early attacks by Hampdens was near Ladbergen, where twin aqueducts, one old and the other newer, carried the waterway over the River Glane, just west of the town. The vulnerability of these raised sections made them the favoured target, along with one on the nearby Mittelland Canal at the point where it crossed the Ibbenbürener Aa River. The rivers passed beneath the canals through large concrete tunnels known in German as a Durchlass, literally let-through or underpass. The 5 Group Operation Order B66 ran to four pages, and was dated the 10th of September 1943. It began with an assessment, that the recent devastation inflicted upon the Ruhr had placed great strains on the transport arteries of north-western Germany, and that an interruption of the water communications connecting the Ruhr to central Germany and the northern ports would further immobilize the region. It identified the Dortmund-Ems Canal as currently the most important inland waterway, and that damage to it would force traffic to be diverted to an already overburdened railway network.

The Operation Order reiterated the vulnerability of the sections contained within the raised banks carrying the canal across low-lying land, and specified the earthen banks south of the twin aqueducts near Greven as the objective. The operation would be carried out by two sections, each of four Lancasters and three Mosquitos, which would proceed to the target in formation by different routes. They were to cross the English coast at 1,500 feet before descending to low level over the North Sea. The Lancasters' Aneroid altimeters were to be set to one hundred feet, and checked by means of the spotlight altimeters as employed during Operation Chastise. Section I was to climb to 1,500 feet four minutes before reaching the Dutch coast to establish its position, and then shallow-dive back to 150 feet. Section II was to rely on a Gee fix to find its planned point to cross the enemy coast. Nine gunners had been posted in on the 10th from 44, 49, 50 and 106 Squadrons and 1660CU for this low level operation, so that all three gun turrets could be occupied throughout. The squadron was to carry the 12,000lb light case bomb for the first time, (not to be confused with the 12,000lb Tallboy of 1944). This was not simply three 4,000lb cookies bolted together, but an entirely new weapon with a larger girth. This would be only the second operation for 617 Squadron over Germany.

The aircraft got away in two sections of four without incident, and set out on their designated courses with the intention of rendezvousing shortly before reaching the target. However, at 00.40 hours, while

A view of the Dortmund-Ems Canal in pristine condition in 1943.

The twin aqueduct section south of Ladbergen, with the camouflaged River Glane passing beneath extreme right.

they were still over the North Sea, a recall signal was sent, following a report from a weather Mosquito of poor conditions in the target area. During the process of turning his heavily laden Lancaster back towards England, Maltby appeared to lose control of JA981, possibly through hitting a slipstream or making contact with the surface of the sea, and the aircraft cartwheeled in, with the loss of all on board. Shannon circled the spot for over two hours, directing the air-sea rescue operation, but no one could be saved. Maltby's was the only body to eventually come ashore, and he lies buried in the village cemetery at Wickhambreaux in Kent. Research by Len Cairns in recent years suggests that Maltby's loss may well have been the result of a collision with a 139 Squadron Mosquito returning from Berlin. DZ598 was lost without trace with the crew of F/L Colledge and F/O Marshall, and could well have been in the same piece of sky as Maltby at that precise moment. This would account for the explosion mentioned on the accident card for this incident, which states, that the aircraft was lost when it hit the sea *"after some obscure explosion and a fire had occurred in the aircraft. It is possible that the pilot partially lost control in a turn……explosion may have been caused by bouncing on the water…… none of the equipment is likely to have exploded in the air."* It also makes the point, that the large bomb doors fitted to accommodate the 12,000 pounder affected the aircraft's stability when lowered.

On the following night, the operation was rescheduled, with Martin taking the place of Maltby. Crew captains and aircraft were; W/C Holden in EE144, F/L Knight in JB144, F/L Allsebrook in EE130, F/L Shannon in EE146, F/L Wilson in JA848, F/L Martin in EE150, P/O Divall in JA874 and P/O Rice in EE131. The route to the target for Holden's formation was almost identical to that of the second wave for Operation Chastise in its initial stages. After taking off they were to adopt a course slightly south of east across the North Sea to Vlieland, some 218 miles and seventy-eight minutes flying time from Coningsby, and then turn onto a south-easterly heading to take them over the Waddenzee and the Ijsselmeer to Stavoren. From here the course deviated from the Chastise route by passing over the Ketelmeer, a small body of water branching inland from the eastern shore of the Ijsselmeer a little to the north of Elburg, and then turning east until reaching the village of Gramsbergen. Here, the formation was to swing to starboard to take up a south-easterly course again, which took it across the frontier into Germany, thereafter proceeding past Nordhorn and continuing on to Wettringen just west of the target, where the intention was to rendezvous with Allsebrook's formation. Allsebrook's route crossed the Dutch coast at a point roughly a third of the way between Den Helder and Egmond, and reached the western shore of the Ijsselmeer near Hoorn. The route then converged on Holden's to cross the eastern shore of the Ijsselmeer at Elburg, remaining thereafter on a more or less parallel course a few miles to the south until just beyond Den Ham, from where it headed directly for Wettringen and the rendezvous. The different routes meant that Section II under Allsebrook would arrive first, and it was his responsibility to drop parachute beacons, or, if they failed, incendiary bombs, at a datum point and two other nearby locations. A decoy beacon was also to be dropped ten to fifteen miles north of the target, and this may have some significance in view of the way in which the operation unfolded.

The force leader, Holden, was to attack first, aiming his bomb within forty feet of the western bank, and then direct the attacks of the others. If his bomb failed to cause a breach, the next in line should attempt to hit the same spot. Once a breach had been confirmed successive aircraft were to deliver their bombs alternately against the western and eastern banks at fifty yard intervals to the north. All attacks were to be carried out from 150 feet at a ground speed of 180 miles per hour, and the 26-90 second fuse would allow aircraft to be clear of the detonation of their bomb. The force leader was to ensure that a minimum of two minutes was allowed between attacks.

Having left Coningsby within a few minutes of each other around midnight and formed up, the four Lancasters of Holden's section dropped down to fifty feet over the sea, and reached Vlieland at 01.15,

giving an average cruising speed of around 170 mph. They climbed to 2,000 feet to get their bearings as they crossed the Dutch coast, before immediately returning to rooftop height. Eleven minutes and thirty-one miles later they arrived at the pinpoint at Stavoren and headed for the Ketelmeer twenty-eight miles and ten minutes further on. The pinpoint at the village of Gramsbergen was reached at 01.48 after a further thirty-five miles, leaving forty miles and fourteen minutes flying time to the rendezvous point at Wettringen. They crossed the Dutch/German frontier with the section of four intact, presumably having navigated accurately up to this point in good weather conditions. It was during this leg that W/C Holden led his formation directly across the small town of Nordhorn some twenty miles and seven minutes further on from Gramsbergen. In their path close to the town centre lay a church and steeple, which, rather than skirting, Holden chose to climb over at around three hundred feet.

Tracer was observed to emanate from the ground from the starboard flank, and EE144 was hit in the starboard inner fuel tank, causing an instant fierce fire to erupt. According to Bob Kellow in Knight's Lancaster, the flak battery was in the grounds of the church, but it was, in fact, on a sports ground

S/Ldr Micky Martin's temporary stint as Squadron Commander did not stand in the way of his continued operational sorties. Martin was ultimately to reach the rank of Air Marshal in the post-war RAF (Crown).

on the edge of the town. Both Kellow and Martin testified that Holden's Lancaster trailed a long ribbon of flame until the tank blew up, causing the aircraft to veer sharply to the left, roll and dive straight down, narrowly missing Knight and Wilson as they broke outwards and upwards to avoid a collision and the anticipated explosion of the 12,000 pounder. The Lancaster struck the ground adjacent to a farmhouse owned by the Hood family, who, on hearing the sound of oncoming aircraft, had taken refuge in their cellar. On board the Lancaster with Holden were Taerum, Spafford, Hutchison and Deering of Gibson's Dams crew, and Powell of Townsend's, plus the mid-upper and rear gunners, F/O Pringle and P/O Meikle. All were initially interred in the Neuer Friedhof cemetery at Lingen, although, it is believed that only Holden and Deering were positively identified. After the war their remains were taken to the Reichswald Commonwealth War Graves cemetery.

Jan and Teupe Hood had seven children, and six of them were at home that night. They all survived the crash within yards of their home, and it was then that the parents went back up into the house to collect additional clothing for the children, so that they could remain in the cellar for the rest of the night. It was as they were preparing to re-enter the cellar that the bomb exploded, having cooked in the fire. The farm house, which had recently been rebuilt after being severely damaged by a bomb blast in 1942, was ripped apart, and when daylight arrived the body of Teupe Hood was discovered in the rubble. The house was totally destroyed, and Jan Hood was hospitalized for a month, which left him unable to attend his wife's funeral.

In this previously-unpublished photograph, Holden's Lancaster EE144 AJ-S lies shattered where it crashed on the outskirts of Nordhorn (by kind permission of Willi Vrielink).

After the formation had passed beyond Nordhorn, Martin described the fog coming down like a wall. They turned earlier than intended, before reaching Wettringen, when the flare path of an airfield, possibly Handorf, was spotted directly ahead. Martin assessed the visibility at this stage as five hundred yards. Had they continued on to the proposed rendezvous with Allsebrook's section at Wettringen, they would then have been eighteen miles and six minutes flying time from the target, which would have lain on an east-south-easterly course. However, this deviation from the planned route took the three Lancasters into the defences of the town of Rheine, which they twice tried to break through, but were forced to pull away and orbit. Finally, Martin led his section round the town on its northern side, thus putting them about ten miles to the north of the target. It was shortly afterwards that Martin lost visual contact with Knight, and became convinced that his friend and fellow countryman had been brought down by the flak from Rheine. The weather was continuing to deteriorate, forcing the crews to stumble around blindly to find a reference on the ground, and Martin guessed that they had probably crossed their pinpoints without knowing.

The beacons dropped at the datum point appear to have been inconspicuous, and it seems that incendiaries were employed. As Les Knight approached the target from the west, having seemingly established its whereabouts, he turned to port to begin flying a box circuit, or one-minute square, as briefed, while awaiting further instructions from Allsebrook. The square required Knight to fly north for one minute, then east, south and west for an equal time, theoretically to arrive back at his starting point. There was apparently some concern about getting too close to the aircraft in front, presumably that containing Martin and crew, which had either been observed visually or at least perceived by its tell-tale slipstream, and Knight decided to lengthen the first and third sides of the square. At the end of the first circuit the canal was not where it was supposed to be, suggesting that they had lost their bearings slightly. During the course of the second orbit, Knight's crew heard Allsebrook direct two other crews, it is believed those of Wilson and Divall, to carry out their attacks. According to an account written by Piet Meijer, "Obie" O'Brien then watched from his vantage point in Knight's rear turret as Wilson's Lancaster sustained flak hits at about this time and crashed in flames next to the canal, and he reported this to the rest of the crew over the intercom. This provides us with a picture of the three Lancasters of Martin's section following in each other's wake, with Martin in the lead, Knight next and Wilson bringing up the rear, although Martin was clearly not aware of Knight's close proximity.

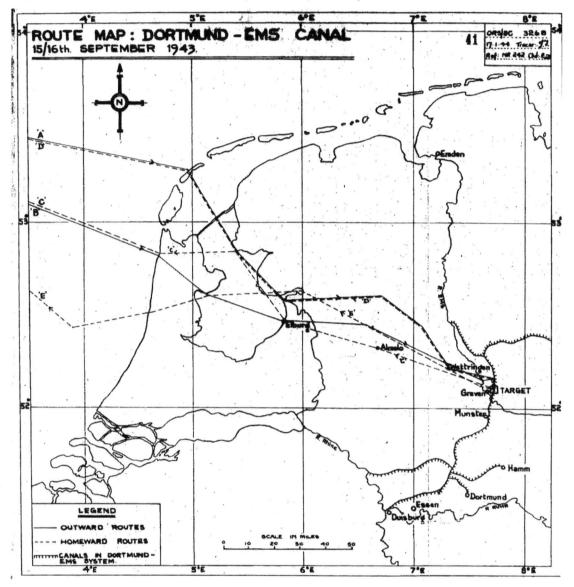

The outward and homeward routes of the Dortmund-Ems Canal raid on 15/16th September. This map is from the original Night Raid Report and shows the complicated routing involved (TNA).

Knight was about to embark on a third orbit, when, according to flight engineer Ray Grayston, someone called "You're too high!" Apparently Knight instinctively pushed the nose down, and almost immediately the Lancaster was rocked by an impact of some sort. After the crew members had regained their composure, "Doc" Sutherland reported from the mid-upper turret that he had seen trees emerge through the swirling mist atop high ground, but had not been able to shout a warning in time. Another member of the crew also believed he had glimpsed one of the beacons or an incendiary at the same moment. Grayston reported rising temperatures on both port engines, which had branches and foliage stuffed in their radiators and soon began to smoke. Knight ordered them to be shut down, and apparently attempted to contact Allsebrook, as the raid controller, for permission to jettison the bomb. As a new weapon, it was undesirable to allow it to fall intact into enemy hands. However, to jettison it live meant exposing Knight and his crew to the risk of destruction in the ensuing blast wave. The safe height in the case of the much smaller 4,000lb cookie was four thousand feet, and clearly, substantially more height would be required for a bomb three times more powerful. There was absolutely no possibility of Knight dragging his wounded Lancaster to a safe altitude, and so he followed protocol by seeking permission from higher authority to let it go unfused, knowing that the enemy would recover it.

In the event, Knight was unable to raise Allsebrook, and turned instead to Martin, his section leader. It has always been assumed, that Knight failed to contact Allsebrook, because Allsebrook and his crew were already dead by this time, and one of the challenges of recording the events of this night is to establish their sequence and timing, particularly with regard to Allsebrook's fate. Let us, therefore, return to Martin's post raid account to attempt to unravel part of the mystery surrounding the time of Allsebrook's loss. Martin states, that five to ten minutes after clearing Rheine, Knight called him up to report that he had lost two engines, and could he have permission to jettison his bomb? Martin replied, "OK, jettison. Good Luck." Martin does not say he heard Knight try to call up Allsebrook first, but does assert, that he heard Allsebrook add his own good luck wishes to Knight, proving that Allsebrook was still alive at this time. We will return later to Knight and his crew, and pick up the story again after his request to jettison the bomb.

As already mentioned, the destruction of F/L Wilson's Lancaster had been witnessed by Knight's rear gunner. Wilson and crew were squadron founder members, and among the first crews to be posted in to 617 Squadron, but they had missed Operation Chastise through a lack of serviceable aircraft and possibly illness. They were all killed when they fell victim to light flak in the manner described above by O'Brien. Two German sources, a local resident and a book detailing the history of Ladbergen, reveal the circumstances of his loss and, in so doing, confirm O'Brien's account. On page 213 of the latter, entitled Land und Lüe, Beiträge zur Heimatgeschichte by Heinrich Stork (Land and lore, contributions to local history), we find the following insight. *For the protection of the Canal a 3.7cm flak battery was established at the start of the war, and between March 1943 and June 1944 it was strengthened by a trained Ladbergen home defence unit (consisting of Hitler youth). On 16.9.43 the aqueduct again became the target for an English special squadron....Although the flak was forbidden to open fire on this day, because of operations over England by Luftwaffe aircraft from (nearby) Handorf, when a fourth approach was made on the aqueduct from such a low level that the aircraft's national markings were identifiable, the battery commander gave the order to fire. After several direct hits the aircraft crashed close to the Canal with the 5 ton special bomb on board, and exploded.*

Herr Wibbeler was a twenty-one year old soldier at the time, at home on leave from the east, and he confirmed this account in a hand-written note sent to Andreas. It translates as follows. *The aircraft was well illuminated (by two converging searchlights), and flew at low level over our farmhouse. It came down about three hundred metres further on. My father and I went to within about eighty metres of the aircraft, which was ablaze. The flames were a couple of metres high and the ammunition was exploding. About fifteen minutes elapsed between the crash and the explosion. The alleged cries for help* (as mentioned in Alan Cooper's book, From the Dams to the Tirpitz) *emanated from my anxious mother, and not from the crew.* Herr Wibbeler confirmed this account in person to me as we stood on the crash site in May 2002.

To these two accounts was added a November 1944 target photograph contributed by Herr Wibbeler, upon which he kindly marked three reference points; a line of trees clipped by the Lancaster, his house, and the crash site, and these enable us to piece together the events of the loss of JA898 KC-X, and the precise location. Wilson had clearly identified the target area, and his was one of the Lancasters passing over the aiming point on a north to south heading. One can imagine the frustration of the battery commander as each of these four passes was made over or close to his position, providing him with ample opportunity to anticipate the line of approach, and it was Wilson's misfortune to be the one that finally tempted him, the only adult member of the unit, to disobey orders and open fire, for which he would later be reprimanded. Searchlight beams suddenly sprang into life ensnaring the Lancaster, which was hit several times and immediately caught fire. It then clipped a line of trees forming a right angle with the eastern bank of the canal at the southern end of the twin aqueduct section, and about a hundred yards after the point at which they merged into a single channel. Continuing in the same direction it passed over the Wibbeler homestead a few hundred yards further on, having to climb to clear the roof, before crashing at around 02.12 a field's width from the canal with the bomb still on board. Just like Holden's bomb, it took around fifteen minutes cooking time before it eventually exploded. A row of houses on the far side of the narrow lane bordering the field sustained heavy damage to roofs and windows from the bomb blast, and one house, according to Herr Wibbeler, actually burned down completely. With Holden and Wilson gone, and Knight out of the picture, Martin was now the sole survivor of the first formation, and we will leave him temporarily as he searches for the aiming point.

Let us now focus on Allsebrook's section, which somehow found itself in the region of the Mittelland Canal. Quite how they all came to be so far north of where they should have been is not immediately apparent, although one of them would have been there legitimately to deliver the decoy beacon. In order to accurately interpret the course of events on this night, it is important to understand the geographical situation, and how it might have appeared to those of Allsebrook's section as they glimpsed the ground briefly and intermittently while searching for their target. The Mittelland Canal approaches the region from the east, although by no means in a straight line, and curves sharply towards the south as it enters the target area. It doglegs to the west immediately north of Gravenhorst, where it crosses the River Aa, before feeding into the Wet Triangle, almost on a due south heading. The Wet Triangle, das Nasse Dreieck, is the meeting point for two major waterways, and it acted then, like today, as a passing zone and a harbour for the canal traffic. During the war it contained typical port installations, like cranes for the loading and unloading of stores, equipment and provisions, and there were also storage facilities for coal. The Dortmund-Ems Canal approaches it from the south, heading almost due north, before veering north-northwest, and then curving onto a westerly heading to feed into it. It leaves the Triangle at its most westerly point, and continues in that general direction.

It is possible, that any of these waterways could be mistaken for the intended target a few miles to the south of Ladbergen, although the compass heading available to the pilot and navigator should have been sufficient to prevent such a misinterpretation. Certainly, though, the latticework of rivers, canals and water junctions in such a small area would have made identification of a precise aiming point from low level in darkness an absolute nightmare even in favourable conditions, let alone in those faced by the crews on this night. What seems to be the case, particularly in view of German timings, is that Allsebrook's section arrived, as planned, in the target area in advance of Martin's, partly because his briefed course was more direct than Martin's, and because it would have been made even more direct if they, like Martin, turned earlier than intended towards the east. A plausible scenario is, that in the prevailing conditions, Allsebrook decided to straighten his track and pass north of Rheine, putting his section ahead

Trees hit by Wilson's Lancaster.

The wreckage of Wilson's Lancaster.

of schedule, possibly having also spotted the airfield flare path close to his briefed route. The defences would have been alerted to the presence of enemy aircraft, but might not have opened up because of the Luftwaffe operations already described. However, on hearing the approach of Martin's section, the defenders then decided to try their luck, and in negotiating his passage round the town, Martin delayed the arrival of his formation in the target area, putting them behind schedule, and increasing the gap between himself and Allsebrook. This is an important fact in establishing a sequence of events to correlate with the German timing of the start of the raid and the loss of Allsebrook. Meanwhile, Allsebrook's new course would have brought him directly over the intersection of the Dortmund-Ems and Mittelland Canals and the nearby River Aa, and he began his search for the target in this area.

We do not know the precise sequence of events, only that Allsebrook and his crew met their end at the point where the Dortmund-Ems and Mittelland Canals join at Bergeshövede in the Wet Triangle. The basin is bordered on its north-eastern quadrant by a chain of hills bisected by the Mittelland Canal. A light flak emplacement and searchlight had been installed in a field beyond the north-facing side of the hill known as the Huckberg on the canal's western bank, and the platoon leader was the husband of the late Frau Erika Kaiser, who lived in the same house on the quayside at Bergeshövede until her death. She was an eyewitness to the recovery of Allsebrook's Lancaster, and she provided the photographs of the event, one of which she appears in. There was also a flak tower in Bergeshövede itself, right on the edge of the Wet Triangle. Frau Kaiser was told, that the bomber had been caught by three searchlights, was on fire, and had lost part of a wing to anti-aircraft fire from one or perhaps both of the above-mentioned positions. It cleared the Huckberg with inches to spare, but was no longer able to fly, and clipped the roof of the end house on the quayside at the south-facing foot of the hill, before colliding with a crane, which toppled over into the water. The Lancaster then flipped onto its back and plunged inverted into the harbour basin at around 02.20. An eyewitness described the burning wreckage slowly rising and falling until finally settling on the bottom, blocking the lock gates. A report written later on the 16th to the head of the Tecklenburg local authority and marked as only for official service use states the following. *Further to the telephone report of earlier today, I now confirm the details on the official proforma. The aircraft was shot down shortly before 4 o'clock, and landed by the small lock in the Dortmund-Ems Canal. More precise information cannot yet be established as the aircraft is lying completely in the water and only two wheels are visible.*

The wreckage was recovered and loaded onto barges on the following day, and, according to some reports, Allsebrook was found strapped in his seat, his hands firmly grasping the control column. However, an article written in 1999 for the local magazine celebrating a hundred years of the Dortmund-Ems Canal states that onlookers were horrified to discover that some members of the crew had been decapitated by the collision with the crane. Another report written on the day of the crash suggests that seven bodies were recovered intact, and that, of the eighth, a leg, ears and pieces of a skull were found floating on the surface of the water. It is quite possible that body parts were recovered from the water, particularly if the cockpit itself came into contact with the crane. The crane was later dragged out of the basin, found to be undamaged, and was put back on its rails and returned to use. A different report has most of the crew as unidentifiable. A more reliable source, though, is the graves register for this crew, which shows five members identified and buried individually, while Phillip Moore, and the rear and mid-upper gunners were initially interred in a joint grave.

The crane hit by Allsebrook's aircraft.

Allsebrook's Lancaster being raised from the water onto a barge.

The satisfaction of the victor is evident from the pose of this German officer standing next to the wreckage of Allsebrook's aircraft.

The flak crew in front of their tower at Nordhorn.

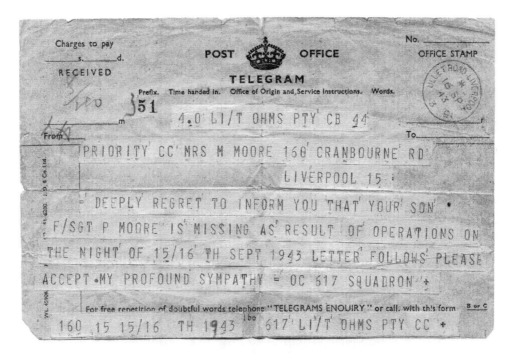

The telegram notifying Phillip Moore's mother of his loss. Such messages were the standard way of delivering the devastating news (Sandra Murphy).

The communal grave for Flight Sergeants Walker, Hitchen and Moore (Sandra Murphy).

What is not in question is the fact that the bomb was not on board the Lancaster at the time of the crash. Precisely what happened to it, though, is less certain. It is possible that Allsebrook intended to drop his bomb on the Durchlass, or underpass, carrying the Ibbenbürener Aa River under the Mittelland Canal at Gravenhorst. The Aa is a smallish river, which, in the conditions, might easily have been mistaken for the aqueduct section of the Dortmund-Ems Canal as it crossed the River Glane between Greven and Ladbergen. On the other hand, and this is equally possible, he jettisoned the 12,000 pounder after being snared by the searchlights and hit by flak. Between November 1944 and February 1945 a number of 5 Group raids on the Mittelland Canal left the Gravenhorst locality in a state of total devastation. The course of the Canal has been altered since the war, but part of the original waterway still exists, and can be traced to the point where it crossed the Aa in 1943. It is northeast of Bergeshövede, and assuming from the events of the final few seconds of Allsebrook's life, that he did, indeed, carry out his attack on a northeast-southwest heading, he would have been instantly in range of the flak battery in the field ahead and to his right. Almost as rapidly he would pass between the hills on either side of the Mittelland Canal, with the Huckberg to his right, exactly at the point where it enters the Wet Triangle, and thus be out of sight of the flak position. In his book, Beyond the Dams to the Tirpitz, Alan Cooper states that Allsebrook called Martin to tell him to hold on a minute, "until I get out of this", possibly referring to the flak or perhaps the low-lying mist. Later still he is said to have reported, that he was returning to base, but this is unconfirmed. The squadron ORB records Allsebrook as carrying out an attack, and this presumably came from other crews during debriefing.

What happened to Allsebrook's bomb? There are no local reports of a huge explosion, and it is inconceivable that it would have gone unnoticed, as there would have been extensive property damage in Gravenhorst. I was fortunate to meet Herr Walter Luth, one of Germany's foremost bomb disposal experts, who has defused many Allied bombs. He alluded to a photo he had seen of an apparent excavation site on one of the canal's banks, which would have been consistent with the unearthing of an unexploded high capacity bomb. He then provided me with a detailed drawing of the very bomb employed by 617 Squadron against the canals on this night. The drawing was made by a German draughtsman shortly after the events here described. Similar in style to the sketch of the Dams bomb produced by the Germans within ten days of that attack, this one of the 12,000 pounder contains the lettering stencilled on the casing, including the date 9/43. The weapon is accurately described, along with its fusing mechanism, and is categorized as "for use at low level against canals, first used 16.9.43." As this ordnance was not employed again until November against the Antheor Viaduct in southern France, and thereafter during December and January against flying bomb sites also in France, it seems likely that the Germans acquired an intact example from the Dortmund-Ems Canal operation. In fact, Allsebrook's was almost certainly one of two examples of the weapon recovered by the Germans on this night. As far as Allsebrook's final moments are concerned, there are two possible scenarios. Firstly, that he jettisoned his bomb in a vain attempt to remain airborne, letting it go "safe" in case it detonated on impact and engulfed the low flying, already damaged Lancaster in its massive shock wave. Secondly, that he did carry out an attack on the banks of the Mittelland Canal, but the bomb failed to detonate. Of course, both offerings are conjecture, and we will never know the truth.

Now let us return to Knight immediately after he had dutifully obtained permission from Martin to jettison his bomb. All Knight could manage on two good engines was a paltry twelve hundred feet, and the aircraft leapt as the massive bulk of the 12,000 pounder fell away in safe condition. According to Martin, three or four minutes elapsed between Knight's request to jettison his bomb and his announcement, "I have successfully jettisoned, and am endeavouring to return to base." Martin heard other pilots wish Knight good luck, and even fellow Australian, F/O Charlie Scherf, chipped in, while flying above in his 418 Squadron Mosquito. Now, as the temperature of the starboard-inner engine began to climb, and they headed west towards the Dutch frontier, Knight ordered everything removable to be thrown out to save weight. He was struggling to keep the aircraft flying straight and level, partly because of the uneven pull of the engines, and partly because of the severe damage to the control surfaces and cables. He called on rear gunner, "Obie" O'Brien, to take up a position in the bomb-aimer's compartment and pull on the starboard rudder pedal to help to ease the pressure on his leg. O'Brien succeeded in doing so, and the Lancaster's nose swung to the right, but it was an intolerable strain also on O'Brien, and he couldn't maintain the pressure for long. One of the port engines was restarted, and seemed to be working, but it soon failed and had to be shut down again. KC-N was now losing height, and as there was no chance of getting home, Knight gave the order to bale out. Someone clipped Knight's chute on as he sat calmly at the controls, and one by one the crew said farewell over the intercom before dropping into the night sky for the very short journey to earth. Such was the pressure required on the yoke and pedals to keep the aircraft upright, that Knight would have known he could not leave his seat, and that his only chance of survival lay in putting the aircraft down under some semblance of control.

During the bale-out procedure, KC-N's path had described a gentle anti-clockwise curve from a south-westerly starting point, and Hobday, Kellow and Johnson left the aircraft as it headed almost due south. By the time that Sutherland and Woollard jumped clear, KC-N was pointing back towards Germany, and was just southwest of the little town of Den Ham. In the few remaining moments left to him, Knight brought the Lancaster over the western edge of the town in what was now a tightening turn to port, and was actually heading a little north of due west as the aircraft, by this time almost totally unfit for flight, clipped trees on the edge of a meadow. This ended all hopes of a controlled forced-landing, and deprived suddenly of its flying speed, the Lancaster plunged nose first into the ground, where the wreckage immediately caught fire. It was 02.46. A mile or two to the northwest his navigator, Bob Kellow, heard the boom of KC-N's end, while he was reeling in the cords of his parachute. The Lancaster had actually come full circle, and was pointing directly at where Kellow was standing as it disintegrated and took Knight's young life. The body of the gallant and highly popular Les Knight was found by local civilians still at the controls, and in defiance of the German authorities they honoured him in a manner befitting his gallantry with a funeral at 18.00 hours that same day.

P/O Divall, who, along with his crew had been the last of the original pre-dams recruits to join the squadron, and who, like Wilson, had missed the dams operation through a lack of serviceable aircraft or illness, was in JA874, and this Lancaster likewise became a victim of the light flak, which was so lethal to low flying heavy bombers. Just as Allsebrook and possibly Rice had done, he was searching an area some distance away to the north of Ladbergen around the Mittelland Canal. Frau Anneliese Brönstrup was ten years old at the time, and lived, as she still did when I spoke to her, in a farmhouse at Steinbeck near the little town of Recke, and right on the north bank of the Canal closest to the point where Divall and his crew perished. She was the only surviving coherent witness to the events, which she heard from the cellar rather than saw, but she was allowed to view one of the bodies on the following morning. This is her story.

An aircraft flew backwards and forwards at low level between Achmer in the east and Bergeshövede in the southwest searching for its target. At each location it ran into flak and eventually made a final approach towards the farmhouse on fire from the general direction of the west. It was on the southern or far side of the canal, and all of the following action took place over a perfectly straight stretch of the waterway of perhaps half a mile between the Kälberberg and Bad Bridges. The aircraft dropped its bomb almost immediately on passing the former, and the weapon landed either in the water or on the towpath. Within seconds of releasing the bomb the aircraft also came down a few hundred yards further along the bank at around 02.15 almost opposite Frau Brönstrup's farmhouse, and was rent by a violent explosion, which flattened the trees lining the canal and flung the rear turret over onto the northern bank with its occupant still inside. The rest of the wreckage was in the water and on the southern bank. When the bomb went up seconds later, its blast also shattered the trees lining the canal, and sent vast quantities of water cascading over the adjacent field, while also causing a collapse of the bank into the water. On the following morning the body of the rear gunner was laid out in the field close to the farmhouse, and apart from a bruise on his forehead, he showed no external sign of injury.

Now we have to interpret these events to piece together the final moments of the crew. Frau Brönstrup speaks of hearing *an* aircraft flying backwards and forwards searching for its target. I believe she probably heard a number of Lancasters, perhaps those of Allsebrook, Divall and Rice, all members of the south-routed and lost second formation. Based on timings examined in detail later in this chapter one can estimate, that aircraft were in the vicinity of the Mittelland Canal and within earshot of Steinbeck for up to roughly twenty-five minutes, culminating in Divall's crash, and this might not have allowed time for a single aircraft to cover the distance repeatedly between Achmer and wherever in search of its aiming point. She might well have heard the drone of Allsebrook's engines, but he flew off to the southwest and was brought down almost immediately some distance away as we have already seen. She may have briefly heard the sound of Shannon's engines, if he were indeed there, before he realised his error and headed south, where he found the correct target area relatively quickly thereafter. We do not know where Rice was at the time, but he probably passed fairly close to Steinbeck at some point. She certainly heard Divall's Lancaster as it flew on fire at very low level towards the farmhouse from the west, appearing to follow the course of the canal. The bomb was dropped on the canal, where we assume it exploded within 26 to 90 seconds.

There is, of course, the question as to whether or not the bomb was delivered, or simply jettisoned live in a last desperate effort to keep the aircraft airborne or in preparation for a forced landing. It must have been apparent to the crew that the Lancaster was finished, and at such low level there was clearly no prospect of them baling out. If the intention had been to jettison the bomb, however, there were plenty of opportunities to do so before the point was reached where it actually fell. There had likewise been many open fields in which to put the Lancaster down under some kind of control. I believe, therefore, that Divall followed the course of the Mittelland Canal, probably at treetop height, and at the point when it became clear to him that the end was at hand, he sought permission from Allsebrook to drop his bomb, and aimed it at the bank as a last resort target. Almost immediately after releasing the weapon the Lancaster crashed further along the southern bank with a violent explosion, killing all on board and flinging the rear turret onto the northern bank to within a few yards of the farmhouse, close to the Bad Bridge. The occupant of the turret was Sgt Daniel Allatson, who had accompanied Brown to the Sorpe Dam in May as a replacement for Brown's own front gunner, who was ill at the time. Divall and his three gunners were the only members of the crew to be positively identified, and all were initially laid to rest in the evangelical cemetery at nearby Bramsche at 16.00 hours on the 18th. The German burial report states that the remains of Divall and two of his unidentified colleagues were interred in one grave, and the other two unidentified men shared another, while the three gunners were given individual graves. After the war their remains were moved to the Commonwealth War Graves Cemetery at Reichswald.

Martin, now, as already stated, the lone survivor of the first section, eventually came upon the Ladbergen stretch of the canal, after initially looking for it ten miles to the north somewhere near the Wet Triangle. Having found it, though, he then experienced the same problems as the others in picking out the aiming point in the conditions. Having declared their position when accounting for Wilson, it was now open season for the flak gunners, and they squirted at Martin every time he came within range, and then gave

Les Knight's Lancaster lies in pieces in this photograph taken by a Dutch person as townsfolk recovered his body for burial in defiance of German regulations.

the same treatment to Shannon when he turned up, he having begun his search some three to four miles to the north. Shannon found that he could only pick up the canal when directly over it at a height of not more than 150 feet, and he eventually released his bomb from that altitude at 02.36. It exploded on the towpath on the eastern bank, and failed to create any breach. Sometime after Shannon had turned for home, Martin called up Rice and told him to abandon his search and return to base, while he continued on alone. It was around forty minutes after Shannon's attack that Martin managed to get a reasonably clear run, after stumbling into searchlights and flak during earlier attempts. In order to make a bombing run Martin needed to meet the canal at the kind of wide angle, which would allow him to turn immediately onto it. The problem was, that like Shannon, he could only catch a glimpse of the water when directly above it, and that was too late for him to make the turn and keep the canal in sight. Finally, he managed to pick it up in such a way as to be able to embark on a timed circuit, which, if judged to perfection, would bring him round exactly onto the track he had been searching for all along. His skill and determination were rewarded as the canal emerged from the mist beneath him and stretched ahead straight and wide, inviting bomb-aimer Bob Hay to press the tit. After a tense moment or two, while the line was adjusted slightly, the 12,000 pounder was dropped from 200 feet, and was seen to explode in the water, apparently without causing damage. Tragically, either Martin's or Shannon's bomb detonated close to a barge carrying ore, killing the Dutch husband and wife crew of Abel and Meetje Stuut from Groningen, who were both just twenty-two years old.

On his way home, according to the ORB, Rice jettisoned his bomb safe in the Waddenzee between the Dutch coast and Terschelling, although in his logbook he cites the Zuider Zee, now known as the Ijsselmeer, as the location. He arrived back at 05.22, having logged a flight of five hours twenty minutes, and Martin touched down a couple of minutes later, reporting the visibility as clearing only once he reached the Zuider Zee. Shannon had been first home, arriving some forty-five minutes before Rice. The Mosquito crews reported reaching the target area shortly before 02.00 hours, and confirmed the poor state of the visibility. F/O Mitchie recorded fairly intense flak, while P/O Woods and F/L Lisson each commented on the searchlight activity as 'little or not troublesome.' For their part, F/Os Scherf and Rowlands each reported being fired upon by flak around the town of Rheine. Only S/L Gibb reported attacking flak positions, and these were around the twin aqueduct section near Ladbergen.

There is now one final mystery to address, a question posed by a Dutch enthusiast some years ago. Did 617 Squadron attack the wrong canal? This arises not out of the bombing of the Mittelland Canal by Divall, but out of the dropping of a large bomb near Denekamp, a small Dutch town about four kilometres southwest of Nordhorn. The Almelo-Nordhorn Canal passes through the centre of Nordhorn, exiting the town at its southern extremity, before arcing towards the west and passing the northern rim of Denekamp. At 04.08 local time, or 03.08 GMT+1 on the 16th of September 1943 a huge bomb, described by residents as an earthquake bomb, exploded in the water close to the canal bank, creating a half-circle crater with a thirty metre diameter and steep sides. The explosion caused serious damage to seven houses and varying degrees of damage to 113 others within a one mile radius. Six people were injured, although none fatally.

There is no doubt what so ever, that this bomb came from a 617 Squadron aircraft, as the only other operation in progress on this night was against a Dunlop Rubber factory in central France. Not only is it highly unlikely that any of the more than three hundred aircraft involved would have strayed over eastern Holland, none of the participants was carrying a 12,000 pounder. The Dutch enthusiast, Jos Knippers, is convinced that the bomb in question was that jettisoned by Knight, but this cannot be the case. The late Ray Grayston, Knight's flight engineer, confirmed to me during an interview that the bomb had been jettisoned safe to prevent its detonation from bringing their crippled Lancaster down. A safe minimum height for the detonation of the much smaller 4,000lb cookie was four thousand feet, and Knight was hovering on the brink of a stall at just a few hundred. Grayston also recalled being interviewed by his German captors, or "goons" as he called them, who questioned him about the bomb they had recovered intact. Although we cannot be absolutely certain whether or not Allsebrook's bomb exploded, it is possible that he flew close to Denekamp on his way to the intended rendezvous much earlier. However, the timings suggest that he and his crew were long dead by the time the Denekamp bomb went off.

Eyewitnesses to the Denekamp incident describe the aircraft as circling a number of times before dropping the bomb, which clearly suggests an attack rather than a jettisoning. If we take into account the approximate time of the crashes of the five Lancasters, those of Holden at 01.55, Wilson at 02.12, Divall at 02.15, Allsebrook at 02.20 and Knight at 02.46, it leaves us with just the three surviving Lancasters as candidates for the Denekamp incident. Shannon recorded the time of his bomb release at 02.36, twenty-two minutes before the explosion at Denekamp, and specified the eastern bank of the waterway as the point of impact. He arrived home at 04.38. The canal at Denekamp has a northern and southern bank, rather than eastern and western, and this would seem to confirm Shannon's account. Martin was within range of ground fire for the duration of his attempt to locate the intended aiming point, and this was not a feature of the testimony from the Denekamp incident eyewitnesses. Martin arrived home at 05.24, forty-six minutes after Shannon. The time of Rice's return to Coningsby is corrupted and undecipherable in the ORB. His log book entry cites 05.22, just a couple of minutes ahead of Martin, although having set off for home some time before Martin bombed, there should have been a longer gap between their arrivals. It is a wartime mystery that will probably never be solved.

David Maltby (centre), flanked by 'Bunny' Clayton and Micky Martin. Having survived the Dams Raid, Maltby perished whilst returning from an abortive attempt to destroy the Dortmund-Ems Canal.

My visit with Andreas Wachtel to the Hood family in Nordhorn in 2002, the release of my original book, Dambusters, The Definitive History, in 2003, and my subsequent visits to Holden's crash site with tour parties generated interest among local people, some of whom were alive at the time of the events described above. I was contacted by Herr Ernst Weege, now in his eighties, who wanted to bring together a group of history enthusiasts for the purpose of compiling their own written record of the wartime experiences of the county of Bentheim, including the events of the night of the 15/16th September 1943. Ernst sought permission to draw on the research of Andreas and myself, and quote extensively from the book. We were delighted to be of assistance, and after some years of hard work, the massive work of some four hundred A4 pages, was brought to fruition. Andreas and I were invited as guests of honour to be present in Nordhorn on the occasion of the book's release on the 16th of September 2013, seventy years to the day from the actual events. The book was released at a venue in the town in a ceremony attended by a few hundred invited guests, and Andreas delivered a speech. Many of us then travelled across the town to the site of Holden's crash adjacent to the Hood farm house, where Herr Hood, who was a six year old in the cellar on that fateful night, was in attendance with his wife, son and daughter-in-law, who now run the farm. The intention had been to unveil a memorial stone and plaque to honour jointly the crew and Frau Teupe Hood, but it was not ready in time, and at the time of writing there is still some dispute as to the wording. Never the less, speeches were delivered by Herr Weege, Gelinde Hood (the daughter-in-law), a local politician and myself (in German), and it is my intention to return to complete the story when the memorial stone is at last dedicated.

The first two operations over Germany had thus cost the squadron fourteen crews, including Maltby, and the squadron took on the reputation of a suicide unit. Acting Squadron Leader Martin assumed temporary command on the following morning, and was anxious to rectify the failure of the previous night's operation by going back immediately. In the light of such extreme losses, however, it was deemed inadvisable to attack such a well defended target so soon. On the principle of getting straight back onto the horse after falling off, it was decided that the remnant should join an element from 619 Squadron that night, the 16/17th, to try to knock out the Antheor Viaduct in Southern France. The operation was led by the 619 Squadron commanding officer, W/C Abercromby, and involved six crews from 617 Squadron, and four from the other unit. The 617 Squadron element consisted of F/L Munro in EE150, F/L Youseman in ED763, P/O Clayton in EE131, F/L Wilson in JB139, F/L McCarthy in ED735 and P/O Brown in EE146. Take-offs were either side of 20.00 hours, and it took over five hours to reach the target area. EE131 suffered from severe icing, and P/O Clayton was forced to jettison his bombs and return home. Visibility in the target area was good, but no results were observed, and the tired crews eventually got back home between 05.56 and 07.30. It transpired that no direct hits had been scored, and near misses were not good enough at this type of target. David Maltby was laid to rest on the 18th in a private plot in the village churchyard at Wickhambreaux, where he and Georgina (Nina) had married. The ceremony was to be attended by F/O Howard of Townsend's crew as the squadron representative, but he arrived late, after the church service had finished. Maltby's son John was just six weeks old.

Successive failures, and the heavy losses recently sustained, no doubt saw the squadron's confidence beginning to ebb. Rebuilding began with volunteers interviewed by Martin, and meanwhile, the squadron got on with the business of training. F/L Kearns arrived on the 20th, to be followed on the 28th by two more crews, those of P/O Weedon from 207 Squadron, and P/O Stout from 9 Squadron. On the following day 49 Squadron contributed W/O Bull, and F/L O'Shaughnessy joined from 619 Squadron on the 30th. Elsewhere, the main force had, by this time, returned to full activity, after forces from predominantly 3, 4 and 6 Groups had conducted a number of operations against French targets in mid-month. A series of four raids on Hanover, spread over the following four weeks, began on the 22/23rd, but despite the commitment of over seven hundred aircraft, stronger than forecast winds badly affected the bombing, and it is likely that most of the effort fell into open country to the south. Mannheim rarely escaped lightly, however, and six hundred aircraft carried out an accurate attack on its northern half on the 23/24th, before the later stages of the bombing spilled across the Rhine into the northern districts of Ludwigshafen. Thirty two aircraft failed to return, and among them was the 49 Squadron Lancaster containing the crew of the recently commissioned P/O Anderson, who were all killed. The second Hanover operation was mounted on the 27/28th, and this cost thirty eight aircraft for little or no return, after most of the bombs again found open country, although this time north of the city. The final operation of the month took place on the 29/30th against Bochum, which, together with its surrounding communities, suffered the destruction of over five hundred houses.

October 1943

Time was up for Townsend and two of his crew, and they were posted to 1668CU on the 2nd of October to take up instructional duties, an occupation considered by many to be more hazardous than operations. P/O Piggin and crew were posted in from 57 Squadron on the 3rd, and were posted back on the 13th, before which, P/O Willsher and his crew had arrived from 61 Squadron on the 5th. The main force Lancaster crews in particular experienced a busy time at the start of the month, finding themselves involved in six operations during the first eight nights. It began on the 1/2nd at Hagen, where Oboe again proved its worth, and the accurate skymarking in the face of complete cloud cover was exploited by the 1 and 5 Group main force. The same two Groups raided Munich on the following night, but the 5 Group time and distance method led to much of its bombing falling short of the target, while a good proportion of the 1 Group effort hit southern and south-eastern districts. The Halifaxes joined in on the 3/4th, and contributed to a partially successful attack on Kassel, where one eastern suburb was consumed by fire, and two aircraft factories were among many buildings damaged in the city's western half. Frankfurt followed on the 4/5th, and this suffered severe damage from the city centre eastwards, where large areas of fire were created, and the docks were also reported to be a sea of flames. After a two night rest, the southern city of Stuttgart hosted an all Lancaster raid by over three hundred aircraft drawn from 1, 3, 5, 6 and 8 Groups. This was the occasion on which 101 Squadron's ABC Lancasters operated in numbers in their RCM role for the first time. Only four aircraft were lost, suggesting, that for the time being at least, the Command had gained a march on the enemy with this device, and the operation itself was moderately successful.

The third raid on Hanover was mounted on the 8/9th, and for the first time at this target, the operation proceeded to plan. The Pathfinders marked the centre of the city, and the main force followed up with accurate and concentrated bombing, with only a relatively short creep-back. The result was that most parts of the city sustained severe damage, and almost four thousand buildings were completely destroyed, while a further thirty thousand were damaged to some extent. Later on the 9th, "Chuffy" Bull hit trees while low flying, but landed safely with no crew casualties. The middle of the month brought minor operations, and a welcome rest for the main force crews. This was ended by the final attack on Hanover on the 18/19th, and this developed into the third failure of the four operations, and cost eighteen of the all Lancaster force. The first major raid of the war on Leipzig followed on the 20/21st, and was attended by appalling weather conditions, which rendered the operation ineffective. The final raid of the month brought a return to Kassel on the 22/23rd, and on this occasion, everything went according to plan. A firestorm developed, which contributed to the destruction of over 4,300 apartment blocks, and a further 6,700 were damaged. This amounted to over fifty three thousand separate dwelling units, or 63% of the city's accommodation, and at least six thousand people lost their lives. 617 Squadron, meanwhile, conducted no operations during the month, and continued its rebuilding process.

Three more crews were installed by the end of the month, the first of which was that of P/O Ross from 1 Group's 103 Squadron on the 22nd. S/L Suggitt came in from 6 Group's 428 Squadron officially on the 26th, having been the commanding officer of that unit for the six weeks immediately prior to his posting, and he would take on the role of B Flight commander. It seems, though, that he actually arrived a few days after the date recorded, and was immediately packed off on a conversion course, which would keep him from the squadron until the 10th of November. Bill Suggitt would prove to be a dour and humourless character, somehow not in keeping with the generally ebullient spirit of the squadron's officer class. P/O Gingles arrived from 432 Squadron, another 6 Group unit, on the 31st, while F/O Stout had gone in the opposite direction to 619 Squadron on the 21st, although he would return.

November 1943

November would bring the resumption of the Berlin offensive, and the next operations for 617 Squadron under a new leader. First, however, over five hundred aircraft were sent to Düsseldorf on the 3/4th, and they inflicted extensive damage on housing and industry. Training continued for the 617 Squadron crews, nine of which were involved in bulls-eye exercises on the 5th. The stabilized Automatic Bomb Sight, or S.A.B.S, had been installed in the squadron's Lancasters, and intensive high level training had been taking place for some time under the watchful eye of S/L Richardson, a bombing expert, who was also known as "Talking Bomb." Chuffy Bull was involved in another incident on the 10th, when flying in Martin's Dams Lancaster, ED909, which suffered an engine fire, but again he landed safely.

The Cheshire era also began on that day, although it appears that he did not actually arrive on station until after the squadron got back from North Africa, following another crack at the Antheor Viaduct on the 11/12th. Eleven crews were detailed for the operation, which was led by S/L Martin in DV246. The others involved were; F/L Shannon in EE146, F/L Munro in EE150, F/L Kearns in ED912, F/L Wilson in ED932, Gibson's Dams aircraft, F/L Youseman in ED735, F/L O'Shaughnessy in ED825, F/O Rice in EE131, F/O Brown in ED763, F/O Clayton in ED906 and W/O Bull in ED886. Shannon lost an engine on take-off, and was forced to abandon his sortie, but the remainder got away safely and headed for southern France. Each was carrying a 12,000lb high capacity bomb, as used at the Dortmund-Ems Canal in September. In the event, despite all crews attacking the viaduct, no hits were scored, although the embankment and track were damaged, and Brown may have bombed a different bridge. At least no casualties were sustained, and the crews flew on the Blida. On the 15th, they flew from Blida to Rabat, and on the 18th, they came home. F/L Youseman failed to arrive, and he and his crew were lost without trace in the Bay of Biscay in ED735. F/L Kellaway, now recovered from his injuries, had been posted to 630 Squadron at East Kirkby on the 15th.

W/C Cheshire had, hitherto, been a 4 Group man to the core. He had begun his operational career as a Flying Officer flying Whitleys with 102 Squadron in June 1940, a squadron also graced by the presence of the late "Dinghy" Young during the same period. On the 12/13th of November, he brought a massively damaged aircraft safely back from Germany, and received an immediate award of the DSO, thus giving an insight into the character which would make him one of the most famous warriors in Bomber Command. With the advent of the Halifax, Cheshire was posted to 35 Squadron in January 1941, to join the likes of Tait and Holden, and was awarded the DFC in March. In early May, while the Halifaxes were grounded for essential modifications to be carried out, he landed a posting to the Atlantic Ferry Organisation and departed for Canada. A surplus of pilots caused him to kick his heels, and he took the opportunity to visit New York. Here he met the retired actress Constance Binney, whom he married in July. He returned alone to the UK soon afterwards to rejoin 35 Squadron, and set about persuading the Foreign Office to allow Constance to join him. This she did in October, and they set up home in a flat in Harrogate. Promotion to Flight Lieutenant came in April, and at the conclusion of his second tour, he was posted as an instructor to 1652HCU at Marston Moor. He returned to operations in mid-1942 as a Wing Commander, and was given command of 76 Squadron, a post which he held until March 1943, when he became station commander at Marston Moor in the rank of Group Captain. Here he and Constance lived in a converted

Meet the new boss. Group Captain Leonard Cheshire became one of the most famous members of Bomber Command. He was an inspirational leader and subsequently devoted his life to charitable work (Crown)

railway carriage, which had had transported to the site. Although throwing himself into his new job, Cheshire was never really happy at being away from the operational scene, and when offered the post at 617 Squadron, he eagerly accepted it, despite having to revert to the rank of Wing Commander.

Later, on the night of the 17/18th, while the 617 Squadron crews were returning from North Africa, an all Lancaster force of over four hundred aircraft went to Berlin, to resume the campaign against the Capital after the autumn break. Harris had stated in a memorandum to Churchill on the 3rd, that he could "wreck Berlin from end to end", if the Americans would join in. They, however, were committed to victory by invasion, where the cameras could record the heroic events, and there was never a chance of securing their support. The attack on this night was scattered across the city, and achieved only modest success, although a diversion at Mannheim by over three hundred Halifaxes, Stirlings and Lancasters produced better results, and helped to restrict losses from the main operation to nine aircraft. 617 Squadron would continue to be exempt from this bitter round of operations through the winter, as other tasks awaited the crews, which were more suited to their particular skills. A maximum effort force of over seven hundred aircraft returned to the Capital on the 22/23rd, and delivered the most destructive raid on it of the war. At least three thousand houses were destroyed, along with twenty three industrial premises, while around two thousand people lost their lives, and a further 175,000 were rendered homeless. A predominantly Lancaster force followed this up twenty four hours later, and guided by the glow of fires still burning beneath the clouds, they delivered another devastating blow. It was Lancasters again on the 26/27th, which carried out a partially successful assault, which fell mainly into industrial areas north-west of the city centre, and thirty eight war industry factories were destroyed.

December 1943

December began for 617 Squadron in frustrating fashion, with a planned operation being cancelled on each of the first three nights. Not so for the Lancaster crews of the main force, however, who found themselves heading back to the "Big City" on the 2/3rd, only to lose forty of their number in return for relatively modest gain. On the following night, Leipzig underwent its most destructive raid of the war at the hands of five hundred Lancasters and Halifaxes, and over eleven hundred people were killed. On the 9th four 617 Squadron aircraft and crews were dispatched to Tempsford in Bedfordshire, the home of 138 and 161 Squadrons, which were engaged in highly secret activities on behalf of the Special Operations Executive (SOE) and the Special Intelligence Service (SIS). Their job was to deliver arms and supplies into the hands of the various resistance organisations fighting the Nazi occupiers, and to land and pick up agents. The crews involved in the detachment were those of W/O Bull in ED886, F/O Weedon in ED825, F/L Clayton in ED906 and F/L McCarthy in EE131. As Lancasters were an unknown quantity at Tempsford, a station familiar predominantly with Halifaxes at the time, a total of sixteen ground crew accompanied the detachment. Bad weather forced the drop over France to be cancelled, and a further attempt was made by three of them, W/O Bull, F/O Weedon and F/L Clayton, on the following night. None of the sorties was successfully completed, and two of the aircraft failed to return, ED886, which had taken Townsend to the dams, and ED825, which had been McCarthy's dams mount.

"Chuffy" Bull had crossed the French coast at 6,000 feet at 23.15, and then lost height to around five hundred feet while trying to establish a pinpoint between Boulogne and St Pol. Light flak was encountered about five minutes later, and Bull made frequent course changes before they were hit, probably in the bomb bay, as the loss card makes reference to a flare igniting. The order to bale out was given immediately as Bull tried to gain some height, and the bomb-aimer was first away, followed closely by the navigator, flight engineer, front gunner and finally Bull himself. Why the wireless operator and rear gunner failed to survive is not clear, but it seems they went down with the aircraft, which crashed a few miles south-south-east of Doullens in the region of the Somme. Bull and three others were soon captured, while the front gunner, F/S McWilliams, managed to evade a similar fate, although their colleagues back home would not learn the happy news of their survival for some time. The occupants of the other Lancaster were less fortunate, though, and F/O Weedon and his crew all lost their lives when they too fell victim to flak while flying at low level in the same general area. Among them was F/S Walters, an American from Pennsylvania, who had enlisted in the RCAF. On the 12th Nicky Ross and crew flew down to Tempsford in JB139, and spent the next few days carrying out practice drops in preparation for another SOE sortie.

Only minor operations had been flown by the Command after Leipzig, and it was not until the 16/17th, that the main force Lancaster crews were recalled to arms. The target was again Berlin, and a late afternoon take-off had almost five hundred aircraft winging their way to the target, timed to arrive overhead at around 20.00 hours. Less than an hour after these had departed for Germany, nine 617 Squadron Lancasters set off for France, their crews briefed to attack a flying bomb site at Flixecourt in the Pas-de-Calais. This gave W/C Cheshire the opportunity to lead the squadron into battle for the first time, flying on this occasion in DV380. Accompanying him were the crews of S/L Martin in DV402, S/L Suggitt in DV382, F/L Kearns in ED912, F/L Shannon in DV394, F/L Wilson in ED932, P/O Willsher in DV393, F/L Munro in DV391 and F/L O'Shaughnessy in DV385. A similar operation was being conducted simultaneously by Stirlings of 3 Group at Tilley-le-Haut, and both forces were provided with Oboe

Geoff Rice with three members of his crew.

Mosquitos to carry out the marking. Oboe had proved decisive at the Ruhr, and for city targets, its accuracy was as good as pinpoint. For small targets, however, an error of just a few hundred yards could prove critical, and this was the case with both operations on this night. The markers for the Stirling raid missed the target by 450 yards, while the single Oboe Mosquito at Flixecourt failed to find the mark by 350 yards. The 617 Squadron crews plastered the markers with their 12,000 pounders, and all brought home an aiming point photograph, only to discover frustratingly, that the target had escaped damage. All arrived back safely, just as the main force crews were leaving the Berlin defence zone having carried out a moderately successful raid for the loss of twenty five of their number. The real problems arose for these as they arrived home to find their stations blanketed in thick fog, many of them with insufficient fuel to reach a diversionary airfield. 1, 6 and 8 Groups were those most seriously affected, and twenty nine Lancasters either crashed or were abandoned by their tired crews during the frantic search for somewhere to land. Around 150 airmen lost their lives in these most tragic of circumstances, when so close to home and safety.

From around 16.20 hours on the 20th, and for the following ninety minutes, 650 aircraft of the main force and Pathfinder squadrons began taking off and forming up for the long slog to Frankfurt. As this was going on at stations from County Durham to Cambridgeshire, eight 617 Squadron crews were preparing to use the main activity as cover for their operation to the Fabrique Nationale gun factory at Liége in Belgium. The FN Company had plants in both Belgium and France, and this site had been manufacturing a variety of weapons from pistols to shotguns and machine guns, including Brownings, for many years. The

American, John Moses Browning, had actually died in Liége in 1926. The 617 Squadron aircraft took off either side of 18.00, with Cheshire again leading his men from the front in DV380, while the other crews were those of S/L Martin in DV385, S/L Suggitt in DV382, F/L Munro in DV391, F/L Kearns in ED912, F/L Wilson in ED932, F/L Rice in DV398 and P/O Willsher in DV393. 8 Group Mosquitos again provided Oboe marking, but the target indicators were not visible through the cloud cover, and after circling for twenty minutes Cheshire ordered the crews to return home with their bombs. Willsher jettisoned his bomb for an undisclosed reason on the estimated position of the target.

They adopted a return route slightly south of due west, which took them across the north-eastern corner of France to the English Channel. This was doubtless to give the defences in and around Brussels to their north a wide berth. Cheshire lost an engine over the Channel, but got back all right, while DV398 did not make it home with the crew of Geoff Rice. It was shot down during the return flight over Belgium, and Paul Brickhill writes that Martin saw a Lancaster going down in flames with one of the gunners still firing at his pursuer. Certainly there would have been night fighter activity in the area where Rice came down, between Charleroi and Mons, because of the Frankfurt raid. However, Rice, himself, on his return to the UK was unsure whether to ascribe the loss of his Lancaster to flak or to a night fighter, and could only report it to have been set on fire before falling into an uncontrollable dive. He gave the order to bale out at 14,000 feet, and recalls Dick MacFarlane handing him his parachute. The volume of wreckage of DV398 led the local people to believe it to be of a twin-engine type, and they reported that it had been blown up by its own bombs.

In fact, Rice had been shot down by Hauptmann Kurt Fladrich, a Staffel Kapitän from 9/NJG/4 based at Juvincourt, near Reims in France. Misidentifying his victim as a Halifax, Fladrich recorded in his logbook that he delivered one attack from below and behind in his BF110G4, and set a fierce fire raging in the bomber's starboard-inner engine. The encounter took place at 20.29 at 4,200 meters, five hundred meters north of Merbes-le-Château, south-west of Charleroi. Fladrich witnessed flames at what he believed was the point of impact on the ground, but it was probably the bomb load going up in the air. It was Fladrich's eighth kill, and he would survive the war with a tally of fifteen. It has been written that the Red Cross claimed F/S Gowrie was captured and later shot by the Gestapo. However, a report by the No2 M.R. & E. Unit refers to a German report describing the removal of six bodies from the crash site and they were interred in Gosselies cemetery in graves numbered 67 to 72. They were just six of more than 47,000 men of Bomber Command killed on operations, but they all had lives, hopes and dreams, and people to mourn their loss. Gunner Tom Maynard was the baby of the crew at just twenty years of age, while Ed Smith, the flight engineer, was twenty-four and had a wife in Berkshire waiting for him to return. John Thrasher and Chester Gowrie had come all the way from Canada to fight Nazism. Bomb-aimer and wireless operator respectively, they were twenty-three and twenty-five years of age. If Martin had, in fact, observed return fire, then it was probably from Sandy Burns in the rear turret. He was just twenty-two, and later that day the dreaded telegram would be on its way to his parents in Dudley. Along with navigator Dick MacFarlane, these were the men whose lives had been extinguished in a fraction of time as an explosion tore their aircraft apart and hurled their pilot out into space. The number of surviving Dams veterans was dwindling fast. We will return shortly to Geoff Rice.

The night's activities were not yet over for 617 Squadron. At 01.15 on the 21st, Joe McCarthy took off from Tempsford in EE131, and headed for France to carry out a drop on behalf of SOE. He was followed fifteen minutes later by "Bunny" Clayton in ED906, at 02.24 by Nicky Ross in JB139 and finally by Ken Brown in EE146 at 02.37. For Ross, who was heading for the Rouen area to make his low-level drop, this was his first operation since joining 617 Squadron and his fiftieth in all. Unfortunately, not one of them was able to locate their assigned target in the conditions, and all were forced to abandon their sorties. It should be

W/C Leonard Cheshire's Lancaster, seen in an unofficial photograph taken by a member of the ground crew.

mentioned, that SOE sorties were highly exacting and dangerous, and required the most precise navigation in order to reach a tiny pinpoint at low-level at night. Even the experienced crews of 138 and 161 Squadrons were frequently forced to bring back their stores and agents, when either the conditions thwarted them or the reception party failed to show. Despite this, these remarkable men from the clandestine "moon" squadrons displayed the most incredible fortitude and persistence to find their drop zones, and successfully completed between them many hundreds of operations during their wartime service.

Rice regained consciousness in a wood at around 08.30 on the following morning, the 21st, more than fourteen hours after taking off from Coningsby, and having "lost" twelve hours since his last memory. His parachute was snagged upon a tree, and pieces of aircraft wreckage lay around him, although of more immediate concern were a broken wrist and a deep gash over his left eye. He deduced, that he had been thrown clear as the Lancaster disintegrated in the air, presumably through an explosion, and this harmonizes with local eyewitness accounts. Protected by an armoured seat, it was not unusual for a pilot to survive in this way, while the rest of the crew perished. Rice, of course, had no knowledge of his crew's fate at this point. Having hidden his parachute in the undergrowth he emerged from the wood into the small village of Binche, where he encountered three farm labourers, who took him to a farm. Here he was washed, fed and re-clothed, before being taken to another farmhouse, where he slept for six hours. He spent that night at yet another location, and moved on again on the following day to a house where he remained for five days over the Christmas period. While there he was taken to a doctor, who first x-rayed and then set his wrist in plaster.

After Christmas he was taken by a gendarme to a kind of hospital run by sisters, and from there to a dentist at La Louviere, who claimed to be English, but was possibly a Belgian being used by the underground to weed out German infiltrators. Rice spent the next four or five days with a French Catholic priest, before returning to La Louviere, where he was given identity and work cards. Moved twice more, he was finally collected towards the end of January, and taken by train to Brussels via Charleroi, where he stayed for ten days with a blind lady. He spent the next seven weeks in the flat of a young married couple, but when one of their friends was arrested, it was decided to move Rice again, this time to the home of a local hospital manager, where he met up with an American bombardier. The latter was sent on to Antwerp, and Rice followed a week later, on the 28th of April, with two more Americans. They were handed over to another man outside of the railway station, who was only able to accommodate two men, the Americans, and Rice was dropped off at a house nearby, where he was met by two other men of about his own age. One of them left to find a safe house for Rice, but returned with members of the secret police, and thus ended Rice's five months on the run. He spent the time from June 1944 to January 1945 at Stalag Luft III, before moving on to Stalag IIIA at Luckenwalde, from where he was liberated by Russian forces on the 21st of April. He finally arrived back in the UK at RAF Cosford on the 26th of May.

Eleven 617 Squadron crews were briefed for an attack on a flying bomb site in the Abbeville-Amiens area on the 22/23rd, and they got away between 20.00 and 20.30 hours. Cheshire was last away in DV380, with ahead of him, Martin in DV402, Suggitt in DV382, Munro in DV391, McCarthy in ME559, Kearns in ED912, Wilson in ED932, Clayton in ED906, Brown in DV394, Ross in JB139 and Willsher in DV393. The target could not be located in the conditions, however, and the operation was abandoned. It is believed, that the Oboe markers were delivered, but they could not be seen, and the most likely cause is their failure to burst. Surprisingly, a force of 3 Group Stirlings operating in the same area against a similar target experienced less difficulty, and carried out an accurate attack. A predominantly Lancaster force attacked Berlin again on the 23/24th, and this was one of the less convincing raids on the Capital, falling mainly into southeastern suburbs, and destroying around three hundred buildings for the loss of sixteen aircraft.

The fifth wartime Christmas came and went in relative peace, and it was on the 29/30th, that the main force conducted its final operation of the year. This was also on Berlin, and was the first of three raids on the city in an unprecedented five nights spanning the turn of the year. Over seven hundred aircraft took off, and they delivered an attack which fell mainly into southern and south-eastern districts, where around four hundred buildings were destroyed. On the following night, 617 Squadron carried out its final operation of the year, with a return to the flying bomb site at Flixecourt by ten aircraft, this time led by the flight commanders, S/Ls Suggitt and Martin, in DV382 and DV402 respectively. They were accompanied by F/L Shannon in EE146, F/L McCarthy in ME559, F/L O'Shaughnessy in DV385, F/L Brown in DV394, F/L Clayton in ME555, F/L Munro in DV392, P/O Ross in ED932 and P/O Willsher in DV393. Six Oboe Mosquitos provided the marking, but the target indicators fell two hundred yards from the site, and this was sufficient to render the attack ineffective. Munro's photoflash failed to release, and McCarthy's camera was inoperative, while Clayton had to take evasive action to avoid another Lancaster, and these were the only three to come home without a snapshot of the aiming point. On the credit side, the frustration born out of these recent failures was to concentrate the minds of a number of squadron notables on overcoming the problem of marking a small target with precision. This brainstorming was to bear fruit in spectacular fashion in the coming year, but in the meantime, matters were not proceeding according to plan for this very special squadron. In May 1943, it had achieved outstanding success, and had passed into bomber folklore, with its deeds splashed across the front pages of the world's press. The remainder of the year, however, had been characterized by gallant failure and bitter losses, and it had to be hoped and expected that better things awaited in 1944.

January 1944

The year began for the main force with a disappointing all Lancaster raid on Berlin on New Year's Night. Very little damage resulted, and twenty eight aircraft were lost, including that of W/C Abercromby, who had led the first Antheor viaduct operation in September when commanding officer of 619 Squadron, but who now lost his life as the commander of the Pathfinder's 83 Squadron. Twenty-four hours later, a similarly ineffective return to the Capital cost twenty-seven Lancasters, and the Pathfinders, in particular, were taking a beating. There is little doubt, that the beleaguered inhabitants of Berlin shared a common hope with the hard-pressed crews of Bomber Command that their city would cease to be the main focus of Harris's attention. However, proud of their status as Berliners first and Germans second, they were a hardy breed, and just like their counterparts in London under the blitz of 1940, they bore their trials with fortitude and humour. During this, their "winter of discontent," they taunted their tormentors by parading banners through the shattered streets, proclaiming, "You may break our walls, but not our hearts." They also sang along to the most popular song of the day, *Nach jedem Dezember kommt immer ein Mai*, (*After every December comes always a May*), the sentiments of which held promise of a change of fortunes with the onset of spring.

617 Squadron opened its 1944 account on the evening of the 4th of January, with an operation by eleven aircraft to a flying bomb site in the Pas de Calais. Cheshire once more took the lead in DV380, and was accompanied on this occasion by the not inconsiderable bulk of the station commander, G/C "Tiny" Evans-Evans as a passenger. This was typical of the man, who had commanded 115 Squadron earlier in the war, and his desire to be one of the boys, and operate against the enemy, would cost him his life in 1945, when the end of the war was tantalisingly close. The other crews involved on this night were those of S/L Suggitt in DV382, S/L Martin in DV402, F/L Shannon in ME555, F/L Brown in DV394, F/L Clayton in ED906, F/L O'Shaughnessy in DV385, F/L Munro in DV391, F/L Kearns in ME559, F/L Wilson in DV932 and P/O Ross in DV393. The crews were airborne either side of 17.30 hours, each standard Lancaster carrying fourteen 1,000 pounders, while the two Type 464 variants contained a reduced load of eleven 1,000 pounders. They all returned less than four hours later, having, they believed, at last delivered an accurate and effective attack.

Cheshire recorded that cloud had made bombing difficult, and that the Oboe-laid red marker was not visible. However, two green target indicators with red candles could be seen intermittently, and he ordered the crews to aim for these. A stick of bombs fell across these target indicators, while others burst within them, but three other sticks were 150 yards wide of the mark. One of the latter may have been from Suggitt, who bombed from 10,300 feet at 19.23¾ with an unserviceable bombsight. Twelve of Martin's bombs went down at 19.15, but two hung up, and these were delivered in a second run five seconds after Suggitt's. Some crews seemed to find a fortuitous break in the clouds straight away, while O'Shaughnessy made five runs before he was sufficiently confident to let his bombs go. Nicky Ross heard Cheshire's order to bomb the green T.Is, but someone else obliterated them before he could comply. He went round again, but by the time he arrived back over the target area, cloud obscured all ground reference, and he brought his bombs home. Subsequent reconnaissance revealed no new damage to this site.

In a welcome break from Berlin, over three hundred Lancasters and a handful of Halifaxes raided Stettin on the 5/6th. As always seemed to be the case at this target, the bombing was accurate, and caused the destruction of five hundred houses, and severe damage to a further eleven hundred, along with twenty nine industrial premises, and eight ships were sunk in the harbour. The main force crews would now enjoy an eight night rest, and during this period, the squadron made its final wartime change of address. This took place over the 8th and 9th, with a move to nearby Woodhall Spa, while 619 Squadron travelled in the opposite direction. The officers were billeted in the elegant Petwood Hotel on the edge of the town, where it stands to this day, resplendent in its extensive and beautiful grounds. Three more crews arrived on posting on the 10th, F/O Stout returning from 619 Squadron along with the American Lt Knilans, and F/O Cooper came from 1660CU. (From this point on, dates of postings will often but not always relate to week ending Friday, and some movements will therefore have taken place a few days before the date cited. It is not possible to be more precise.)

Hubert "Nick" Knilans was to become one of 617 Squadron's characters, and unusually, he remained at Woodhall Spa for his entire operational career of two tours. Born in Wisconsin in 1917, Knilans joined the RCAF in October 1941, before America entered the war. After basic training as a pilot in Canada, Knilans arrived in the UK to continue his training, initially in Scotland, and then at 1660 CU at Swinderby. Here he gathered a crew around him, and was posted to 619 Squadron at Woodhall Spa in June 1943. His first two operations, against Cologne and Turin in July, were flown as second dickey to experienced pilots. The Ruhr campaign had by this time almost run its course, and the Battle of Hamburg was about to begin. The first of the already described four major operations against Germany's second city became Knilans's first as crew captain on the night of the 24/25th. On return, a faulty or wrongly set altimeter almost ended the crew's career, but Knilans managed to fly his way out of trouble, and the Lancaster was soon repaired. They went to Essen on the following night and returned on three engines, and on the 27/28th they participated in the firestorm raid on Hamburg. In September Knilans was commissioned as a Pilot Officer, and in early October his rear gunner was killed by a night fighter during an operation to Kassel. Soon afterwards he was transferred to the USAAF, but was allowed to remain on attachment to the RAF, although sporting an American uniform in the rank of 1st Lieutenant. Knilan's first tour took him to Berlin on a number of occasions during November and December, and his final operation was the above-mentioned one against Stettin on the night of the 5/6th of January 1944. This coincided with the departure of 619 Squadron from Woodhall Spa to make way for 617 Squadron, and Knilans volunteered to remain in comfort at the Petwood to carry out a second tour with the Cheshire boys, rather than be posted to a training unit or the American 8th Air Force.

Ten crews were detailed for operations on the 10th, but this was cancelled, and the same thing occurred on the 14th. That night, 496 Lancasters and two Halifaxes set of for Brunswick, to carry out the first major operation against this town in central Germany. There was no doubt relief among the crews at briefings that Berlin was not the target, but Brunswick lay a little to the east of Hanover, and the memory of trying to crack that difficult and expensive nut during the autumn was still fairly fresh. It was a target which was to have some significance for 617 Squadron in the future, but on this night, it escaped with light superficial damage, while the attackers paid for the failure with thirty eight aircraft, eleven of them Pathfinders. In just two weeks since the turn of the year, 156 Squadron alone had lost fourteen crews from just three operations.

On the 13th, the squadron welcomed to its bosom F/L Bill Reid, who had been awarded a Victoria Cross for his courage during the raid on Düsseldorf on the 3/4th of November, while he was serving with 61 Squadron. A 617 Squadron operation planned for the 20th was cancelled, and six crews carried out low level bombing practice at Dusk over the sea. During the course of this, ED918, the Lancaster flown to the Sorpe Dam by Ken Brown, bounced off the surface of the water before careering onto the beach at Snettisham and hitting a breakwater. F/L Tom O'Shaughnessy and his navigator, F/O Holding lost their lives, and two others sustained injuries, those of F/O Kendrick, the bomb-aimer, so serious that it would take him a year to recover and return to operations. As this tragedy was taking place, over seven hundred aircraft were arriving over Berlin, to deliver an attack on the Capital through complete cloud cover, and the crews were unable to make an immediate assessment of the results of their efforts. It was later learned that the main weight of the attack had fallen into the hitherto less severely damaged eastern districts, where moderate damage was inflicted. Thirty five aircraft failed to return, and the Halifaxes sustained disproportionately high casualties.

Finally, on the 21st, two and a half weeks since the squadron's last operation, W/C Cheshire led a force of twelve aircraft back to the flying bomb site in the Pas de Calais, one of six similar targets for the night. He was again in DV380, and the other crews were those of S/L Martin in DV402, S/L Suggitt in DV382, F/L Munro in DV391, F/L Shannon in DV403, F/L Wilson in JB139, F/L McCarthy in ME559, F/L Kearns in ME557, F/L Clayton in ME560, F/L Brown in DV394, P/O Willsher in DV392 and P/O Ross in ME562. They took off shortly after 17.00 hours, with Cheshire carrying seven spot fires and six 30lb incendiaries along with his 1,000lb bombs, and Martin had some 500 pounders as well. After an initial reference was provided by two Oboe Mosquitos from 8 Group, Cheshire was able to obtain a clear site of the wood, wherein lay the target, but his bombing run at 7,000 feet was hampered by flares bursting directly ahead. They were in bomb-aimer Keith Astbury's line of sight at the critical moment, and he dropped a salvo rather than a stick, recognising that the markers were going to overshoot. Cheshire observed the salvo to burst in the north-eastern corner of the wood, before pulling away to circle and monitor the rest of the bombing. He saw six or seven night fighters to the south, but none came closer than five miles. F/L Wilson brought some of his bombs home after the spot fires burned out before he could complete a second run, and Brown and Willsher did likewise, but the others plastered the site, taking advantage of the clear visibility. Reconnaissance revealed considerable damage to the site, and this was in reality the first effective attack by the squadron against this type of target.

Fifty-six 3 Group Stirlings and twelve Lancasters from 617 Squadron returned to the Pas-de-Calais late on the 25th for another crack at the flying bomb sites. The Lancasters and crews were as per the last operation, except that F/L Brown was replaced by Lt Knilans, who was on his first operation with the squadron and flying in ME561, while Wilson was flying in DV385. This time it was a late take-off, between 22.10 and 22.31, and they were at the target in less than two hours. The first Oboe marker was right on the mark, but went out almost immediately, and red spot-fires dropped probably by Martin were assessed as on or near the aiming point. Partial cloud cover was encountered, which made it impossible to mark from above, but difficult also from below because of the speed of the flares drifting across the target. Kearns bombed first at 23.53 from 12,000 feet, and Cheshire last at 00.39 after coming down to 5,300 feet. Some delivered all of their bombs in one stick, while others made two runs, but the general impression was of an accurate attack, and all returned safely either side of 02.00 hours. Post raid reconnaissance revealed craters to the northwest of the target area and blocked approaches, but it was not possible to attribute specific damage arising from this operation. Canadian P/O Duffy was posted in towards the end of the month, but he would need to undergo conversion training at 5 LFS before being declared operational.

Although 617 Squadron had now completed its operations for the month, the main force still had a daunting schedule ahead of it. An unprecedented three Berlin operations in the space of four nights began on the 27/28th, when five hundred Lancasters slogged their way to the Capital, and delivered a scattered attack, which spread into dozens of outlying communities, something which had become a feature of the campaign. Twenty thousand Berliners were bombed out of their homes, and thirty three Lancasters were missing. On the following night, the Halifax brigade joined in and contributed to a destructive raid, which hit mostly the western and southern districts, but many public and administrative buildings were damaged, and a further 180,000 people were rendered homeless. The cost, at forty six aircraft, was high,

'Micky' Martin and crew on the roof of the Air Ministry in London after receiving awards for their part in Operation Chastise. Left to right: Flt Lt Jack Leggo (Bar to Distinguished Flying Cross), Flt Sgt Tammy Simpson (Distinguished Flying Medal), Flt Lt Bob Hay (Bar to DFC), Pt Off Toby Foxlee (DFM) and Ft Lt HBM 'Micky' Martin (Distinguished Service Order) (Crown)

but only one night's rest was allowed to lick the wounds, before over five hundred aircraft returned on the 30/31st. This was another destructive assault, which hit many parts of the city, including the centre, and large areas of fire were created, and a thousand people were killed. The heavy losses continued, however, and on this night they totalled thirty three aircraft. Although the crews were not aware of the fact, this was the final concerted effort to destroy Berlin. Had the weather obliged, Harris would have mounted another major operation early in February, but in the event, it would be mid-month before another one could take place, and this would prove to be not only the penultimate raid of the campaign, but the penultimate one of the war by RAF heavy bombers. There is no question, that Berlin had been sorely afflicted during this series at the end of January, but it remained a functioning city, and the seat of government, and nowhere were there signs of imminent collapse.

February 1944

Smoke billows from the Gnome & Rhone engine factory at Limoges. This photo was taken by the crew of F/L Brown in DV394.

On the 2nd news came through from the Red Cross that "Chuffy" Bull, his bomb-aimer, F/S Batey and his flight engineer, Sgt Wiltshire, were safe and on extended leave in Germany. The news, that the navigator, Sgt Chamberlain, was also in captivity, would filter through later. Nine aircraft took part in a secret bombing practice on the 7th, and what they learned was put into effect on the night of the 8/9th, while the main force was still grounded by the weather. The operation gave Cheshire an opportunity to demonstrate just what 617 Squadron could achieve, and it proved to be a turning point. He and Martin had unofficially developed a system of delivering markers with pinpoint accuracy by diving a Lancaster towards an aiming point, and releasing the spot fires from low level before pulling out. This was a somewhat hairy exercise in a Lancaster, and the effort of pulling out almost tore the wings off. The idea was then presented to the ever-receptive AVM Cochrane, the 5 Group AOC, who cautiously gave the green light for a live trial to take place.

The target selected for the trial was the Gnome & Rhone aero engine factory at Limoges, and twelve crews were briefed accordingly. They were, W/C Cheshire in DV380, S/L Suggitt in ED763, S/L Martin in DV402, F/L Shannon in DV403, F/L Clayton in ME560, F/O Knights, recently arrived from 619 Squadron, in DV385, F/L Brown in DV394, Lt Knilans in ME561, F/L Wilson in ME559, P/O Ross in ME562, F/L Kearns in ME557, and F/O Willsher in DV392. Take-offs were between 21.07 and 21.25, and the target was reached shortly before midnight. On his fourth run across the target, having given the workers ample warning to vacate the factory, Cheshire dropped his incendiaries into the centre of the factory roof from under a hundred feet, and Martin backed up with his spot fires and incendiaries some four minutes later. Five crews waiting above at 8,000 to 10,000 feet were carrying 12,000 pounders, Shannon, Clayton, Brown, Ross and Willsher, and four of these were direct hits, while Willsher's undershot by about 150 yards. The remaining five crews carried eleven 1,000 pounders each, and most of these fell across the target, although Wilson reported his bombs to have fallen at least fifty yards to the left after the plug on the control switch was found to be pulled out. The operation was an outstanding success, and the dramatic events were captured on cine-film. A photograph of Cheshire's markers cascading onto the factory was released to the press, and the actual footage has found its way into many documentary films since. Reconnaissance photographs showed immense damage to the target, with nine medium bay sized workshops and a large multi-bay building all suffering heavily. Twenty-one out of forty-eight bays were destroyed, and a further twenty were badly damaged. Other buildings in the target area were also affected, and even the bays remaining intact had sustained internal damage from blast.

F/L Kit Howard and his crew had been posted in from 17 OTU on the 7th, and five days later, they joined Duffy and crew, who were already undergoing conversion training at 5 LFS at Syerston. On the 12/13th, eleven aircraft took off for a reunion with their old friend, the Antheor Viaduct, Cheshire, as always, leading from the front. This time, it is believed, he was in ME559, while his own DV380 was undergoing servicing, and they refuelled at Ford on the way. The other crews were those of S/L Martin as deputy leader in DV402, S/L Suggitt in DV382, F/L Munro in ME557, F/L Shannon in DV403, F/L Clayton in ME560, F/O Knights in DV385, F/L Brown in DV394, Lt Knilans in ME561, F/L Wilson in ED763 and P/O Ross in ME562. The crews were airborne before 22.00 hours, having refuelled at Ford on the way. A heavy flak defence greeted the force, and this and the searchlights hampered the efforts of Cheshire and Martin to mark at low level. Martin's aircraft was hit in the nose while in the act of marking, and his bomb aimer, F/L Bob Hay was killed. He had been with Martin since their days at 455 and 50 Squadrons, and had been the 617 Squadron bombing leader from the start, almost a year earlier. The flight engineer, F/L Ivan Whittaker, also sustained injuries to his legs, while the Lancaster was seriously damaged. Martin was forced to abort his sortie and make for Sardinia, jettisoning the 12,000 pounder en-route. A safe landing was made on a small American airstrip with a very short runway, and Whittaker was carted off to hospital. Meanwhile, Cheshire had been unable to pick out the viaduct visually, and could only make out the line of the foreshore. Despite repeated attempts to approach the aiming point, he was beaten off by the fierce ground fire, and ultimately dropped his markers onto the beach. The following crews were instructed to adjust their aim accordingly, and one bomb fell within fifteen yards of the target, but as they withdrew towards home, the viaduct was still standing. The operation was another gallant failure, and the crews were all back at Ford by 05.35. The weather closed in shortly afterwards, but Suggitt judged that he could make it back to Woodhall Spa, and took off sometime after 08.00 hours poor weather. Ten minutes later, the Lancaster struck high ground ten miles north-east of Chichester, and seven of the eight men on board were killed instantly. Among them were the squadron intelligence officer, S/L Lloyd, and F/S Pulford DFM, who had been the flight engineer in Gibson's dams crew. His death, along with that of Hay the night before, reduced still further the number of dams survivors. Suggitt was found alive and delirious still strapped in his seat, but he never regained consciousness, and lost his fight for life at Chichester hospital at 16.00 hours on the 15th. He was replaced as B Flight commander by Les Munro. Reconnaissance photos of the viaduct taken later that day revealed new craters and a very near miss, but the structure remained intact.

This day brought an influx of new crews to the squadron, ten of the Group's other units contributing one each. F/L Hadland arrived from 9 Squadron, F/L Edward from 50, F/L Fearn from 57, F/L Williams from 61, F/L Poore from 106, F/L Pryor from 207, F/O Kell and P/O Stanford from the RAAF's 463 and 467

Squadrons respectively, F/O Hamilton from 619, and P/O Cheney from 630. The remainder of the month was occupied with the funerals arising from Suggitt's crash, and intensive flying training for the new crews, although, one happy note was the arrival back from Sardinia of Martin on the 23rd, and he was sent straight off on leave. On the afternoon of S/L Suggitt's death, 891 crews were attending briefings for what would be a record breaking operation that night. The Command was rested and replenished after two weeks on the ground, and this enabled Harris to assemble the largest non-1,000 force yet, and of course, the largest force ever sent against Berlin. It would be the first time that over five hundred Lancasters and three hundred Halifaxes had operated together, and they would deliver a new record 2,600 tons of bombs onto the Capital. Much of this was put to good use in central and south-western districts, where a thousand houses were destroyed, along with over five hundred temporary wooden barracks. Almost twelve hundred fires were started, and many important war industry factories sustained damage, but forty three aircraft failed to return from this penultimate raid of the war by RAF heavy bombers on the "Big City".

The heavy brigade sat out the next three nights, before over eight hundred aircraft set out for Leipzig, and the greatest disaster to afflict the Command to date. Matters began to go awry as early as the Dutch coast outbound, when the bomber stream was met by a proportion of the enemy night fighter force. These maintained contact all the way to the target, which some aircraft reached ahead of the Pathfinders through wrongly forecast winds. They were forced to mill around in the target area, while they waited for the markers to go down, and collisions and the local flak batteries accounted for about twenty four of them. The operation itself was inconclusive in the face of complete cloud cover, and when all those aircraft which were going to return home had done so, there was a massive shortfall of seventy-eight, a new record loss by a clear twenty one aircraft. The Halifax percentage loss rate was the final straw for Harris, and the Merlin-powered Mk II and V variants were withdrawn from future operations over Germany, as had been the Stirlings in November.

Despite the losses over the last two operations, almost six hundred aircraft took off for Stuttgart on the 20/21st, and delivered a scattered but destructive raid, which hit central districts, and suburbs from the north-west to the north-east. Only nine aircraft were lost, although a number of others crashed in England on return. A new tactic was employed for the next two operations, the splitting of the force into two waves separated by two hours, in the hope of catching the night fighters on the ground refuelling and rearming. It was tried first at Schweinfurt on the 24/25th, and while the operation itself suffered from undershooting and was a failure, the second wave lost 50% fewer aircraft than the first, in an overall loss of thirty three. On the following night, Augsburg fell victim to one of those fairly rare occasions beyond the range of Oboe, when all facets of the plan came together in perfect harmony. Accurate Pathfinder marking was exploited by the main force, which produced concentrated bombing of the city centre. The heart of this beautiful and historic old city was torn out by fire, and centuries of culture were lost forever. Almost three thousand houses were reduced to rubble, along with many public and architecturally important buildings, and around seven hundred people lost their lives. Twenty one aircraft failed to return, and this suggested that there was some merit in dividing the forces.

At 617 Squadron the second half of February had been taken up with the funerals arising from Suggitt's crash, and intensive flying training for the new crews. One happy note was the arrival back from Sardinia of Martin on the 23rd, and he was sent straight off on leave. One interesting piece of 617 Squadron trivia concerned Joe McCarthy's original Dams Lancaster, ED915, Q-Queenie, which had become unserviceable on the very threshold of immortality. Joe's personal Lancasters always bore the code Q, and although he never actually carried out an operation in ED915, he regularly used it for testing and exercises right up to the end of February 1944, almost as if it were his own private taxi.

March 1944

March was to bring unprecedented activity for 617 Squadron, and it should have opened its account on the night of the 1/2nd, but in the event, the operation was cancelled. Not so for the main force, however, which returned to Stuttgart, and inflicted substantial damage in central, western and northern districts, for the remarkably low loss of four aircraft. 617 Squadron's opportunity came on the following night, when a B.M.W. aero-engine factory and the adjacent G.S.P. machine tool works at Albert in France were selected for attention. Cheshire led the operation in DV380, carrying S/L Moyna to operate the cine camera. The other crews were those of the newly promoted S/L Munro in DV391, F/L Wilson in DV246, F/L Kearns in ME557, F/L McCarthy in ME559, F/L Cooper in DV394, F/L Poore in DV403, F/L Clayton in ME560, F/L Williams in EE131, F/O Stout in ED763, F/O Kell in ME555, F/O Knights in DV385, F/O Willsher in EE146, Lt Knilans in ME561 and F/O Ross in ME562. Cooper, Poore, Williams, Stout and Kell were all flying their first operations with the squadron, and for Poore it would be his twentieth in all. Cheshire, Munro and Wilson were carrying a mostly incendiary bomb load, while eleven others had a 12,000 pounder in the bomb bay, and Poore was the odd man out with fourteen 1,000 pounders. They got away either side of 19.00 hours, and reached the target some two hours later. Cheshire was unable to mark the target because of an unserviceable bomb site, but Munro dropped two spot fires right on the button from 6,000 feet, and the factory was plastered by most of the other crews, all under the watchful gaze of the station commander, G/C Philpott, who was flying with F/O Ross. An on the spot survey carried out in February 1945, when the factories were back in French hands, revealed such severe damage to the G.S.P. plant, that no attempt had been made to use it again, while the former B.M.W. works was still capable of only 10% of its former level of production.

A raid on the Ricamerie needle-bearing factory at St Etienne on the 4th was aborted when the crews encountered ten-tenths cloud over the target, and Cheshire was unable to make a positive identification. This would have been the first operation for the crews of F/L Hadland and F/O Duffy, but their turn would come at the same target next time round. This occurred on the 10th, when the full list of crews was; W/C Cheshire in DV380, S/L Munro in DV391, F/L Shannon in DV403, F/L Kearns in ME557, F/L McCarthy in ME559, F/L Wilson in JB139, F/L Clayton in ME560, F/L Cooper in DV394, F/L Hadland in EE146, F/O Duffy in ME555, F/O Knights in DV385, F/O Stout in DV246, Lt Knilans in ME561, F/O Willsher in DV393, F/O Ross in ME562 and F/O Stanford on his first operation with the squadron in EE131. Stanford, a genial South-Australian born in 1917, was working as a bank clerk when a RAAF recruiting train stopped at the Murray River town of Tailem Bend. He volunteered at once, but was rejected on medical grounds after it was discovered, that a severe blow to the head by a cricket ball some time earlier had left him concussed and potentially at risk at altitude. Four months later he presented himself at the recruiting centre at Adelaide, and by keeping mum about his injury, passed the physical with ease. After training in Australia and England he joined 467 Squadron RAAF just as the main phase of the Berlin campaign was getting into full swing. He flew eight times to the "Big City" as captain and once as second pilot.

Unlike many trips to France, this one to St Etienne was to be a long one, for which take-off began with Cheshire at 19.27, and ended with Shannon at 20.05. The target was reached shortly after 23.00, and similar conditions were encountered to those thwarting the previous attempt. Cheshire went in at 1,700 feet, and managed to mark the western and eastern edges of this 170 X 90 yard target, setting it alight with incendiaries. Munro also went in low, before Cheshire ordered the main force to drop their 1,000 pounders on the glow of the fires visible through the cloud. Some crews were able to identify the target visually, while others bombed the fires as instructed, but it was not possible to assess the extent of the damage with any accuracy. Stanford's bombsight had become unserviceable during the outward flight,

86

and Cheshire told him to hang about until the other crews had bombed. He was then called in downwind to avoid the smoke now emanating from the target, which was actually 1,200 feet above sea level, and he bombed visually from an indicated 3,000 feet. After his return at 03.48, Munro reported, that one small factory building appeared to be wrecked, and he thought he could see four bomb holes in the roof of the main building. Any doubts about the effectiveness of the operation were vanquished by the reconnaissance photos, which revealed every building but one in this important plant to have been destroyed or extensively damaged. The main weight of the attack had fallen on the eastern part of the target area, and the multi-bay building had been destroyed by a combination of blast and fire. In addition, two long sheds had been almost totally destroyed, and others severely damaged.

An abortive operation to Woippy by sixteen aircraft on the 15th gained some success, when Duffy's aircraft, ME560, was repeatedly attacked by night fighters. The rear gunner, F/S McLean, claimed two destroyed and two probables, and after the war it was confirmed that he, with assistance from the mid-upper gunner, W/O Red Evans, had, indeed, despatched all four. F/L Edward flew with the squadron for the first time on this night, but like all the others, he was forced to bring his bombs home. The main force, meanwhile, returned to Stuttgart on this night, the first time it had operated in numbers since going there two weeks earlier. This time the attack was less successful, and most of the bombing fell into open country. Night fighters arrived in the target area at the same time as the bomber stream, and thirty seven aircraft were brought down.

The Michelin rubber works at Clermont Ferrand provided the target for sixteen 617 Squadron crews on the following night, and they were W/C Cheshire in DV380, S/L Munro in DV391, F/L Shannon in DV403, F/L McCarthy in ME559, F/L Kearns in ME557, F/L Wilson in JB139, F/L Cooper in ME562, F/L Hadland in ED763, F/L Edward in DV246, F/O Willsher in DV393, F/L Williams in ME555, Lt Knilans in ME561, F/O Kell in DV402, F/O Knights in DV385 and F/O Duffy in ME560. The crews became airborne either side of 19.30 hours, and on arrival at the target, Cheshire, Munro, Shannon and McCarthy all dropped spot-fires or target indicators along with 30lb incendiaries from very low level in a four minute window to 22.50. One stick of incendiaries from Cheshire's aircraft undershot by up to a mile, but Munro's marking was spot on again, and with the target well alight the waiting crews were ordered to bomb on his spot-fires. Ten 12,000 pounders were delivered with great accuracy between 23.03 and 23.17, and Edward's load of incendiaries went down with the last one. Cheshire reported a huge explosion in the target area at about 23.40, and the operation was declared to be another outstanding success, which was again captured on film by S/L Moyna, who was now a regular passenger in Cheshire's Lancaster. Cheshire and Shannon were the only two not to mention obtaining an aiming point photograph. Reconnaissance photos confirmed that all buildings had been damaged, except for the canteen. The largest building, measuring some 900 X 480 feet was hit by two 12,000 pounders, which demolished most of the structure and stripped the roof. Half of the inner tube plant was destroyed and workshops and power stations damaged, mostly by blast rather than fire, as the low-level dropping of incendiaries tended to lead to concentration rather than a spreading throughout the target area.

On the 18th, thirteen crews were detailed for an attack on the Poudrerie Nationale powder factory at Bergerac. They were Cheshire in DV380, Munro in DV391, Shannon in DV403, McCarthy in ME559, Clayton in ME560, Wilson in JB139, Kearns, this time in ME562, F/L Pryor on his first operation with the squadron in ED763, Cooper in EE146, Knights in ME555, Willsher in DV393, Kell in Martin's beloved DV402 and Knilans in DV246. They all got away safely in a twenty minute slot from 19.28, with Cheshire carrying spot-fires and 30lb incendiaries, and what could now be described as the "Old Firm", that is Munro, Shannon and McCarthy, with similar loads plus a target indicator or two, to ensure that the target remained well marked. 12,000 pounders were borne aloft by Clayton, Wilson, Kearns, Knights, Willsher and Kell, while

Post-raid reconnaissance photo of the Michelin works at Clermont Ferrand, following the visit of 617 Sqn and colleagues on 16/17th March 1944 (Crown).

the remainder were to deliver incendiaries. Clayton's brief required him to conduct an experiment using a 1,000 pounder to detonate his 12,000 pounder as an airburst over the explosives storage area. Apparently it worked, because the entire dump went up, lighting the sky for ten seconds. Kearns was unable to release his bomb either mechanically or manually despite making four runs across the target. He pulled away, closed the bomb doors and the bomb-aimer plugged in the electrical circuit again. On re-opening the bomb doors some ten miles east south east of the target the 12,000 pounder and flares fell out. Visibility was good, and the factory and storage buildings were clearly seen to be well ablaze after a number of large explosions. All participants landed safely back at Woodhall Spa between 02.02 and 02.30 from what was a completely successful operation. Again, the extent of the damage, particularly that caused by the blast, was confirmed by reconnaissance photos.

This night brought the first of two hugely destructive raids by the main force on Frankfurt. Over eight hundred aircraft destroyed or seriously damaged six thousand buildings, most of them houses, and over 55,000 people were bombed out of their homes.

The nitro-cellulose explosives works at Angouleme followed for 617 Squadron on the 20th, when fourteen crews were detailed to take part. On duty on this occasion were Cheshire in DV380, Munro in DV391, Shannon in DV403, McCarthy in ME559, Kearns in ME562, Wilson in JB139, Clayton ME560, Williams in DV246, Cooper in DV385, Hadland in ED763, Edward in EE146, Willsher in DV393, Kell in DV402, and F/O "Mac" Hamilton on his first operation with the squadron in ME555. Cheshire was first off at 19.18, and with the exception of Williams, the rest got away within twenty minutes. Williams's take off was timed at 20.03, after he was forced to switch to the spare aircraft, when his own declared itself unserviceable. He also had a different bomb load from the others. With the exception of Cheshire and the "Old Firm", who carried a single 8,000 pounder plus spot-fires or TIs, all of the others were loaded with one 8,000 pounder and one 1,000 pounder, while Williams had eight 1,000 pounders in his bomb bay plus eight red spot-fires. Munro dropped his store at 22.14 from 6,400 feet, and the others followed up over the next fifteen minutes or so from heights ranging from 6,000 to 10,700 feet. Most of the bombing was accurate, causing explosions and large fires, and Cheshire described the target as wrecked. He was right. Most of the plant's buildings were completely destroyed, and nearly all of those that weren't were damaged to some extent.

On the 21st, Martin, one of the founder members of the squadron, was posted to take up duties with 100 Group, which had been formed in November to co-ordinate radio counter measures, and also to use the Mosquito borne Serrate device to hunt down and destroy enemy night fighters. It would not be long before Martin was flying one of these with 515 Squadron. The second main force raid on Frankfurt was carried out by almost eight hundred aircraft on the 22/23rd, and it was even more devastating than that of four nights earlier. All parts of the city were hit, but western districts suffered most grievously, and half of the city was without Electricity, gas and water for an extended period. Almost fourteen hundred people died over the two nights, and this major victory was achieved for the combined loss of fifty five heavy bombers.

On the following night 617 Squadron sent fourteen aircraft to attack an aero engine factory at Lyons. The crews involved were Cheshire in DV380, McCarthy in ME559, Shannon in DV403, Kearns in ME557, Clayton in ME560, Cooper in DV394, Wilson in JB139, F/L Fearn on his twenty-second sortie in all and first since joining 617, in DV385, Williams in EE131, Edward in EE146, Hadland in ED763, Willsher in DV393, Stanford in ME555 and Ross in ME562. Take-off time was as for the previous three operations, and they reached the target area sometime after 23.00 hours. The non-marking element of the force were each carrying eleven 1,000 pounders, while Cheshire and Shannon were loaded with six each in addition to their spot-fires, TIs and flares, and McCarthy had nine. Cheshire had been ordered not to mark from low level, and this should not have been a problem as a flare force provided by 106 Squadron was to illuminate the area for the 617 Squadron markers. Unfortunately, the flare force illuminated the wrong area, initially four miles too far north, then ten miles to the south and finally ten miles north again. 617 had to use its own flares, and the fact that they were too few added to the difficulties in identifying the target in the hazy conditions. Cheshire instructed the crews to overshoot the spot fires, but as the bombs had been fitted with delay fuses, they turned for home unable to determine the results of their efforts. Cheshire, though, remained behind in the target area to observe the outcome. Ross failed to pick up a divert signal on the way back, and he alone landed at Woodhall Spa, while the others all put down at Tangmere on the south coast. This was not the first occasion that difficulties had been encountered with flares, or that their performance had proved to be unsatisfactory. They were designed to burst at 4,000 feet, and drift slowly to earth, but some ignited at 8,000 feet, while others only did so on impact with the ground. This also happened if they were parachute flares and the parachute failed to open. Flares igniting at ground level created copious amounts of smoke as they burned out, and could easily obscure the aiming point.

The squadron would return to this target on the night of the 25/26th, but before that, the 24th was momentous for a number of reasons. Firstly, Shannon and McCarthy were made A and C Flight commanders respectively, and were recommended for the acting rank of Squadron Leader, Munro having already been installed as a flight commander some time earlier. Secondly, that night the main force conducted the nineteenth and final raid of the long-running campaign against Berlin, and the final raid of the war on the city by the RAF's heavy brigade. Over eight hundred aircraft took off, and they encountered unusually strong winds from the north at cruising altitude, which pushed them continually south of track, and broke the cohesion of the bomber stream. This led to scattered bombing at the Capital, and over a hundred outlying communities were afflicted. The south-western districts received most of the bombs, and housing was the chief victim. The jet stream wind continued to dog the crews on the way home, and many aircraft were driven over heavily defended areas of Germany, where they fell within range of predicted flak. A massive seventy-two aircraft failed to return, and over two thirds of them were brought down by ground fire. Also on the 24th a B17 arrived at Woodhall Spa with its American crew, who were to spend a few days with their 617 Squadron counterparts in an exchange arrangement.

On the following night sixteen 617 Squadron aircraft returned to Lyons for a second crack at the aero-engine factory. W/C Cheshire again took the lead in DV380, with S/L Shannon in DV403, S/L McCarthy in ME559, Kearns in ME557, Wilson in JB139, Clayton in DV394, Fearn in the now departed "Mickey" Martin's DV402, Edward in EE146, Poore in DV391, Williams in EE131, Hadland in ED763, Pryor in DV385, Hamilton in ME555, Ross in ME561, Willsher in DV393 and Stanford in ME554. Cheshire carried F/S Pengelly as an additional gunner on this night to occupy the front turret, and an F/S Kimberley was also on board as the cine-camera operator. The usual take-off time had them arriving in the target area around 23.00 hours, and Cheshire, Shannon and McCarthy went in at low-level to deliver their spot fires and TIs. McCarthy is recorded in the ORB as dropping his from 50 feet. Unusually for 617 Squadron, there seemed to be some confusion concerning the accuracy of the markers, and Pryor aimed his twelve 500 pounders at the red spot fire to the east in accordance with instructions from Cheshire. Most of the others, he noticed, seemed to be bombing the wrong marker, and he described the raid as appearing to be very scattered. Certainly, Wilson admitted to misunderstanding the instructions and bombed the wrong spot fire. By the time that Hadland dropped the last bombs at 00.06, almost an hour after the raid began, smoke in the target area made it impossible to determine whether or not the factory buildings had been hit. Cheshire recorded fires covering approximately one square mile, and added that there was no attempt at photography. In fact, the bombing had been concentrated around the southwest of the factory. Stanford landed at Ford with an unserviceable wireless, and some kind of a leak from his starboard-inner engine. The American visitors had watched the squadron depart for the operation, and now they were invited to sit in on the debriefing.

Although the Berlin offensive was now over for the main force, the winter campaign still had a week to run, and two more major operations for the crews to negotiate. The first of these was delivered by almost seven hundred aircraft upon Essen on the 26/27th, when over seventeen hundred houses were destroyed, and forty-eight industrial buildings were seriously damaged. Thus was continued the remarkable run of successes against this once elusive target since the introduction of Oboe to main force operations a year earlier. On the 27th Cheshire went to Coleby Grange to receive instruction in a Mosquito, and two examples of the type were subsequently taken on squadron charge that day. The third attempt to nail the aero engine factory at Lyon was carried out by fifteen aircraft on the 29/30th. The crews were those of Cheshire in DV380, Kearns in ME557, Clayton in ME560, Ross in ME562, Knilans in ME561, Stout in ME559, Duffy in DV394, Stanford in ME554, Hamilton in DV403, Wilson in JB139, Poore in DV391, Pryor in DV402, Edward in EE131, Fearn in DV246 and Knights in DV385. They carried an unusual variety of bomb loads, Cheshire's consisting of spot-fires, T.I.s and two 500 pounders, while Kearns had T.I.s and eight 500 pounders on board, Clayton spot-fires, T.I.s and five 500 pounders, Ross, Knilans, Stout, Hamilton, Wilson, Poore, Pryor and Knights one 8,000 pounder and two 1,000 pounders, and Duffy, Stanford, Edward and Fearn fourteen 500 pounders. This time most of the hardware seemed to find the mark, and Clayton reported seeing the main factory building to be well alight with its roof gone. It was later assessed, that sixteen of twenty-two key buildings had been destroyed. Fearn's Lancaster was hit by heavy predicted flak, but no serious damage resulted. This proved to be the final operation of the month. On the following day Cheshire went solo for the first time in a Mosquito, and he would use his new skills to good effect in the coming months.

The month's activities were not quite over for the main force crews, who had just one more operation ahead of them, before they would turn their attention to an entirely different campaign. The night of the 30/31st was to be devoted to a standard, deep penetration, maximum effort raid on the birth place of Nazism, Nuremberg. The only departure from standard routine was the selection of a 5 Group inspired plan, in place of that offered by 8 Group, which normally prepared the details of an operation. The Pathfinder AOC, AVM Bennett, threw a fit when he learned of the route, which would take the bomber stream in a long straight leg from Belgium across Germany, to a point about fifty miles north of the target, from where the final run-in was to commence, and he predicted a disaster. There were some doubts about the weather, and it was half expected that the operation would be scrubbed, but it was not to be. 795 aircraft took off, and climbing for height, the crews were struck by some unfamiliar features about the conditions. The moon, though fairly new, cast an unusually bright light, and the visibility possessed a crystal clarity which had rarely before been encountered. The forecast cloud at cruising altitude failed to materialize, but a layer formed beneath the aircraft, to silhouette them like flies on a table cloth. To add insult to injury, condensation trails formed to further advertise the aircrafts' presence, and the jetstream winds which had so adversely effected the Berlin raid a week earlier, blew this time from the south. This again broke the cohesion of the bomber stream, and spread it out over a vast area.

The combination of the route and the conditions handed the force on a plate to the night fighters, which were waiting at their control beacons almost in the path of the approaching bombers. The carnage began over Charleroi in Belgium, and the ground from there to Nuremberg was littered with the burning wreckage of RAF aircraft. Over eighty aircraft fell before the target was reached, and those crews who either failed to notice the strength of the wind, or refused to believe the evidence, were blown up to fifty miles north of their intended track, and turned towards Nuremberg from a false position. This demonstrated a flaw in the "windfinder" system, which used selected crews to check wind speed and direction and report it back to HQ. Having never encountered such strong winds before, the navigators were loath to accept what the evidence told them, and modified the figures before sending them. At group even the modified figures were disbelieved and were modified down again for re-broadcast to the bomber stream. As a result more than a hundred aircraft bombed Schweinfurt in error, and thus further reduced the numbers attacking the intended target, which escaped with modest damage. Ninety-five aircraft failed to return home, and many more were written off in crashes, or with battle damage too extensive to repair.

April 1944

As far as the main force was concerned, what now lay ahead of the crews was in marked contrast to that endured by them over the winter months. The new priority was the pre-invasion campaign, the main component of which was the Transportation Plan, the systematic dismantling by bombing of the French and Belgian railway networks. This would require attacks on all of the main railway centres with marshalling yards, along with the locomotive depots and repair and maintenance facilities. This had, in fact, already been put into practice by the Halifax and Stirling squadrons during March, with attacks on railway yards at Trappes, le Mans, Amiens, Laon, Aulnoye, Courtrai and Vaires. Now that the entire main force had become available, the crews could look forward to shorter-range hops to France and Belgium in improving weather conditions, in place of the long slog to Germany on dark, often dirty nights. These operations would prove to be equally demanding in their way, however, and would require of the crews a greater commitment to accuracy to avoid unnecessary casualties among friendly civilians.

The main fly in the ointment as far as the crews were concerned was a policy from on high, which decreed that most such operations were worthy of counting as just one third of a sortie towards the completion of a tour, and until this flawed idea was rescinded, an air of discontent pervaded the bomber stations. Despite the prohibitive losses over the winter, the Command was in remarkably fine fettle to face its new challenge, and Harris was in the enviable position of being able to achieve what had eluded his predecessor. This was to hit multiple targets simultaneously with forces large enough to make an impact. He could now assign targets to individual Groups, to Groups in tandem or to the Command as a whole as dictated by operational requirements, and spread his Pathfinder crews around to provide a sprinkling for each raid. Also, while he was at the helm, his favoured policy of city busting would never be entirely shelved in favour of other considerations, and whenever an opportunity arose to strike against the cities, he would take it.

On the 2nd of April Cheshire was awarded a second Bar to his DSO, and celebrated the event on the 5/6th by going to war for the first time in a Mosquito. This would also be the first time that 617 Squadron marked for 5 Group, and it was to be a defining moment. A force of 144 Lancasters was made ready, seventeen of them provided by 617 Squadron, and the full squadron order of battle was; Cheshire in ML976, with F/O Kelly as navigator, Munro in LM482, McCarthy in LM492, Clayton in ME560, Cooper in DV394, Edward in EE146, Poore in DV391, Pryor in DV380, Fearn in LM485, Ross in ME562, Knights in DV385, Knilans in ME561, Stout in ED763, F/O Cheney on his first operation with the squadron, in DV393, Kell in DV402, Duffy in ME555, Stanford in ME554 and Hamilton in DV403. The main target was an aircraft repair factory at Toulouse, which Cheshire was to mark from low level in the Mosquito, while Munro and McCarthy were on hand to back up with spot fires from medium level, before joining the others in delivering 8,000 pounders. The other 617 Squadron aircraft were, in fact, carrying six 500 pounders in addition to their blockbuster.

Part of the main force element was to attack three other targets on Toulouse airfield. After an outward flight for the Lancasters of almost four hours, Cheshire went in in the Mosquito at 00.17 at 800-1,000 feet, and lobbed two red spot-fires onto the factory buildings with such accuracy, that it was not necessary for Munro and McCarthy to back up. Three minutes later Munro watched his 8,000 pounder fall into a large repair hangar from 10,000 feet, while McCarthy dropped his from a thousand feet higher. The non-marker crews from 617 Squadron delivered their attacks from between 15,000 and 17,800 feet, while their 5 Group colleagues were assigned to lower flight levels, and all the attacks were completely successful, costing between them just one 207 Squadron Lancaster. S/L Moyna was on hand in Munro's aircraft to record the scene for posterity. All crews were diverted to Wescott on the way home, and when Pryor finally got back to Woodhall he ran off the perimeter track, damaging his rear turret, fuselage and tail-plane. On learning of the success of the Toulouse operation, carried out as it was by ordinary crews from squadrons of the line without special training, Harris authorized 5 Group's independence from the rest of the main force.

Later on during the 6th six H2S Lancasters arrived on temporary detachment from other 5 Group squadrons complete with air and ground crews. The aircrews were to remain permanently, but the ground crews would stay only while the aircraft were on charge. P/Os Castagnola and Ian Ross came with JB370 and ND472 respectively from 57 Squadron, P/O Carey brought ND339 from 106 Squadron, P/O Sanders came from 49 Squadron with ND683, P/O Watts and ND554 arrived from 630 Squadron, and P/O Levy and ND631 were posted in from 44 Squadron. Also posted in at the same time was F/L Fawke from 1660CU. Freddie Watts and his crew had begun their operational career with a trip to Berlin at the end of January. They didn't see the mighty city through the impenetrable cloud cover, but they made it home after a seven-hour trip to contemplate the fact that they now only had another twenty-nine operations to negotiate. The second and third came at Schweinfurt and Augsburg on consecutive nights at the end of February, while March brought two trips to Stuttgart, two to Frankfurt, and the disasters of the final Berlin raid and Nuremberg. With a number of other operations in the bag this brought the crew's time with 630 Squadron to an end on a total of eleven. During its time with 630 Squadron the crew's Lancaster ND554 was coded LE-C, "Conquering Cleo", and bore a painting of a lion tearing up a swastika. Ian Ross had joined 57 Squadron from 1654CU, where his flight commander had been Drew Wyness. His first operation was a trip to Brunswick in mid-January as second dickey to Arthur Fearn, and six nights later he took his own crew to Berlin and returned on three engines. Berlin was the destination three more times in four nights at the end of the month, the second one again resulting in the loss of an engine, while the third one ended in an early return. The final raid of the winter campaign, the Nuremberg catastrophe, was the crew's fourteenth and last sortie with 630 Squadron.

P/O Levy had arrived at 44 Squadron with his crew as a Sergeant pilot on the 3rd of February, during the two-week stand-down in main force operations preceding the penultimate Berlin raid. The crew's first operation was the Leipzig disaster on the 19/20th, when technical problems forced them to return early and land at the emergency strip at Woodbridge on the Suffolk coast. Five nights later they completed the trip to Schweinfurt, before participating in the destruction of Augsburg twenty-four hours later. Levy was commissioned on the last day of the month, the 29th as it was a leap year, and celebrated with a raid on Stuttgart on the following night. During the final third of March Levy and his crew attacked Frankfurt on the 22/23rd, took part in the final attack on Berlin on the 24/25th, went to Essen two nights later and survived Nuremberg on the 30/31st. Bill Carey was a diminutive Australian who came to the squadron with eleven operations under his belt.

The new offensive got into full swing on the night of the 9/10th of April, when separate forces attacked railway targets at Lille and at Villeneuve-St-Georges on the outskirts of Paris. The former was directed at the Delivrance goods station by elements of 3, 4, 6 and 8 Groups, and it succeeded in destroying over two thousand items of rolling stock, while also causing damage to buildings and track. Sadly, and almost inevitably, the collateral bombing of adjacent residential districts caused over four hundred civilian deaths. The latter operation was aimed at the marshalling yards by a contingent from all of the Groups, and whilst this attack was believed to be moderately successful, almost a hundred fatal casualties were inflicted on civilians here also. On the following night, five railway yards were attacked in France and Belgium, of which the marshalling yards at Tours were assigned to 5 Group. Only one of the night's targets escaped serious damage, but stray bombs at Ghent killed over four hundred Belgian civilians.

On the same night 617 Squadron dispatched seventeen Lancasters and a Mosquito to a signals equipment depot at St Cyr. The crews were Cheshire in ML976, Munro in LM482, McCarthy in LM492, Clayton in ME560, Wilson in LM485, Poore in DV391, Fearn in DV393, Pryor in EE146, Cooper in DV394, Williams in EE131, Knilans in ME561, Duffy in ME555, Stanford in ME554, Stout in ME559, Cheney in JB139, Kell in ME557, Ross in ME562 and Knights in DV385. New pilots, Carey, Castagnola, Sanders and Levy, along with some other crew members, flew as passengers to observe the squadron's bombing techniques in operation, and S/L Moyna again set up his camera in Munro's Lancaster. They took off in a thirty-minute slot, Cheshire the last to depart at 23.59, and one hour and fifty-six minutes later he began his dive from 5,000 to 1,000 feet to deposit two red spot-fires onto the western edge of the main target. He then called in Munro to place his markers more accurately on the centre of the target, but they fell some distance away. The Operations Record Book records Munro's spot-fires falling at 02.02, and while this was going on the other 617 Squadron crews had to wait, finally coming in to bomb as the first markers had almost burned out.

In his post raid report Cheshire described the first stick of bombs falling onto the northwest corner of the factory and starting fires. This was fortuitous, as it, in effect, remarked the aiming point. This first stick to fall was delivered from 9,300 feet at 02.06 by Lt Knilans, who himself witnessed the resultant immediate conflagration. Cheshire then ordered the other crews to aim for these fires. The spot-fires carried by McCarthy were not required, but his single 8,000 pounder was, and this would soon join the 8,000 and 500 pounders carried by the remainder of the squadron. Munro mentions his own bomb falling into the centre of the fires already burning in the target area. Smoke rose to 8,000 feet, and hampered any further assessment of the results. All aircraft returned safely to Woodhall Spa, and with the exception of Clayton and Williams, whose cameras failed to function, each brought back an aiming point photo. Later in the day, Australian F/O "Bunny" Lee and his crew arrived on posting from 106 Squadron, with which they had completed a tour of twenty-nine operations

Over three hundred aircraft drawn from 1, 3, 5 and 8 Groups delivered Aachen's most serious raid of the war on the 11/12th, as a result of which, more than fifteen hundred people lost their lives, and this was followed by a period of minor operations. On the 14th, Bomber Command officially became subject to the dictates of SHAEF in preparation for the forthcoming invasion, and would remain thus shackled until the Allied armies were sweeping towards the German frontier at the end of the summer.

The end of an era came on the 15th, when most of the remaining original Type 464 Provisioning Lancasters were flown out to Metheringham for storage. The intention was to fly them occasionally and maintain them sufficiently to allow their return to operations should the need arise. On the following day S/L Shannon and F/Ls Kearns and Fawke were declared operational on Mosquitos, and their crews were unceremoniously put up for disposal, although Shannon retained the now F/O Sumpter as his navigator, while F/O Barclay performed that function for Kearns, and F/O Bennett for Fawke. On the 18th matters came to something of a head between Cochrane and Bennett, when 5 Group welcomed back into the fold two of its most prestigious former squadrons, 83 and 97. To add insult to injury it had already taken delivery of 627 Squadron with its Mosquitos three days earlier. All three squadrons were on permanent detachment from the Pathfinders, much to the chagrin of Bennett, who was infuriated at having three of his finest units taken from him, particularly so, as 5 Group was the recipient. The squadrons remained officially part of 8 Group, and the crews retained their ranks and coveted Pathfinder badge, but to all intents and purposes they were now 5 Group.

Much has been written about the alleged animosity between Bennett and AVM Cochrane at 5 Group, and whatever the truth, they were two of the most brilliant men to serve Bomber Command during the entire war, both having a tactical awareness and intellect beyond the aspirations of most. It was simply a case of differences of opinion concerning the best way to mark a target, and both viewpoints had equal merit. Bennett considered low-level marking to be suicidal, and would not ask it of his crews, while Cochrane would consider any reasonable idea to improve accuracy. In fact, low-level marking in a small, fast Mosquito was relatively safe, as events would demonstrate. Certainly, neither of these group commanders would allow their differences to be aired in public, nor to interfere with their prosecution of the war. The transfer of the squadrons was, however, an indication of the success of the low level visual marking method pioneered by Cheshire and Martin, and 627 Squadron was to be dedicated to this role, with the two heavy squadrons providing the illumination.

The transfer of these squadrons was not a reflection on Bennett, who had achieved remarkable success in bringing his Group to a peak of performance and efficiency. Rather, it was an indication of the success of the low level visual marking method pioneered by Cheshire and Martin. It was unfortunate, though, that the arrival of the two heavy squadrons at Coningsby was marred by the attitude of the base commander, Air Commodore Sharp. As the crews climbed out of the buses, already disgruntled at being removed from what they saw as an elite status at 8 Group, they were summoned to a lecture by Sharp, a man with no relevant operational experience. Instead of welcoming them as brothers-in-arms, he harangued them about their supposedly bad 8 Group habits, and told them to buckle down to learning 5 Group ways. This was an insult to battle-hardened airmen, for whom the new role of target illuminating would be a piece of cake compared with the complexities of their former job. It left a sour taste, and it would be a considerable time before a grudging loyalty developed to 5 Group. Whatever the circumstances leading to this situation, for the remainder of the war 5 Group had its own target marking force, with 83 and 97 Squadrons acting as the flare force and heavy markers, while 627 Squadron, after a bedding-in period, would take over the low level visual marking role from 617 Squadron. From this moment also, 5 Group would be referred to in 8 Group circles somewhat disparagingly as the "Independent Air Force", or the "Lincolnshire Poachers", and the former appellation, at least, would prove to be an accurate description.

That night 617 Squadron operated four Mosquitos for the first time, accompanied by nineteen of its Lancasters to mark the marshalling yards at Juvisy for the Group. It is not possible to be certain which Mosquitos were in use from this point, as the ORB entries often differ from those in logbooks, and the squadron kept changing its aircraft. Where there is major doubt, therefore, the Mosquito serials will be omitted from the narrative. The Mosquito pilots for this operation were W/C Cheshire, S/L Shannon, F/L Kearns and F/L Fawke, and they were guided to the target by three Oboe Mosquitos from 8 Group. The Lancaster crews were those of Munro in LM482, McCarthy in LM492, Wilson in LM485, Ross in ME562, Cooper in DV394, Knights in DV385, Willsher in DV393, Duffy in ME555, Stout in JB139, Poore in DV391, Pryor in EE146, Stanford in ME554, and seven crews on their first operation with the squadron. These were W/O Gingles in LM489, F/L Howard in ED763, F/L Reid in ME557, P/O Sanders in ND683, P/O Carey in ND339, P/O Ian Ross in JB370, and P/O Levy in ND631. 617 Squadron's heavy brigade got away between 20.25 and 20.46 carrying a mixture of 1,000 and 500 pounders and flares, while Munro, McCarthy, Wilson and Nicky Ross also had red spot-fires on board. The Mosquitos left Woodhall Spa in a three-minute slot to 21.30, and they arrived in the target area shortly after 23.00 hours. The three 8 Group Oboe Mosquitos provided the initial reference for the 617 Squadron Lancaster element, and Stanford, Reid, Sanders and Levy all dropped their flares at 23.12, to be followed by the others over the ensuing five minutes.

Despite the illumination Cheshire experienced difficulty in identifying the first aiming point, and called on which ever of the other Mosquito pilots who could see it to go in and mark. Fawke answered the call and dived down to 800 feet at around 23.20. Cheshire then ran in to mark the second aiming point at 23.21, diving from 5,000 to 2,000 feet to deliver four spot-fires. Unfortunately, they all hung up and had to be brought home. Shannon and Kearns stood in reserve for the second batch of flares, but were not needed, and Cheshire ordered the other squadron Lancasters with spot-fires to back up those delivered by Fawke. Apart from one or two wild sticks of bombs the attack by around 180 Lancasters of the Group seemed to be accurate and concentrated, and was witnessed by A/C Sharp from his vantage point in Duffy's ME555. Post raid reconnaissance confirmed the accuracy and concentration of the operation, which left track, rolling stock and engine and carriage repair sheds extensively damaged. The main lines were also severed at many points, but collateral damage was inflicted upon residential districts northwest of the target.

83, 97 and 627 Squadrons did not participate at Juvisy. No doubt incensed by their treatment at the hands of their new masters, the commanding officers refused to allow the crews to operate on the basis that they had not yet assimilated the techniques of the 5 Group method. In the event they did not have long to wait for their 5 Group baptism. A two-phase operation was planned against the marshalling yards at la Chapelle, north of Paris, to take place with an hour between the attacks. It would be mounted on the night of the 20/21st, and would be the first fully orchestrated performance by the newly independent Group. The plan called for 8 Group Mosquitos to drop cascading flares by Oboe to provide an initial reference, and for six Mosquitos of 627 Squadron to lay a screen of Window ahead of the approaching main force Lancasters. Once the target had been identified, the first members of the 83 and 97 Squadron Lancaster flare force were to provide illumination for the low-level marker Mosquitos of 617 Squadron. These would then mark the first aiming point with red spot-fires for the main force Lancasters to aim at, and the whole process would be repeated an hour later at a second aiming point. The 617 Squadron element for the first phase consisted of Cheshire and Fawke in Mosquitos, Munro in LM482, with Air Commodore Satterly on board as an observer, McCarthy in LM492, Wilson in LM485, Duffy in ME555, Stout in ME559, Knilans in ME560 and Ian Ross in JB370. For the second phase Shannon and Kearns represented the Mosquito element, while the Lancasters were those of Howard in ED763, Reid in ME557, Stanford in ME554, Carey in ED817, Levy in ND631, Sanders in ND683, and P/O Watts, on his first operation with the squadron, in ND554. All of the squadron's Lancasters were loaded with twelve 1,000 pounders.

Zero hour was set for 00.05, and this required the first phase Lancaster brigade to depart Woodhall Spa either side of 22.00 hours, to be followed half an hour later by Cheshire and Fawke, while the second phase Lancasters became airborne around 23.15, with Shannon and Kearns bringing up the rear in their Mosquitos at 23.45 and 23.47 respectively. Two minutes before zero hour six 627 Squadron Mosquitos began Windowing from high level, and continued to do so for seventeen minutes until the arrival of the main force. Drifting downwards in still air at the rate of five hundred feet per minute, the Window would provide cover throughout the period of the main force's presence in the target area. The Pathfinder Mosquitos turned up on time, but their target indicators failed to cascade on impact on the first or southern aiming point. This eventuality had been anticipated, however, and it meant, that the first element of four flare-carrying Lancasters had to orbit, while plan B was put into action. A second batch of four aircraft arrived a minute or so later, and two of them dropped flares by Oboe, which allowed the remaining six flare carriers to deliver theirs. It was at this point, that the original Pathfinder target indicators began to burn on the ground.

The only problem resulting from this hitch was the reduction in time for the low-level marking to take place. Rather than having an interval between the two elements of four flare-carrying aircraft, which would have allowed for an extended period of illumination, they all went down at once. In the event, this did not prove to be a problem for Cheshire, who released four spot-fires from 1,200 feet at 00.16, and Fawke backed these up four minutes later. A VHF communication problem between Cheshire and the main force controller, W/C Dean of 83 Squadron, caused the opening of the attack to be delayed for a minute or so, but this was quickly sorted, and the initial bombing was accurate and concentrated. Smoke soon obscured the spot-fires, however, and Dean found it necessary to remark the aiming point. At 01.11 Shannon marked the second or northern aiming point, and his spot-fires were backed up by Kearns two minutes later. The second phase proceeded smoothly, and both halves of the railway yards were severely damaged. Reconnaissance photos taken on the following day again confirmed the remarkable concentration of the bombing, and the devastation around both aiming points. A bridge at the southern end of the yards was also severely damaged. While this raid was in progress, elements of 1, 3, 6 and 8 Groups were conducting a punishing assault on Cologne, which suffered the destruction of over eighteen hundred houses, and damage to hundreds of industrial and business premises.

Thus far the Group's low-level visual marking technique had not been tried out against a heavily defended target in Germany, and this would provide the real test. Brunswick had been attacked by the Command for the first time in numbers in mid-January, and had escaped relatively lightly. As events were to prove, it would continue to be a difficult nut to crack until late in the year. This large town was selected as the proving ground for the 5 Group method just forty-eight hours after the La Chapelle operation, and a maximum 5 Group effort was called. As the target lay beyond the range of Oboe, there would be no Pathfinder involvement on this occasion, and 54 Base would have to provide all of the marking. The only non-5 Group participants were ten ABC Lancasters from 1 Group's 101 Squadron, which were to provide an RCM screen as well as carry a full bomb load. The Group carried out its own weather reconnaissance prior to the operation, and as the report from this was not encouraging, it was decided to send two 627 Squadron Mosquitos to the target area thirty minutes before zero hour. If they encountered cloud cover over the target, thus rendering the low-level marking method ineffective, they would inform the approaching flare force from 83 and 97 Squadrons to prepare skymarkers for the main force crews to aim at. The two Mosquitos were then to rejoin the main force and carry out a dive-bombing attack. Ten 627 Squadron Mosquitos were to begin dropping Window six minutes before they reached the target, arriving three minutes before zero hour, while the flare carrying Lancasters were to arrive five at a time at one minute intervals to provide seven minutes of illumination for the low-level element. This entire complex operational plan depended on good VHF communication, and sadly, this would prove to be the night's Achilles heel.

Munro was at the controls of the first 617 Squadron Lancaster to take off from Woodhall Spa at 23.15. He was in his usual aircraft, as was McCarthy, and the others were, Nick Ross in ME562, Duffy in LM489, Cooper in DV394, Stanford in ME554, Willsher in DV393, Poore in DV391, Stout in ME559, Fearn in DV246, Hamilton in DV403, Shannon's former chariot, Reid in ME557, Knights in DV385, Sanders in ND683, Ian Ross in JB370, Levy in ND472, Watts in ND554 and Carey in ED817, the second prototype Dams Lancaster. Watts was the last away at 23.35. Some of these were carrying six 1,000 pounders with spot-fires to back up the marking if required, while others were loaded with nine 1,000 pounders and a 2,000 pounder, or a 2,000 pounder plus clusters of the new "J" bomb incendiaries. The Mosquito element was as for the previous operation, and these faster-flying aircraft left just before midnight, arriving in the target area about ninety minutes later. Ian Ross was back at Woodhall Spa less than two hours after taking off. An astro comparison showed the D.R and P4 compasses to be unreliable, and on the way home they dumped their 2,000 pounder in the sea. Communications difficulties had already manifested themselves by the time of Cheshire's arrival in the target area, interference on the VHF frequency preventing the weather Mosquito crews from contacting the flare force. The problem would eventually be traced to a single VHF set incorrectly fitted in a 617 Squadron Lancaster.

The initial flares were released over the town of Wolfenbüttel, five miles south of the intended location, and as Cheshire searched in their light at low level, he found only suburbs and open country. He withheld his spot-fires and waited for the next batch of flares, which were a little to the north of Brunswick's centre, but close enough for Gerry Fawke to identify the aiming point and mark it with four red spot-fires. Cheshire verified the accuracy of Fawke's work, and ordered Kearns to back up with a further four red spot-fires, while Shannon held off and ultimately was not needed. This had now set the timing back by seven minutes. Cheshire called in the main force to bomb, and the initial salvos fell squarely into the town centre. However, the first spot-fires began to burn out around four minutes after the opening of the attack, and Geoff Stout aimed his load at their estimated position. His incendiaries went down, but the 2,000 pounder hung up and was eventually jettisoned. Green target indicators were dropped to replace the extinguished red spot-fires, in accordance with instructions at briefing, but unfortunately, they fell southwest of Brunswick, and inevitably began to attract later bomb loads. Cheshire was unable to communicate directly with the main force because of interference, but managed to get through to Munro, who could pass on his message by W/T. In the event, Munro apparently misheard Cheshire's message because of the interference, and he retransmitted instructions to bomb the green TIs. This was carried out by many of the remaining main force crews, and at least 50% of the night's effort was directed away from the intended aiming point. Never the less, some useful damage was inflicted, and on the credit side, the losses were restricted to a very modest four aircraft. Meanwhile, the other Groups were busy over Düsseldorf, destroying or seriously damaging two thousand houses and dozens of industrial buildings, and while the Independent Air Force had got off lightly at Brunswick, twenty-nine aircraft failed to return from the Ruhr.

Having failed to prove conclusively the 5 Group method at Brunswick, it was decided to try again at the much bombed and consequently well-defended southern city of Munich. Just two nights after Brunswick 234 Lancasters and sixteen Mosquitos of 5 Group, accompanied by ten ABC Lancasters from 101 Squadron, set out for southern Germany. 617 Squadron dispatched the same four Mosquitos and crews, who departed Woodhall Spa around midnight, a remarkable three hours after the twelve Lancasters. The latter were led by Munro, unusually in LM485, and McCarthy in LM492, while the rest of the heavy element consisted of Cooper in DV394, Williams in EE131, Fearn in DV246, Reid in ME557, Hamilton in ME555, Stout in ME559, Stanford in ME554, Knights in DV385, Duffy in LM489, and Nick Ross in ME562. All of the Lancasters were carrying "J" clusters and standard 30lb incendiaries alone. Taking off at the same time were six other of the squadron's Lancasters, whose purpose was to provide a diversion for the main raid by dropping flares and target indicators over Milan. This contingent included four of the H2s equipped Lancasters, and the crews were Edward in ME560, Watts in ND554, Levy in ND631, Carey in ED817, Ian Ross in JB370 and Sanders in ND472.

As the 5 Group main force approached southern Germany via south-western France, feinting towards Italy, eleven 627 Squadron Mosquitos made for the target area by a more direct route to commence windowing two and a half minutes ahead of the flare force. Cheshire and Co also flew directly to the target, although skirting to the south of the well-defended city of Augsburg, and running the gauntlet of a continuous flak barrage. Munich boasted around two hundred light flak guns and many searchlights, all of which seemed to greet Cheshire's arrival as the first flares were on their way down at 01.40. Cheshire dived through the murderous curtain of steel to release his markers from 1,500 feet squarely onto the aiming point, before screaming across the city at little more than rooftop height to make good his escape. The other three Mosquitos attempted to back up over the succeeding fifteen minutes, but Fawke's markers failed to release. Never the less, the 5 Group heavy brigade plastered the markers, and over eleven hundred buildings were destroyed, mostly in the central districts of the city. It was on this trip that the squadron suffered the year's first operational loss of a crew, that of F/L Cooper, whose Lancaster,

DV394, was shot down by a JU88 R-2 night fighter of 1/NJG2 on the way home southwest of Ulm. The bomb-aimer, F/O Harden, was killed, while the remainder of the crew survived to fall into enemy hands. They had been undone by Hauptmann Gerhardt Raht, a twenty-three year-old ace operating out of Langensalza, for whom it was the thirty-first kill in a tally that would reach fifty-eight by war's end. Bill Reid arrived home with a hole in his starboard-inner nacelle courtesy of predicted flak, and a night fighter attacked Geoff Stout during the camera run without effect. The operation was declared an outstanding success, and it was probably this raid above all, which sealed the award of the Victoria Cross to Cheshire at the eventual end of his operational career of one hundred sorties.

While this operation was in progress, six other of the squadrons Lancasters, including four of those equipped with H2s, were carrying out a spoof raid on Milan as a diversion, dispensing flares and TIs to attract night fighters away from Munich, and all of these, five of the crews recently posted in, and led by F/L Edward in ME560, returned safely. At the end of the month, F/L Hadland was posted to 5 LFS for instructional duties. The southern German city of Karlsruhe was the target for the other Groups on this night, but strong winds pushed the attack towards its northern half, and much of the bombing fell into open country.

617 Squadron had now closed its month's account, but the main force continued to pound its way across Germany and France, and three operations were laid on for the 26/27th. The main effort was directed at Essen, and returning crews claimed a successful outcome. The Independent Air Force went to Schweinfurt, where 627 Squadron carried out the low level marking for the first time as successors to 617 Squadron. Sadly, its maiden effort was not blessed with success under difficult circumstances and a spirited defence, and much of the bombing fell into open country. The other target was the railway yards at Villeneuve-St-Georges, part of which was accurately bombed by Halifaxes of 4 and 6 Groups. Aircraft from 1, 3, 6 and 8 Groups carried out a very successful raid on the highly industrialized town of Friedrichshafen on the 27/28th, where the night's principal targets were tank engine and gearbox factories. Over 60% of the town's built-up area was estimated as destroyed, and tank production suffered a serious setback. The remainder of the month was devoted largely to railway targets, although small forces from 5 Group attacked a number of factories in France and Norway. F/L Hadland concluded his tour at the end of the month, and was posted to 5 LFS for instructional duties.

April ended on a sad note for the squadron with news of the death of F/O Brian Jagger, who had been Shannon's front gunner on Operation Chastise and a regular in the mid-upper turret from then on until his posting to the Bombing Development Unit at Newmarket on the 6th of March. He had flown his last operation with Shannon on the 25/26th of January, and his commission had come through in February backdated to October. He had already advanced another rank since then, and at the time of his death he was still on the strength of the BDU. F/L Healey DFC, a 49 Squadron pilot, took off from Binbrook in the afternoon of Sunday the 30th for a proving flight in 460 Squadron's ND553, with a 460 Squadron crew on board and F/O Brian Jagger DFM. The purpose of the flight was to trial the new "Village Inn" system, also known as AGLT - Automatic Gun Laying Turret, with an RAF fighter making dummy attacks on the Lancaster to test the new system. The Lancaster was being thrown around the sky in evasive action, and it was during these strenuous manoeuvres that the dinghy began to inflate while still in the Lancaster's wing. It broke free from its stowage in the wing, when it had inflated too much to remain contained. It burst out with disastrous consequences, tangling around the tail and forcing the Lancaster over onto its back, and despite the best efforts of the pilot, the aircraft crashed near Witchford at 16.55. In the light of similar incidents involving dinghies and Lancasters during this period, it was decided to reduce the pressure in the CO_2 bottles used to inflate the dinghy. Such was the secrecy surrounding AGLT at the time that the accident card referred to the flight simply as fighter affiliation.

May 1944

Just one operation involved 617 Squadron during May, and even then it was only the Mosquito crews who were called upon. It was mounted on the 3rd, the day that saw 617 Squadron original F/L Ken Brown posted to 5 LFS as an instructor, having been preceded on the 1st by Foxlee and Simpson of Martin's Dams crew. The target for that night for 346 Lancasters of 1 and 5 Groups was the Panzer training camp and motor transport depot at Mailly-le-Camp in France. As home to the 21st Panzer division it was believed to hold many thousands of troops, and was one of the foremost tank training establishments outside of Germany. As such it was considered to be a threat to the forthcoming invasion, and a priority target, therefore, for elimination. It lay deep inside France, well to the east of Paris, around 130 miles from the nearest German frontier and three hundred miles from the bomber stations in Lincolnshire. The plan was for 617 Squadron Mosquitos to mark two aiming points, one for each Group, before handing the target over to the master bomber, and although the site was expected to be well defended, it was not thought to be an unusually difficult operation. Cheshire was to act as marker leader, while W/C Deane of 83 Squadron was the overall controller. They attended separate briefings, and it seems that neither was fully aware of the complete picture, which included a separate aiming point for 1 Group's Special Duties Flight from Binbrook. Cheshire and Shannon got away from Woodhall Spa within a minute of each other shortly after 22.00 hours in, it is believed, ML976 and NS993 respectively, while Kearns and Fawke took off at 22.21 and 22.23 in Mosquitos DZ525 and DZ521, which had been borrowed from Woodhall Spa co-residents 627 Squadron.

Cheshire and Shannon were in position before midnight, and as the first flares from the 83 and 97 Squadron Lancasters illuminated the target below, Cheshire released his two red spot fires onto the first aiming point at 00.00½ from 1,500 feet. Shannon backed them up from 400 feet five and a half minutes later, and as far as Cheshire was concerned, the operation was bang on schedule at this stage. A 97 Squadron Lancaster also laid markers accurately to ensure a constant focal point, and Cheshire passed instructions to the main force controller to call the bombers in. It was at this stage of the operation that matters began to go awry. A communications problem arose, when a commercial radio station, believed to be an American forces network, jammed the VHF frequencies in use. A few crews from 9, 207 and 467 Squadrons heard the call to bomb, and did so, but for most the instructions were swamped by the interference. Deane then attempted to control the operation by W/T, but this also failed, and the wireless transmitter in his Lancaster was later found to be sufficiently off frequency to prevent the call to bomb from reaching the main force crews. Post raid reports are contradictory, and it is impossible to establish an accurate course of events, particularly when Deane and Cheshire's understanding of the exact time of zero hour differed by five minutes. Remarkably, it also seems, that Deane was unaware that there were two marking points, or three, if one includes 1 Group's Special Duties Flight. Cheshire, initially at least, appeared happy with the early stages of the attack, and describes the bombing as concentrated and accurate. It seems certain, however, that many minutes had passed between the dropping of Cheshire's markers and the first main force bombs falling, during which period Deane was coming to terms with the fact, that his instructions were not getting through. A plausible scenario is, that in the absence of instructions, and with red spot fires clearly visible in the target, some crews opted to bomb and others followed suit. These would have been predominantly from 5 Group, but as the 1 Group crews became increasingly agitated at having to wait in bright moonlight with evidence of enemy night fighters all around, some of them inevitably joined in.

Now a new problem was arising. Smoke from these first salvoes was obliterating the entire camp, and Cheshire had to decide whether to send in Fawke and Kearns to mark the second aiming point. His feeling,

An aiming point photograph of Mailly-le-Camp from an unidentified aircraft. It also captures the image of a Lancaster (bottom right) in distress having lost its port inner engine.

and that of Deane, as it later transpired, was, that it was unnecessary. The volume of bombs still to fall into the relatively compact area of the target would ensure destruction of the entire site. By 00.16, the first phase of bombing should have been completed, leaving a clear run for Fawke and Kearns across the target. In the event, the majority of 5 Group crews were still on their bombing run, a fact unknown to Cheshire, who asked Deane for a pause in the bombing while the two Mosquitos went in. As far as Cheshire was concerned, there was no response from Deane, who would, anyway, have been confused by mention of a second aiming point of which he was unaware. In the event, Deane's deputy, S/L Sparkes of 83 Squadron, eventually found a channel free of interference, and did, in fact, transmit an instruction to halt the bombing, both by W/T and R/T, and some crews reported hearing something. While utter chaos reigned, Kearns and Fawke dived in among the falling cookies at 00.23 and 00.25 respectively to mark the second aiming point on the western edge of the camp. At 2,000 feet, they were lucky to survive the turbulence created by the exploding 4,000 pounders, when 4,000 feet was considered to be a minimum safe height. They were not entirely happy with their work, but F/O Edwards of 97 Squadron dropped a stick of markers precisely on the mark, and S/L Sparks was then able to call the 1 Group main force in. Meanwhile, the night fighters continued to create havoc among the Lancasters as they milled around in the target area. As burning aircraft were seen to fall all around, some 1 Group crews succumbed to their anxiety and frustration, and in a rare breakdown of R/T discipline let fly with comments of an uncomplimentary nature, many of which were intended for and, indeed, heard by Deane. Despite the confusion the operation was a major success, which destroyed 80% of the camp's buildings, and 102 vehicles, of which thirty-seven were tanks, while over two hundred men were killed. Forty-two Lancasters failed to return, two thirds of them from 1 Group. The operation created a great deal of acrimony, and controversy abounds to this day. The fault lay with the inaccurate and contradictory information given at the various briefings, but much of the venom instigated by the heavy losses has unjustly been directed at Cheshire.

For the remainder of the month, the squadron was engaged in intensive training for a special operation in connection with the invasion. So secret was it that the Operations Record Book refers only to limited

Post-raid reconnaissance photo showing the effects of saturated bombing of the target at Mailly-le-Camp. This came at a heavy cost to the attacking force as night fighters and flak took their toll.

flying training. Some of the activity took place off the Scottish coast, where captured German radar installations had been set up at Tantallon Castle, and scientists were able to work out how best to create a ghost invasion fleet. Mostly, though, the squadron's tactics were worked out in trials against the Bempton radar at Flamborough Head on the Yorkshire coast near Bridlington, where a final trial was flown without informing the controllers. Their report of a large coastal convoy on their screens confirmed the effectiveness of the plan. As navigation was the critical aspect of the operation, however, the crews spent the bulk of their time concentrating on this using Gee sets. As far as the Command in general was concerned, railway yards and ammunition dumps occupied elements on the 6/7th, and airfields, coastal batteries and ammunition dumps were targeted on the 7/8th. Over four hundred aircraft were sent against coastal batteries in the Pas-de-Calais on the 9/10th, to maintain the deception concerning the true location of the forthcoming invasion, and then it was back to railway installations at five sites on the 10/11th. 5 Group attacked a military camp at Bourg-Leopold in Belgium on the 11/12th, but haze forced the Master Bomber to halt proceedings part way through. Later on the 12th, Mosquito NT205 suffered an oleo leg collapse when it swung on take-off with Shannon at the controls.

On the 16th a party was held to celebrate the anniversary of Operation Chastise, and all ex-members of the squadron who took part in the famous operation were invited. Gibson was unable to attend, but he was there for a further celebration in the form of an all-ranks squadron dance on the 19th. Railways and coastal batteries continued to dominate main force activity for the remainder of the month, but Duisburg received its first major raid for a year on the 21/22nd, and Dortmund was similarly honoured twenty-four hours later. A 5 Group contingent participated in the former, but while the latter was in progress, the Independent Air Force returned to Brunswick, and again failed to deliver a telling blow. An attack by elements from all but 5 Group on two railway yards at Aachen on the 24/25th developed into an area raid, while small 5 Group forces were assigned to factories at Eindhoven and Antwerp, although neither of these operations was satisfactorily concluded. Other Dams veterans to depart during the course of the month of May were Johnson of McCarthy's crew, Clay of Munro's, Goodale of Shannon's and Whittaker of Martin's.

June 1944

June was to be another busy month for the Command, and the first four nights brought attacks on coastal batteries, signals and radar stations and communications ahead of D-Day. Over a thousand aircraft were aloft on the night of the 5/6th, D-Day Eve, to target ten coastal batteries, while support and diversionary operations involved others. At briefings crews were not informed of the significance of the night's operations, but there was a strict ban on jettisoning bombs over the sea, and all were ordered to maintain briefed flight levels. 617 Squadron's contribution was perhaps the least spectacular of all its operations, although one of the most exacting and arduous, and certainly, one of the most important. Sixteen aircraft were detailed for Operation Taxable, the purpose behind all of the secretive training in May. As already mentioned, this was a "spoof", an exercise designed to simulate an invasion fleet on enemy radar screens. The intention was to divert the enemy's attention away from the actual landing grounds along the Normandy coast, by making them believe the invasion was destined for the Pas-de-Calais, thus reinforcing an already long-held German conviction. A similar operation conducted at a different location by 218 Squadron Stirlings under the code name, Operation Glimmer, would compound the deception. No details of this highly secret operation were made available for entry into the Operations Record Book.

Each 617 Squadron Lancaster carried two pilots, and up to twelve other crew members. Cheshire led the operation and the first of two sections in LM482 as second pilot to Munro, while the McCarthy/Shannon combination headed the second section in LM492. The other participating pilots and aircraft were; Reid/Kearns in ME557, Clayton/Carey in ME560, Wilson/Sanders in LM485, N Ross/Fearn in ME562, Edward/I Ross in EE131, Kell/Cheney in DV402, Stout/Watts in ME559, Willsher/Howard in DV393, Lee/Fawke in DV246, Knights/Poore in DV385, Williams/Stanford in ME554, Hamilton/Levy in DV403, Duffy/Gingles in ME555, and Knilans/Castagnola in ME561. In order to give the impression of a fleet of ships advancing at eight knots towards the French coast at Cap d'Antifer, sixty miles east of the Normandy beaches, eight 617 Squadron Lancasters had to fly line abreast two miles apart at 180 miles an hour dispensing Window at the rate of one bundle every five seconds. After heading for the French coast, all aircraft turned to port to complete an elliptical circuit lasting seven minutes. Each new circuit advanced the forward travel of the formation by one minute. The second section would take off later to be in place to relieve the first section after two hours. Any deviation from the detail of the plan, particularly with regard to timing, would be detected on the enemy radar screens, and would raise suspicions. The operation began with the departure of the first eight aircraft from Woodhall Spa shortly after 23.00 hours to take up their starting position off the Sussex coast at around midnight. Each aircraft remained airborne for four and a half hours, two of which were spent windowing, and the crews flew their routines flawlessly, if unspectacularly. As dawn's early light began to break, all returned safely from their contribution to the landings on Fortress Europe. There was no reaction from the German side, but the operation had been just one of many designed to deceive and confuse, and in this, history shows it to have been successful.

A further thousand aircraft were employed against road and railway communications targets on D-Day Night, and it was similar fare, although in smaller numbers, on the 7/8th and 8/9th. The latter occasion provided the squadron with an opportunity to renew its association with Barnes Wallis, when using his 12,000lb Tallboy deep penetration bomb operationally for the first time. The shark-like projectile had to withstand an impact velocity, if dropped from its optimum height of 18,000 feet, of 750 m.p.h., after falling for thirty-seven seconds. In order to achieve this without breaking up, it boasted a case thickness near its nose of more than four inches, and carried a charge weight of 5,200lbs of Torpex. The depth of penetration into the earth depended upon the fuse delay time from 0.025 seconds upwards. At deepest penetration it was estimated to be capable of displacing one million cubic feet of earth, and creating a crater requiring five thousand tons of earth to refill it. An instantaneous detonation, on the other hand, would produce a crater twenty-five feet in depth, and more than eighty yards across. The fact that it proved able to penetrate many feet of reinforced concrete was an unanticipated bonus yet to be discovered.

The target on this night was the Saumur Tunnel in France, through which an important rail link passed. The operation got under way with the departure of the Lancaster element, beginning with Kearns at 22.45. The crews involved in the main operation were those of Cheshire in NT202, Shannon and Fawke, it is believed in DZ418 and DZ421 respectively, although there is some dispute, Munro in LM482, McCarthy in LM492, Wilson in LM485, Kearns in DV246, Edward in EE131, Clayton in ME560, Poore in DV391, Reid in ME557, Duffy in ME555, Stanford in ME554, Stout in ME559, Cheney in JB139, Knights in DV385, Hamilton in DV403, Willsher in DV393, Nick Ross in ME562, Fearn in DV380, Kell in DV402 and Knilans in ME561, all of whom carried a Tallboy. A second element, consisting of Sanders in ED909, Martin's original Dams Lancaster, Levy in ND631, Watts in ED933, Castagnola in ND472, Ian Ross in JB370 and Carey in EE146, took off at the same time with a load of eight 1,000 pounders and six seven inch clusters each to use against the nearby Saumur bridge. This operation would bring another milestone in the distinguished career of Nicky Ross, his seventieth sortie. In addition to the 617 Squadron effort, four 83 Squadron Lancasters were on hand to provide the illumination for this hurriedly prepared operation. Shannon's sortie was over almost as soon as it began, after an over-speeding port engine forced him to return some twenty minutes or so after take-off. The others arrived in the target area around 02.00 hours, and Cheshire delivered his spot-fires at 02.06 after diving onto the southern aiming point from three thousand to five hundred feet. He complained that the flares were dropped too far to the south and the east, and only the last two or three were of any use. Sometime later Fawke dropped three red spot-fires onto the northern end of the tunnel, where the bridge was situated, and had time to witness the bombing of Cheshire's markers before his fuel situation demanded he turn for home.

Cheshire reported copious amounts of smoke as a result of the bombing, but considered that further backing up would not improve the situation. He observed 50% of the bombs falling within a hundred yards of the markers, with just one or two very wide of the mark. Munro recorded that the markers were in the cutting, and that most of the bombs fell around them, and he saw one direct hit. Bombing altitudes for those with Tallboys ranged from Hamilton's 8,200 feet to McCarthy's 10,500, while those with 1,000 pounders attacked from between 3,000 and 6,500 feet. Sanders reported seeing a direct hit on the bridge five minutes before he bombed, and Watts thought the last three bombs of his stick fell directly onto it. One direct hit was scored on the tunnel, which blew a hole in the roof, and, it was hoped, that this might have brought tons of earth crashing down onto the track. Wilson made several runs across the southern aiming point, but found the marker extinguished before he was able to bomb. He finally released his Tallboy at the bridge, and saw it impact about a hundred yards from the markers, observing many blue sparks near the bomb burst. Photographic reconnaissance showed an 85-foot diameter crater in the roof of the tunnel, and a total of seventeen others of varying dimensions within 220 yards of the southern entrance. The tracks were cut around one hundred yards from this entrance, while a near miss on a road/rail intersection some distance away had cut all tracks and damaged the road. There was also a large crater blocking a road 180 yards east of the northern entrance.

The evidence pointed to an entirely successful operation, and it seemed at least, that the tracks were still blocked up to two months after the operation. However, documentation surfaced after the war to suggest

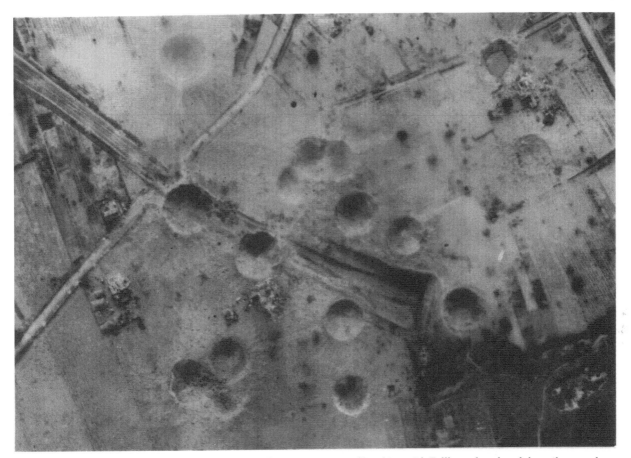

A reconnaissance photo of the Saumur tunnel shows the concentration of bombing with Tallboys that closed the railway, at least for a limited period. The crater on the roof is 85 feet in diameter.

that the tunnel had been quickly returned to use by the Germans, but that the appearance of devastation was allowed to remain to give a false impression and discourage a further attack. This was a ploy later used at the Dortmund-Ems Canal. Whatever the truth, it was a very creditable performance by the crews, considering the absolute minimum of training allowed them. The entire month of May and first week of June had been taken up with the training for Operation Taxable, leaving just two days to prepare for Saumur. Once the crews became accustomed to the routine of delivering Tallboys, the margin of error would reduce to a matter of a few dozen yards.

On the 9/10th the emphasis for the main force was switched to four airfields south of the beachhead, Flers, Le Mans, Laval and Rennes, which were bombed by elements of 1, 4, 6 and 8 Groups to prevent them from being used by the enemy to bring up reinforcements. The six H2s equipped Lancasters returned to their former squadrons on the 10th, and with them went the ground crews, while the aircrews remained at 617 Squadron. Railway targets featured for the main force on the next three nights, and on the last of these, the 12/13th, a new oil campaign began at Gelsenkirchen. Elements of 1, 3 and 8 Groups carried out a highly accurate attack on the Nordstern refinery, and halted all production for several weeks at a cost to the enemy of a thousand tons of aviation fuel per day.

The 14th brought the Command's first daylight operations since the departure of 2 Group twelve months earlier. The raid took place in two waves against the fast, light marine craft moored in the harbour at le Havre, which posed a threat to Allied shipping supplying the Normandy beachhead. The first phase was a predominantly 1 Group affair, which took place in the late evening, and included the participation of what amounted to a maximum effort by 617 Squadron. Its contribution involved three Mosquitos and twenty-two Lancasters, whose crews were to aim their Tallboys at either the E-Boat pens or at the E-Boats themselves moored in the harbour, and the whole operation was conducted under the umbrella of a fighter escort. The Mosquito element again consisted of Cheshire, Shannon and Fawke in NT202, DZ484 and DZ418 respectively, and the Lancaster crews assigned to the E-Boat pens were those of Munro in LM482, Poore in DV391, Clayton in ME560, Williams in EE131, Edward in EE146, Kearns in DV246, Nick Ross in ME562, Duffy in ME555, Hamilton in DV403, Kell in DV402, Stout in ME559, and Cheney in JB139. Those briefed to attack the E-Boats were McCarthy in LM492, Wilson in LM485, Fearn in DV380, Reid in ME557, Howard in ED763, Knilans in ME561, Knights in DV385, Stanford in ME554, Willsher in DV393 and Gingles in LM489.

A time on target of shortly after 22.30 had the Lancasters taking off between 20.10 and 20.25, while the Mosquito crews stayed at home for another hour. Cheshire records the squadron arriving at the target a little early, but going straight in to mark. He delivered his offset spot-fires in between the two aiming points at 22.30½ after diving to 7,000 feet through fierce light flak, and within seconds the Tallboys were raining down onto the aiming points from 15,500 to 19,000 feet. Shannon and Fawke remained on standby to remark the aiming point if required, but this proved to be unnecessary. The offset method of marking allowed the spot-fires to remain visible even though the aiming points themselves became obscured by smoke, part of which emanated from defensive smoke installations belonging to the occupiers. All of the crews reported the bombing as accurate, with a number of direct hits on the pens and two enormous explosions at around 22.26, and McCarthy saw sticks of 1 Group bombs fall across the jetties. The raid was successfully concluded without loss to 617 Squadron, although Knights and Knilans returned with flak damage, and Sgt Crosby in Knilans's mid-upper turret collected a piece of shrapnel in his thigh and was admitted to station sick quarters. A predominantly 3 Group force followed up as darkness was falling, and few, if any of the enemy craft remained unscathed.

On the following evening an operation was mounted against a similar target at Boulogne by elements of 1, 4, 5, 6 and 8 Groups, but thick cloud over the target created problems, which were compounded by heavy and accurate flak. Cheshire was in NT202, the lone 617 Squadron Mosquito in action, and the Lancaster crews were those of Munro in LM482, McCarthy in LM492, Kearns in DV246, Clayton in ME560, Wilson in LM485, Howard in ED763, Poore in DV391, Fearn in DV380, Reid in ME557, Edward in EE146, Williams in EE131, Stout in ME559, Willsher in DV393, Knilans in ME561, Stanford in ME554, Knights in DV385, Nick Ross in ME562, Duffy in ME555, Hamilton in DV403, Cheney in JB139, Kell in DV402 and Gingles in LM489. Cheshire followed hard on the heels of the Oboe Mosquitos, and confirmed the accuracy of their target indicators for the 1 Group attack. However, recognising that the 617 Squadron Lancaster crews would not be able to make a visual identification of the aiming point because of the cloud, he retained his own red spot fires. Munro, meanwhile, had assessed the conditions as unfit for bombing, and ordered the squadron to return home, but Cheshire immediately called to say, that it was clear below 8,000 feet. Munro descended, having rescinded his instruction, but on encountering poor visibility and enemy opposition at the lower altitude, he reinstated the order to go home.

By this time Wilson, Howard, Poore, Stout, Willsher, Knilans, Stanford, Knights, Hamilton and Gingles had bombed from between 8,000 and 12,000 feet, but with one exception, the others brought their precious Tallboys home. McCarthy was thrown off course by the heavy flak during his bombing run, and having gone round for a second go, discovered that his Tallboy had already fallen off somewhere. On his way out of the target area at 22.45, Cheshire dropped two 500 pounders from 6,000 feet onto a flak position. The cloud also brought darkness earlier than on the previous night, and Stout made the point, that an earlier attack would have improved the bombing conditions. Despite the difficulties the raid was assessed as a great success. The pens were hit several times, and many of the dock facilities were severely damaged by the main force attack. There was also much loss of shipping, and rail facilities were disrupted. The port arsenal was almost entirely razed to the ground, and, inevitably, the town itself suffered severe damage. Hamilton's Lancaster was damaged by flak on this occasion, and he landed at West Malling, where his bomb-aimer, F/O Duck, was admitted to hospital with serious injuries.

The night of the 16/17th brought the start of another new campaign for the increasingly stretched resources of the Pathfinder and main force squadrons, this one against flying bomb launching and storage sites in France. The Command was to make a heavy commitment to eliminating this threat, and that of the other V-Weapons over the succeeding two and a half months, and 617 Squadron was to play a major role. The squadron was not involved on this first night, when elements of 1, 4, 5, 6 and 8 Groups accurately bombed four sites. Also on this night, 1, 4, 6 and 8 Group aircraft continued the assault on the enemy's oil industry with a scattered attack on the refinery at Sterkrade/Holten. The offensive against railways would also continue throughout the summer, and the bulk of the aircraft operating on the 17/18th were assigned to three such targets in France.

A concrete structure that was originally intended as a V-weapon storage and launching site at Watten became the objective for two 617 Squadron Mosquitos and nineteen Tallboy-carrying Lancasters in daylight on the 19th. Attacks on the site during 1943 had caused so much damage, that its purpose had been changed to the production of liquid oxygen for V-2s, which were to be launched from elsewhere. The construction was still in progress, and the site was not operational by this stage. Cheshire and Shannon led in NT202 and DZ421 respectively, while the Lancaster crews were those of McCarthy in LM482, Wilson in DV380, Poore in DV391, Clayton in ME560, Duffy in ME555, Cheney in JB139, Hamilton in DV403, Gingles in LM489, Edward in EE146, Reid in ME557, Williams in EE131, Howard in ED763, Knilans in ME561, Nick Ross in ME554, Knights in DV385, Stout in ME559, Willsher in DV393 and Kell in DV402. Nine Oboe Mosquitos provided the initial marking, before Cheshire delivered two red spot-fires at 19.40 after diving to 3,000 feet. He was unable to see any result, though, and assumed that they had failed to ignite. Despite this, Shannon was not called in to back-up. The squadron was supposed to bomb in three waves, but the attack became a collection of single aircraft. As Knilans made his bombing run his bombsight became unserviceable, and all switches were put to "safe". Twenty seconds later the Tallboy fell off, and impacted about two and a half miles south of the target. This was observed by Jimmy Castagnola, who was not on the order of battle, but was flying with Knilans as a passenger, while some members of his and other crews did likewise in other aircraft. Kit Howard's Tallboy hung up, and he brought it home. The conditions thwarted the crews' best efforts, and no Tallboys fell closer to the concrete structure than fifty yards, although an immediate post raid report suggested an aiming point photo had identified one hit.

A similar operation was attempted on the following day at a V-Weapon store at Wizernes, for which three Mosquitos and seventeen Lancasters were dispatched, but this had to be aborted because of excessive cloud. A second attempt launched on the 22nd was again frustrated by cloud, but it was only delaying the inevitable. On the 24th Cheshire and Fawke led another operation against the target at Wizernes in NT202 and DZ415, and the sixteen Lancaster crews were those of Munro in LM482, McCarthy in ME559, Edward in DV403, Kell in DV402, Howard in ED763, Nick Ross in ME561, Reid in ME557, Williams in EE131, Wilson in DV380, Cheney in JB139, Willsher in DV393, Stanford in ME554, Gingles in LM489, Knights in DV385, Poore in DV391 and Clayton in ME560. The Lancasters took off in a ten-minute slot to 16.30, and both Mosquitos were in pursuit within twenty-five minutes. The Mosquitos were carrying four smoke bombs and two red spot fires, but Cheshire found he was unable to release either because of technical problems. Fawke delivered his at 17.50 after diving from 17,000 to 6,000 feet, and then watched the Tallboys winging down from either side of 17,000 feet. Bomb bursts were observed all around the target, on the railway line and near the mouth of the tunnel, and Bill Reid saw one Tallboy penetrate the roof, and appear to burst inside causing an eruption but no smoke. A number of very near misses were claimed, and, as Barnes Wallis was to assert, a near miss with an earthquake bomb was probably more effective than a direct hit, and would destroy a concrete structure by its shock wave effect.

It was on this operation that the squadron suffered its first loss since April, when DV403 was shot down by flak over the target right in the middle of the attack. The Lancaster was seen by other crews to be hit in a wing, and to lose height slowly as fire took hold, before falling out of control and exploding above the ground. A number of parachutes were reported, and three of the crew, navigator F/O Pritchard, bomb-aimer F/S Brook and wireless operator F/S Hobbs, did survive. Sadly, F/L Edward DFC, his flight engineer and two gunners were killed, while the Canadian mid-upper gunner, P/O Johnston DFC, succumbed to his injuries shortly afterwards.

On the 21st a P51D Mustang, HB837, had arrived on the station to act as the personal chariot of Cheshire, and on the morning of the 25th Cheshire climbed into it for the very first time to prepare to lead a squadron contingent against a V-Weapon storage site at Siracourt, a target that had been attacked by a main force element a few days earlier. HB837 is believed to have been assigned an AJ-N code, but photographic evidence suggests that it actually bore no squadron markings, although it did have D-Day stripes. Also operating were two Mosquitos, NT205 and NT202, in the hands of Shannon and Fawke respectively, and seventeen Lancasters. These contained the crews of Munro in LM482, McCarthy in ME559, Clayton in ME560, Williams in EE131, Poore in DV380, Wilson in LM485, Howard in ED763, Reid in ME557, Nick Ross in ME561, Gingles in LM489, Kearns in ME554, Knights in DV385, Stanford in ME555, Carey in EE146, Kell in DV402, Willsher in DV393, and F/O Lee in JB139, on his first operation with the squadron.

For the first time in his operational career Cheshire would have to navigate himself to the target, and this he managed to do, before diving from 7,000 to 500 feet to deliver his two spot fires at a few seconds after 09.00. The ORB suggests that Shannon put down smoke bombs and red target indicators, but Fawke's were not required. Shannon estimated three direct hits on the aiming point, and Fawke reported at least two, Williams claiming one of them, and Gingles suspecting that he scored another. Howard and Reid both suffered hang-ups on their first run, but released successfully on their second. The concentration of bombing around the aiming point was excellent, and the target was left wrecked. A number of accounts suggest, that Cheshire's first landing in his new Mustang had to be undertaken in darkness. This is not so. The Command devoted the 25th to operations against flying bomb related targets, and all took place simultaneously in the morning, three other sites in the Pas-de-Calais coming under attack by around three hundred aircraft from 1, 4, 6 and 8 Groups. The 617 Squadron ORB shows Cheshire landing at 10.18, in time for an early lunch, and even had the timings been transposed by twelve hours to the evening, with double summertime in force, 22.18 would still have been in daylight. Towards the end of the month, P/O Castagnola, a Maltese, was posted back to 57 Squadron, but it was a temporary move, and he would return in August. The remainder of the month was devoted to the same round of operations by the main force against railways and V-Weapon sites, while 617 Squadron, despite remaining on standby from the 27th to the 30th, stayed at home.

July 1944

July opened as June had closed, with 617 Squadron crews standing by for operations on each of the first three days. It was similar fare also for the main force crews in terms of targets, flying bomb sites providing employment for over three hundred aircraft on both the 1st and 2nd. It was the 4th before the Independent Air Force was next invited to re-enter the fray, when it was called upon to attack a V-Weapon storage site in caves at St-Leu-d'Esserent, some thirty miles north of Paris. The caves had originally been used for growing mushrooms, and they were protected by some twenty-five feet of clay and soft limestone, to say nothing of the anti-aircraft defences brought in by the Germans. There is some confusion concerning the timing of the operation, which involved not only seventeen Lancasters, a Mustang and a Mosquito from 617 Squadron, but also 231 Lancasters and fifteen Mosquitos from the Group, and a number of Pathfinder aircraft, which were probably Oboe Mosquitos to provide an initial reference point. Some accounts suggest that 617 Squadron attacked early in the evening, and was followed by the Group later on. However, the squadron's ORB shows the Lancaster element taking off either side of 23.30 hours on the 4th, and this coincides with the departure times for the rest of the Group. There were, in fact, two aiming points, the area dump for the main force, and the tunnel complex at Creil, a settlement three miles northeast of St Leu for 617 Squadron.

Cheshire got away in the Mustang at 00.15, four minutes after Fawke in NT205. The Lancaster crews were those of Munro in LM482, McCarthy in LM492, Wilson in LM485, Howard in ME557, Stout in ME559, Poore in DV391, Ian Ross in ME560, Knilans in ME561, Duffy in ME555, Sanders in DV385, Watts in ED763, Willsher in DV393, Williams in EE131, Lee in JB139, Kell in DV402, Pryor in ME562 and Gingles in LM489. At 01.30 Cheshire dived to eight hundred feet to deliver two red target indicators, but was unable to take any further part in the operation because of an unserviceable VHF set. Perhaps this accounts for Fawke not being invited to back up the markers, although he may not have been called in anyway. Twelve of the squadron's crews sent their Tallboys to earth from between 17,000 and 18,700 feet, but smoke began to obscure the aiming point, and five others, Poore, Ross, Sanders, Watts and Williams, brought their Tallboys home. There were no casualties among the 617 Squadron element, but the main force lost thirteen Lancasters, most of them to night fighters. The attack was a success on all counts, with a large section of earth measuring some 200 X 400 feet receiving a large number of hits and collapsing into underground workings. Railway tracks leading to the target were also cut by at least twenty-five craters, and a railway bridge over the River Oise was hit and partially destroyed. The attack was concluded without loss, and was followed up by the Group that night, and again on the 7/8th, when night fighters exacted a heavy toll.

On the 5th, having disposed of one enemy threat, the squadron took on 627 Squadron in a cricket match, and disposed of them also! On the 6th over five hundred aircraft were engaged on operations against V-Weapon targets, and 617 Squadron was assigned to a V-3 super gun site at Mimoyecques. Although Cheshire did not know, this was to be his final operation, not only with 617 Squadron, but also of the war in Europe. He took off in the Mustang at 14.23, and was followed a minute later by Fawke in Mosquito NT205. Seventeen Lancasters had already departed up to forty-five minutes earlier, and they were captained by Munro in LM482, Wilson in LM485, Stout in ME559, Ian Ross in ME560, Kell in DV402, Lee in JB139, Pryor in DV385, Fearn in DV380, Gingles in EE146, Poore in DV391, Willsher in DV393, Watts in ME557, Stanford in EE131, Howard in ED763, Nick Ross in ME562, Duffy in ME555 and Knilans in ME561. The target was difficult to identify because of all the craters from previous attacks, and even after Cheshire had opened the proceedings with a dive to eight hundred feet to deliver two red spot fires at 15.24, they did not show up well in daylight. Fawke was carrying two 500 pounders, and he dropped these onto a flak position in the target area. Arthur Kell lost an engine during his first run, so he went round again, while Lee was forced to jettison his bomb in the target area after being hit by flak. Paddy Gingles's bomb-aimer was unable to draw a bead on the target during the first run, and as they approached the aiming point for the second time he found it obscured by smoke and debris, so their Tallboy was dutifully returned to the bomb store. Freddie Watts and Nicky Knilans also brought their Tallboys back, the former after failing to identify the aiming point in time, while the latter had his bombsight fail. Again, a number of direct hits were scored, Duffy claiming one of them, and provisional reconnaissance revealed four deep craters in the immediate target area, one causing a large corner of the concrete slab to collapse. Seven other large craters were seen in the immediate vicinity of the target.

Not only was this Cheshire's final operation, it also signalled the end for Nick Ross on a grand total of seventy-seven. He would be signed out on posting to 1661CU by 617's new commander, James Tait, on the 15th with the endorsement in his logbook, *"This officer has had an outstanding operational career. His courage and competency are worth the highest praise."* As confirmation of this he was awarded the DSO. On the 12th Cheshire was posted from the squadron to 5 Group HQ, having now completed one hundred operations in a glittering career, which was to be capped by the award of the Victoria Cross. Cheshire was succeeded by the highly experienced W/C James Tait, who was apparently known to some as "Willie". In keeping with commanders since Gibson, Tait had 4 Group blood coursing through his veins, and had served previously with a number of its leading squadrons. It was no easy matter to find an officer of the appropriate stature to command such an elite body of men, who could step easily into the shoes of someone as unique as Cheshire. Tait was such a man. He had commanded 51 Squadron briefly between December 1940 and January 1941, before leading the Bomber Command contribution to the earlier-described ill-fated Operation Colossus from Malta, the airborne undertaking by the SAS in Italy in February 1941. He was posted to 35 Squadron shortly after its reformation to introduce the Halifax to operations, and took command of 10 Squadron in April 1942, as stand-in for W/C Don Bennett, now A-O-C the Pathfinders, who was evading capture to return home from Norway after a failed assault on the Tirpitz. Tait then moved on to the command of 78 Squadron in July, and remained in post until November. Thereafter he completed a spell at 22 O.T.U., before joining 5 Group as Base Operations Officer at Waddington, where he apparently managed to notch up a number of further operations. Also departing during the month were the three flight commanders and squadron founder members, Shannon, Munro and McCarthy. It was the end of an era. Munro went to 1690 BDTF on the 13th, McCarthy to 61 Base on the 20th, and Shannon to 27 OTU on the 24th.

On the 17th W/C Tait led the squadron for the first time in a return to Wizernes. He was in the Mustang, and according to the ORB, so was S/L Danny Walker as navigator. As the Mustang is a single-seater he must have been sitting either on the tail or on Tait's lap! Fawke took off first in NT202 at 11.28, a minute before his boss, but both had been preceded by the Lancaster element, which consisted of the crews of Knights in DV385, Pryor in LM485, Stanford in ME554, Lee in LM492, Fearn in DV380, Gingles in LM489, Kell in DV402, Willsher in DV393, Watts in DV246, Sanders in ME562, Knilans in ME561, Stout in ME559, Duffy in ME555, Hamilton in EE146, Cheney in LM482 and Levy in ED763. Fifty-nine minutes after take-off Tait dived to five hundred feet to release two red spot fires onto the aiming point, and a minute and a half later Fawke did likewise from three thousand feet. Over the next sixteen minutes the Tallboys rained down, and bomb bursts were seen all around the structure. One direct hit on the concrete dome was claimed by Bob Knights, but this proved to be an error, as photo reconnaissance revealed that no direct hits had been scored. There were, however, two large craters in an adjoining quarry, which caused a minor landslide, and evidence of other hits on the railway track and the tunnel entrance. It was a very successful operation, which sealed once and for all the fate of the site, although this was not at the time appreciated, and further operations against it would take place.

An impressive amount of damage was caused to the periphery of the V2 storage facility at Wizernes although the main concrete dome was not hit on this occasion. The operation on 17th July was later determined to have forced the closure of the facility.

Early on the following morning over nine hundred aircraft took off to lend support to Operation Goodwood, an armoured advance by the British Second Army in the Caen area. Five fortified villages to the east of the town were attacked in carefully controlled operations, which also involved elements from American units, and Bomber Command delivered 5,000 of the total of 6,800 tons of bombs dropped. This day also saw the arrival on posting to 617 Squadron of F/L Oram and his crew from 50 Squadron, and the appointment of Gerry Fawke as C Flight commander in place of Joe McCarthy. On the 20/21st W/C Tait led the squadron back to Wizernes, this time in Mosquito DZ484 with Danny Walker as navigator, with Fawke and Tom Bennett in DZ534, but adverse weather conditions prevented an attack from taking place, and the fifteen Lancasters all returned with their Tallboys. Later on the 21st ED936, Rice's Chastise Lancaster, crashed at Woodhall Spa, presumably on landing after a training flight or an air-test, and it was subsequently struck off charge. F/L Tony Iveson, a future flight commander, came from 5 LFS on the 22nd, while F/L "Bunny" Clayton went to 1663CU on the 23rd, at the conclusion of his tour.

On the morning of the 25th the Mustang and Mosquito NT205, with Tait and Fawke respectively at the controls, led sixteen Lancasters against the V-Weapon site at Watten. The Lancaster crews were those of Knilans in ME561, Poore in DV391, Hamilton in LM485, Sanders in ME562, Ian Ross in ME555, Williams in LM489, Reid in ME557, Howard in ED763, Stanford in ME554, Fearn in DV380, Levy in DV402, Watts in LM492, Knights in DV385, Stout in ME559, Cheney in DV393, and Carey in LM482. Even for the lumbering Lancasters this was an operation of less than three hours duration, and Tait would be back home in under two. The heavy element took off either side of 07.30, while Fawke got away at 08.10 and Tait eight minutes later. On arrival over the target Tait found marking to be unnecessary, and all but two of the

Tallboys went scything down in a ninety second slot from 09.09½. "Mac" Hamilton was the first to bomb, and he claimed a direct hit, while a second bull's eye was registered by Poore. Heavy and accurate flak was encountered, which damaged a number of aircraft, including Cheney's, and in the confusion caused by the loss of the intercom, his mid-upper gunner, Sgt McRostie, baled out and fell into enemy hands. The Tallboy was jettisoned a short distance south-south-east of the target, and the aircraft returned safely along with the rest of the squadron participants. There was much smoke and dust over the target area after the bombing, and the Tallboys had ½ hour delay fuses, preventing an immediate assessment of the outcome, but later reconnaissance showed at least two direct hits.

On the 31st 617 Squadron led a raid by ninety-seven Lancasters and six Mosquitos from 5 and 8 Groups on a V-weapon storage site in a railway tunnel at Rilly-la-Montagne. The 617 Squadron contingent consisted of Tait in Mosquito NT202 with Danny Walker in the right hand seat, Duffy in NT205 with F/O Don Bell beside him, and the crews of Sanders in ME562, Ian Ross in LM489, Knights in DV385, Reid in ME557, Poore in DV391, Stanford in ME554, Hamilton in LM485, Stout in ME559, Willsher in LM492, Cheney in JB139, Howard in ED763, Fearn in DV380, Levy in DV402, Knilans in ME561, Williams in EE131 and Carey in DV246. Tait again decided, that the target was clearly visible after marking by Pathfinder Oboe Mosquitos, and the main force was called in without further marking being required. Two aiming points were employed, one at each end of the tunnel, and the 617 Squadron crews were divided between them. Ross, Knights, Williams and Carey were unable to pick up the aiming point in time, and brought their Tallboys home. The others went down within two minutes of each other from 20.18, while the 5 Group main force also peppered the site.

A partially successful conclusion to the operation was marred by the loss of F/L Reid VC and his crew in ME557, which was struck by bombs from one of these 5 Group Lancasters flying well above. It happened only seconds after the Tallboy was released, and caused severe structural damage to the central fuselage, and tore out an engine on the port side. The gaggle was operating at between 16,000 and 17,000 feet at the time, and it took four minutes for the Lancaster to crash, after eventually breaking up in the air. Only Reid and his wireless operator, F/O Luker, survived, and they both fell into enemy hands. This was the day that brought another new arrival to the squadron in the form of F/L Cockshott from 1660CU, and he would be promoted to squadron leader to become a flight commander.

August 1944

August's operations began for the squadron with an intended attack on a V-Weapon site at Siracourt in the late afternoon of the 1st. This was just one of numerous operations during the day against similar targets involving over seven hundred aircraft, most of which ended with a recall, presumably through unfavourable weather conditions. Tait led the flight out in Mosquito NT202 accompanied by fifteen Lancasters, but on arrival in the target area he found the target obscured by thick cloud and sent the squadron home. Attacks by daylight on flying bomb sites dominated the first six days of the month, but 617 Squadron's next target would be a bridge at Etaples on the morning of the 4th. In the meantime, though, on the 3rd, F/L Kearns was posted to 17 OTU at the conclusion of his tour. Tait was back in the Mustang for the Etaples Bridge, while Duffy flew NT205 as the lone Mosquito. The Lancaster crews were those of Howard in ED763, Poore in DV391, Fearn in DV380, Knilans in ME561, Oram on his first trip with the squadron in LM485, Stout in ME559, Willsher in LM492, Cheney in JB139, Kell in DV402, Levy in DV246, Williams in EE131, Ian Ross in ME554 and Gingles in LM489. Tait dived to fifteen hundred feet to deliver a smoke bomb as a marker, and Duffy attempted to do likewise at the southern end of the bridge, but nothing happened. Unusually, the Lancasters were each carrying twelve 1,000lb bombs, and these went down in a hail either side of 10.58. A number scored direct hits, while a few others straddled the structure, but the majority seemed to overshoot, possibly as a result of the cloudy conditions, and the bridge remained intact.

This had been Cheney's thirty-eighth sortie in an operational career spanning twelve months and three squadrons. After completing basic training in his native Canada he arrived at 29 O.T.U. at North Luffenham in England's smallest county of Rutland on the 16th of March 1943. His first operational flight was a nickeling trip to Paris in a Wellington on the 1st of July, and six weeks later he was posted to his first squadron. He arrived at 106 Squadron at Syerston on the 17th of August, and was posted from there to East Kirkby on the 15th of November to join the newly formed 630 Squadron. Three nights later Harris began the second and main phase of his Berlin campaign, and remarkably, ten of Cheney's eleven operations with 630 Squadron were to the "Big City". An excellent record gained him and his crew an invitation to join 617 Squadron. This they agreed to do, and on the 15th of February 1944, the posting took place, thus probably sparing them from participation in the penultimate raid of the campaign on Berlin that very night. It was the 31st of March before Cheney got his hands on JB139 for the first time, the Lancaster which was to become his "own", although at the time it was coded KC-X, rather than KC-V, to which it would be recoded on the 4th of April to become "Dark Victor". His first operation with 617 Squadron, and his twenty-third in all, was to Toulouse on the 5/6th of April in DV393.

Early on the morning of the 5th the crews were briefed for an attack on the U-Boot pens at Brest. Tait took Mosquito NT202 for this operation, while Fawke was back in NT205. The fifteen Lancasters were carrying their more familiar Tallboys, and contained the crews of Howard in ED763, Poore in DV391, Fearn in DV380, Knilans in ME561, Oram in LM485, Knights in DV385, Sanders in ME562, Stout in ME559, Willsher in LM492, Cheney in JB139, Kell in DV402, Levy in DV246, Williams in EE131, Gingles in LM489, and Iveson in ME554, on his first operation since joining the squadron. The crews were on board their aircraft and at their positions by 08.50, and a green flare signalled engine start shortly afterwards. Take-off was without incident, and was followed by the long climb to bombing altitude. "Paddy" Gingles lost an engine while outbound near Bristol and was forced to abort his sortie, but the others pressed on in near perfect weather conditions, with visibility recorded by Tait as extreme. It was a few minutes before noon when Tait dived towards the aiming point, releasing his smoke markers from 4,500 feet. Fawke's markers were not required, and he was able to sit on top and watch the show. He described the bombing as very concentrated, and observed the pens to be covered in bomb bursts and smoke. Two stray Tallboys were seen to fall into the water in front of the pens, but six direct hits were scored on the concrete roofs, two of them claimed by Knights and Stout. Hit by flak shortly after bombing, JB139 suffered severe damage and crew casualties, and following dramatic activity inside the doomed aircraft, all baled out over the sea. Four of the crew failed to survive, but Cheney and two others were rescued by the French, who passed them on to the Americans, and they were home by the first week of September. The eighth crew member was captured, and subsequently released by the American infantry also in September. During the course of the 5th F/L Wilson left the squadron on a posting to 1661CU.

The squadron was back in action again on the evening after Brest, for an attack by two Mosquitos and twelve Lancasters on the U-Boot pens at Lorient. Tait and Fawke were in NT202 and NT205 respectively, and the Lancaster crews were those of Knights in LM492, Knilans in ME561, Fearn in DV402, Sanders in ME562, Oram in LM485, Iveson in ME554, Gingles in LM489, Carey in PD238, Howard in ED763, Stout in ME559, Willsher in LM492 and Kell in DV246. Tait released two red target indicators from 8,000 feet at 20.23½, and watched as the Tallboys fell in a rapid salvo at around 20.28 onto the easily identifiable target. Smoke prevented an accurate assessment of the bombing, but Tait saw none fall wide, while Fawke observed one direct hit and two very near misses. Bob Knights again claimed a bull's eye, as did Fearn, whose Tallboy was the first to go down. Howard thought his bomb struck the north-western corner of the pens, but this was where Fearns' impacted, and he may have been mistaken. What was not in doubt, however, was that it was another very impressive display of high level precision bombing. Only three crews missed out, Ross and Hamilton failing to take off because their aircraft had not been made ready in time, and Carey, who jettisoned his Tallboy five miles from the target and two miles out to sea because of an electrical problem. F/O Duffy did not participate in this operation, having completed his tour, and he now awaited a posting. Instead, he took Mosquito NT202 for a spin over the Wainfleet bombing range, accompanied by F/O Ingleby. Tragically, the aircraft crashed following structural failure, and both were killed.

The squadron's campaign against U-Boots and other targets nautical continued with a raid on La Pallice on the 9th. Tait was in NT205 on this occasion, with F/S Gosling in the right-hand seat. The latter was one of four new arrivals from 83 Squadron on the 10th of July, and they would eventually crew up with S/L Cockshott. The Lancaster crews were those of Howard in ED763, Pryor in ME561, Fearn in DV380, Oram in DV391, Iveson in ME554, Knights in LM482, Kell in LM492, Watts in DV246, Sanders in ME562, Hamilton in PD233, Gingles in PD238 and Ian Ross in ME555. These were to attack the U-Boot pens, while seventeen other Lancasters from the Group went for an oil depot. The target was a good deal further south than those recently attacked, and it took three hours to reach. Tait was carrying two 120lb smoke bombs, but decided not to use them. The first salvo of Tallboys headed towards the aiming point at 13.01 from an average of 17,000 feet, and the consensus was, that the first one missed very narrowly, probably hitting the dock gates, while the second one, claimed by "Mac" Hamilton, was a direct hit right in the centre of the roof. Kell also saw his bomb strike the aiming point, but then smoke and the generally poor weather conditions made it impossible to identify individual bomb bursts. In his post-raid report Tait referred to some loose bombing due to misidentification, but described the performance as good on the whole, and confirmed, that there appeared to be two direct hits. Reconnaissance confirmed a direct hit on the southeast corner of the pens, causing the collapse of a large section of roof, and three other direct hits with possible penetration.

On the 11th Duffy was laid to rest at the Stonefall Cemetery in Harrogate, in the beautiful section reserved for Canadian airmen, and the service was attended by members of his former crew as representatives of the squadron. The squadron returned to La Pallice that afternoon, with Tait in NT205 accompanied once

The formidable strength of the U-Boot pens at Brest is apparent in this photograph (Crown).

more by Danny Walker. The heavy brigade consisted of S/L Cockshott in PD238 for his maiden operation with the squadron, Williams in EE131, Pryor in LM485, Oram in DV391, Fearn in DV380, Howard in ED763, Carey in ME554, Hamilton in PD233, Gingles in LM489, Sanders in ME562, Knights in LM492, Kell in ME561, Watts in DV246 and Willsher in LM482. Ian Ross was also supposed to be taking part, but his sortie was scrubbed when it proved impossible to bomb his Lancaster up in time. Possibly because of a shortage of Tallboys, the Lancasters were each carrying six 2,000lb armour-piercing bombs, and having become accustomed to loading just one Tallboy, this probably tested the armourers. The main force took off in a twenty-minute slot before noon, to be followed by Tait at 12.29. He arrived in the target area ahead of the Lancasters, which were delayed by ten minutes because of a change in the forecast winds. Fearn was not among them. He had lost his starboard-outer engine a little under two hours into the flight, and turned back after jettisoning his bombs over the sea. The others achieved an accurate and concentrated bombing performance with numerous direct hits, and although the operation was written up as a success, later photographic reconnaissance showed four hits but no penetration, and also demonstrated the futility of throwing conventional bombs at reinforced concrete.

The busy round of operations continued with an attack on the U-Boot pens at Brest on the 12th, this time with Tallboys in the bomb bays, and with W/C Tait flying a 617 Lancaster, DV380, for the first time. It should be remembered, that, as a former 4 Group man, all of his many previous operations in heavy bombers, other than those during his time on the Base staff at Waddington, had been flown in Whitleys and Halifaxes, so Fearn donated his own crew to look after the commanding officer. Fawke flew the lone Mosquito, NT205, to photograph the operation, and the other Lancaster crews were those of Cockshott in PD238, Pryor in LM485, Oram in DV391, Ian Ross in ME555, Hamilton in PD233, Gingles in LM489, Sanders in ME562, Watts in DV246 and Kell in ME561. Cockshott was last but one away at 07.01, but he was first back three hours and fifty minutes later with his Tallboy still attached after developing engine trouble. Hamilton's Tallboy was the first to go down onto the aiming point at 09.45¾, and was a direct hit followed immediately by two more. Fawke had a good view of the proceedings from 7,500 feet, and reported all but one of the bombs hitting the target, the errant one falling as a near miss into the water

Damage to the U-Boot pens at Brest shows up in a post-raid reconnaissance photo (Crown).

on the open side of the pens. Reconnaissance confirmed two direct hits with penetrations and another causing a crater on the roof.

The morning of the 13th brought a return to Brest, with Tait flying in EE146, which would become his personal transport. With him this time were four members of Kell's crew, one of Paddy Gingles's and F/L Larry Curtis, formerly of Mick Martin's crew. Fawke flew in NT205 as the camera Mosquito, taking off at 09.19, by which time Tait had been on his way for fifty minutes. The 617 Squadron element of thirteen Lancasters was joined by fourteen others from 9 Squadron, in the first of what would become a series of joint Tallboy operations. Some crews were briefed to attack the U-Boot pens, and others the derelict French cruiser Gueydon. This was one of a number of ships, which, it was thought, the enemy might use to block the harbour entrance ahead of advancing American forces, and it was decided to sink them in safe positions. The rest of the squadron contingent consisted of the crews of Cockshott in PD238, Willsher in ME561, Lee in LM482, Ian Ross in ME555, Oram in DV391, Pryor in LM485, Howard in ED763 and Sanders in ME562, all assigned to the vessel, and carrying twelve 1,000lb bombs each. The crews of Williams in DV385, Hamilton in PD233, Knights in LM492, Watts in DV246 and Tait were briefed to attack the pens with Tallboys. From his vantage point, Fawke described the Tallboy bombing as good, and estimated three direct hits. Williams claimed one of them from 16,900 feet at 10.59½, and Hamilton another, which struck the northern edge of the roof. The Gueydon was straddled by a number of sticks, but there were no confirmed hits, and she was still afloat as the force withdrew.

The 14th was a day of high activity for the Command, which began at Woodhall Spa either side of 08.30 with the take-off of thirteen 617 Squadron Lancasters, and a single Mosquito, NT205, with Fawke at the controls. They were again accompanied by a contingent from 9 Squadron for another tilt at the Gueydon at Brest, and the payload for each aircraft on this occasion was six 2,000lb armour-piercing bombs. Tait reverted to DV380 for this trip, and retaining Gallagher and Curtis in his crew, he added four others, including bomb-aimer Keith Astbury, who had been flying with Munro, and wireless operator Arthur Ward, who was on his ninth operation since returning to the squadron in April after recovering from the injuries received in the crash in January as a member of O'Shaughnessy's crew. Cockshott was in PD238, Pryor in LM485, Oram in DV391, Fearn in ME561, Howard in ED763, Williams in DV385, Sanders in ME562, Watts in DV246, Lee in LM482, Willsher in DV402, Ian Ross in ME555 and Knights in PB415. Fawke took up his position at 8,000 feet to photograph the proceedings, and he spotted one bomb appearing to hit the stern of the ship. Only Lee among the others was able to confirm this and other hits, while a number of crews commented on near misses. The consensus, though, was that the bombing had generally overshot the mark. Kit Howard saw what he believed to be a hole in the ship's side, which caused air bubbles and a lightening of the water. Heavy flak was encountered over the target, and Williams and Willsher were too busy evading it to notice where their bombs fell. A number of aircraft were hit, among them Lee's and Pryor's. The former sustained an ankle injury as a result, but he brought the Lancaster home to a safe landing at Beaulieu. The latter's bomb-aimer, F/O Pesme, was killed instantly by a splinter of shrapnel when right over the aiming point, and the bombs were jettisoned. Reconnaissance showed both vessels to be still afloat.

F/O Castagnola returned from 57 Squadron on the 15th, and was joined by New Zealander F/O Joplin from 51 Base, whence also came F/L "Benny" Goodman on the following day. 617 and 9 Squadrons joined forces again on the 16th for what became an abortive operation against the U-Boot pens at La Pallice. Tait was in EE146, and he continued to chop and change his crew, this time adding Terry Playford and Gerry Witherick as navigator and rear gunner respectively, who had formally flown with the now tour-expired Dickie Willsher. The Tallboy element consisted of Cockshott in PD238, Pryor in LM485, with F/O Woods as his replacement bomb-aimer, Sanders in DV402 and Knights in PB415. Those, like Tait, carrying six 2,000 pounders were Howard in ED763, Fearn in PD233, Oram in DV391, Carey in ME554, Ross in ME555 and Watts in PB416. A late afternoon take-off brought them to the target at 20.00 hours, and Tait identified what he thought was the U-Boot pens through a gap in the cloud. He released his six 2,000lb bombs, only to discover a few seconds later through a second gap, that he had been mistaken. Fawke was on hand in NT205, but photographs were impossible in the conditions, which also allowed no chance of a successful attack, and the remaining ten aircraft were sent home with their bombs.

617 and 9 Squadrons returned to La Pallice on the 18th with Fawke in Mosquito NT205 to record the event, and Tait in EE146, Oram in EE131, Knights in PB415, Watts in DV402, Knilans in PD238 with Joplin as a passenger, and Pryor in LM485 each carrying a Tallboy. The others, Fearn in PD233, Howard in ED763, Levy in PB416, Ross in LM489 and Carey in ME555 had six 2,000 pounders in their bomb bays. Tait and Fearn were the first to release their bombs at 15.08, at which point Fearn's Lancaster was hit by flak. He immediately took violent evasive action, and as a result of the gyrations, he and his crew were unable to observe the fall and impact of their bombs. Tait saw a Tallboy burst on the southwest corner of the pens, and another slightly overshoot to the north. The others confirmed the accuracy of the bombing, and Pryor reported a second direct hit right in the centre of the aiming point, but smoke was beginning to obscure the target, and a final assessment was not possible. Fearn brought his extensively damaged Lancaster safely home along with the others. Reconnaissance pictures showed at least one and maybe two direct hits by Tallboys, but no penetrations.

Unfavourable weather conditions helped to keep the squadron's crews on the ground for the next few days, and it was not until the early afternoon of the 24th that they were next called into action. At briefing they learned they were to attack the E-Boot pens in the Dutch port of Ijmuiden. There were actually two major structures in the port to house the Schnellboote, those referred to in British intelligence reports as the old one and the new one. The Germans knew the old one as Schnellbootbunker AY, and the new one as 2 or BY. The letters A and B represented 1 and 2, and Y was the code for Ijmuiden. The pens close to the mouth of the basin were the new ones, and were still under construction. The old pens occupied the northern end of the basin, and this was the structure selected as the squadron's target for today. Fawke was in NT205, the lone Mosquito, and in keeping with his role ever since Tait had reverted to a Lancaster, he was on hand for photographic reconnaissance, rather than to mark the target. Only eight 617 squadron Lancasters were involved in this joint operation with 9 Squadron, and they contained the crews of Tait in EE146, Howard in ED763, Iveson in PD238, Pryor in PD233, Carey in LM489, Ross in EE131, Watts in PB415 and Levy in PB416. All were armed with Tallboys as they took off between 12.14 and half past the hour, and they arrived at the target two hours later in good bombing conditions. Fawke took up a position at 4,000 feet, and recorded two hits in the water to the north, one near the southeast corner and another fifty yards to the south. He witnessed a very large explosion on the centre of the pens at 14.28, and the last three bombs fell into the smoke created by this. Ross and Watts were the first to bomb within seconds of each other, the former observing a direct hit in the centre of the roof, and his own bomb striking the northwestern corner. Watts, on the other hand, saw the first four Tallboys go down, and thought the first hit the south-western corner, while the second and third fell into the docks about a hundred yards from the mouth of the pens, and the fourth caused the large explosion in the centre of the roof. Whatever the individual impressions, the consensus was again that the operation had been concluded successfully.

In fact, at least one direct hit had caused a large portion of the roof to collapse, and the rear of the pens was badly damaged. A later report determined that E-Boot pen A had received the 617 Squadron Tallboys, while 9 Squadron's efforts hit Ijmuiden West railway station, where six tracks and overhead lines were damaged and one man was killed. The office of a fishing company used by the Germans was also demolished, and various warehouses were either damaged or destroyed. Four German naval vessels were sunk, although one was later raised. In all eight Kriegsmarine personnel were killed and nineteen seriously wounded.

617 Squadron carried out its last operation of the month on the 27th, when shipping was attacked at Brest, again in concert with 9 Squadron. The ORB is not specific about the ships involved, but they were a freighter and a hulk. With Allied ground forces close by, one or both of the vessels were possibly intended for strategic sinking by the enemy to block access to the port and prevent its immediate use. Some accounts describe them as "Sperrbrecher", the German word for blockade-runner, intending to portray the meaning of a blockage or artificial reef, but they are employing the wrong word. Twelve Lancasters were involved in the operation, crewed by Tait in EE146, Howard in NF923, Watts in DV246, Knights in PB415, Levy in PB416, Stout in LM482, Castagnola in DV402, Pryor in LM489, Hamilton in PD233, Iveson in PD238, Joplin in ME554 and Goodman in EE131, the last two mentioned operating with the squadron as crew captains for the first time. All carried twelve 1,000 pounders for this afternoon foray, and Fawke was again on hand in NT205 to photograph the results. Assessment was difficult, but one vessel seemed to be down by the bows as the force withdrew, and Fawke complimented 9 Squadron on the quality of its bombing. The hulk was not visible on reconnaissance photos, and it was believed, therefore, to have sunk, while the freighter appeared to be damaged. By this time two more postings-in had taken place. S/L Wyness, a contemporary of Martin and Knight at 50 Squadron in 1942, arrived from 57 Squadron on the 25th to assume the role of flight commander, and F/O Huckerby came in from Cheshire's former command, 4 Group's 76 Squadron. The latter's posting is something of a mystery, as he was an experienced pilot, but carried out no operations with 617 Squadron before his posting out in February 1945.

September 1944

Tirpitz, pride of the Kriegsmarine, feared by Churchill and kept out of the war by 617 Squadron.

The Command would de vote much of its effort during September to removing pockets of resistance from around the three major French ports still in enemy hands. Operations were mounted daily against Le Havre between the 5th and the 11th, although those on the 8th and 9th were severely restricted by the weather conditions. British ground forces followed up, and within hours of their attack the German garrison surrendered. At Woodhall Spa, meanwhile, the first ten days of the month brought more rumour than flying, as the crews were kept on standby for a special operation. Further crew movements took place during the period, which brought F/O Martin from 61 Squadron and F/L Sayers from 467 Squadron on the 1st, while the long-serving F/O Willsher departed for 5 LFS at the same time. 5 LFS retaliated by sending F/O Leavitt, an American, in the other direction on the 8th, but not to be outdone, the squadron dispatched F/L Poore there on the 13th at the conclusion of his tour. Phil Martin was another Australian who had joined 61 Squadron after a spell flying Wellingtons at 17 O.T.U., at Silverstone during December 1943 and January 1944, while the Berlin campaign was at its height.

For the first ten days of September there was more rumour than flying, as the crews were kept on standby for a special operation. Further crew movements took place in the meantime, which brought F/O Martin from 61 Squadron and F/L Sayers from 467 Squadron on the 1st, while F/O Willsher departed for 5 LFS at the same time. 5 LFS retaliated by sending F/O Leavitt in the other direction on the 8th, but not to be outdone, the squadron despatched to them F/L Poore on the 13th. On the 11th, twenty crews again joined company with 9 Squadron, and departed Woodhall Spa for the gruelling flight to Yagodnik in the Archangel area of Russia, from where the first of the squadrons' three epic Tirpitz raids was to be launched. Laid down in October 1936, the mighty battleship Tirpitz, sister ship of the Bismarck, represented a major leap forward in warship design, and was the means by which the Kriegsmarine intended to wrest control of the seas from the Royal Navy. She was launched in January 1939 in a blaze of publicity at a ceremony attended by Hitler himself and the entire Nazi hierarchy. A standard displacement of 41,700 tons, and a main armament of eight fifteen inch guns was complemented by a

On the first operation against the Tirpitz S/L Wyness ran out of fuel in ME559, KC-Y, and was forced to crash-land in Russia. The aircraft was written off.

design speed with a full load of thirty knots, and by 1944 a crew of more than nineteen hundred officers and men was on board. At over eight hundred feet long Tirpitz was larger, faster, better armed and better protected than her British contemporaries, and these aspects alone would enable her to impact the war and British thinking without her ever engaging other surface vessels in combat at sea.

On the 11th twenty crews departed Woodhall Spa, and set off for the gruelling flight to Yagodnik in the Archangel region of north-west Russia, from where Operation Paravane, the first of the squadrons' three epic attacks on the Tirpitz was to be launched. This was to be another joint operation with 9 Squadron, which dispatched eighteen Lancasters. The 617 Squadron element consisted of Tait in EE146, Gingles in LM489, Ross in EE131, Carey in NF920, Iveson in ME554, Hamilton in PD233, Cockshott in PD238, Fawke in DV405, Sanders in ME562, Howard in NF923, Watts in LM485, Knights in DV391, Kell in LM482, Stout in ME561, Castagnola in PB415, Pryor in DV246, Levy in PB416, Knilans in LM492, Wyness in ME559 and Oram in ED763. Take-off began at 18.36 DBST, and Stout was last away at 19.37. Remarkably, and as a result of expert navigation, all the aircraft arrived in the general vicinity of Yagodnik, only to be thwarted by fog and the absence, through misinformation, of a guiding beacon. Carey's NF920 was damaged by flak over Finland en-route, and would not take part in the operation, and F/O Ross and S/L Wyness in EE131 and ME559 respectively, were compelled by fuel shortage to crash-land, and wrote off their aircraft. Four 9 Squadron aircraft also crash-landed and were damaged beyond repair. The remainder landed safely, although not all at Yagodnik. Lt Knilans's lobbed LM492 down in a field as his fuel was about to give out, and Iveson soon joined him. Tait arrived sometime later as a passenger in an ancient Soviet biplane, and found his crews being entertained by Russian soldiers, male and female, in a wooden hut. Iveson had sufficient fuel to reach Yagodnik, and took off without incident. The Russians put some petrol into LM492, and Knilans flew it out, cutting a hundred yard long swathe through the treetops bordering the field in the process. A smashed Perspex nose caused discomfort to the crew by allowing in a howling gale, and an engine overheated after foliage blocked the radiator. However, the weather was to delay the operation long enough to allow repairs to be successfully completed, and LM492 would take its place on the order of battle.

It was the 15th before the 617 and 9 Squadron operation could be launched from Russian soil against the pride of the German fleet, which lay at anchor in Kaa Fjord in Norway. Approaching from the land south-east of the target shortly before 13.00 hours double British summer time, the crews were able to observe the ship in the distance as it gradually became swallowed up by the smoke from smoke-pots, and it had become completely enveloped by the time that the first bombs went down. A gaggle of Tallboys was released at 12.56 DBST (13.56 local time) by Tait, Howard, Kell, Stout, Pryor and Oram from between 14,200 and 17,400 feet, and those of Fawke, Castagnola and Knilans followed during the next nine minutes. Hamilton suffered a hang up, and after three abortive runs, finally parted company with his Tallboy, either intentionally or involuntarily four miles south of the target at 13.15, while Gingles, Cockshott and Knights were unable to establish an aiming point, and took their bombs back to Yagodnik. Johnny Walker mines were delivered by Iveson, Sanders and Watts from between 11,000 and 12,000 feet, Iveson using those ferried to Russia by Carey, after being forced to jettison his own during the flight from England. One large explosion was witnessed by a number of crews, but it was impossible to assess the results. After the attack the crews returned to Yagodnik to prepare for the flight home. Nine crews arrived back on the 17th, but F/O Levy failed to return, PB416 having crashed in mountains in Norway, killing all nine men on board, including two of S/L Wyness's crew. Another five crews returned to Woodhall Spa on the 18th, F/L Oram on the 19th, F/O Carey on the 20th, and F/L Knights was the last home on the 21st.

What was not at that time appreciated was the fact that Tirpitz had suffered damage from a direct hit right on the bows ahead of the anchor cable holders. The Tallboy, almost certainly the one delivered by Tait, passed through the ship and exploded about thirty-five feet from the stem below keel level, tearing a 32 x 48 foot hole in the starboard bow. This allowed the forward section of the ship to take on 1,500 tons of seawater, and such damage, along with that caused internally by a number of near misses, was sufficient to prevent her from returning to sea in the foreseeable future. German engineers reported that repairs would take nine months if there were no interruptions, but a committee chaired by Admiral Doenitz on the 23rd declared the vessel to be beyond repair. It was decided that she would be drafted into the new defensive line being prepared in the Lyngenfjord area, where her main armament could be put to good use. As a result, she would be towed to a new location at Tromsö in October for use as a floating fortress. To the Allies, however, she still appeared to offer a threat as a "fleet in being". Her new anchorage placed her two hundred miles closer to the northerly British airfields, and just within range of the Lancaster force.

Following a 1 and 5 Group operation to the twin towns of Mönchengladbach and Rheydt on the night of the 19/20th, news came through that Gibson was missing. After the war it was confirmed that his Mosquito, in which he had been performing a Master Bomber role, had crashed on the outskirts of Steenbergen in Holland with fatal consequences. On the evening of the 23rd 617 Squadron joined others of 5 Group to attack the River Glane underpass section of the Dortmund-Ems Canal near Ladbergen, the scene of the tragic events of twelve months earlier, when five out of eight crews had failed to return. Eleven of the 136 Lancasters were provided by 617 Squadron, and they contained the crews of Tait in LM485, Stout in NF923, Sanders in ME562, Martin in DV380 on his first operation with the squadron,

Cockshott in LM489, Iveson in ME554, Hamilton in ME555, Wyness in DV402, Sayers in LM482, Castagnola in ME559, and Oram in DV393. All 617 Squadron aircraft were carrying Tallboys, and these were primed and ready to go as the target was approached in 7/10ths cloud at around 21.40 hours. Iveson reported being able to see the red TIs clearly from 16,000 feet at 21.42, but they disappeared frustratingly beneath the cloud just fifteen seconds before the release point was reached, and despite making two further runs, he could not pick up the aiming point again. He brought his Tallboy home, as did Sayers, who was over the target for thirty minutes, and seems to have had the TIs in sight throughout. His efforts were hampered by an unserviceable compass, however, and as he made his sixth run the TIs burned out. Wyness started his bombing run from 14,000 feet with the TIs in view, and had three good runs thwarted by cloud at the crucial moment. He was ordered to come down to 12,000 feet, and if unable to see the aiming point, to return to base with his bomb, and this is what he did. Sanders also brought his Tallboy home. Tait dropped his from 7,500 feet at 22.04, and Phil Martin followed suit from 8,000 feet eight minutes later during his sixth run. In between these, Cockshott, Hamilton and Castagnola delivered their bombs also from 8,000 feet, which was clearly the optimum altitude for the occasion, and Oram concluded the 617 Squadron effort from an even lower 7,000 feet at 22.16. He also commented on a good concentration of thousand pounders from the 5 Group main force, but no one was able to determine the effects of the bombing.

In fact, it had been a highly successful operation, which left both branches of the canal breached, and a six-mile stretch of this vital waterway drained, bringing a halt to all through-navigation until the 21st of October. On the debit side it had been an expensive operation, in which eleven Lancasters came to grief, and among them was one from 617 Squadron. Geoff Stout was on his way home with his Tallboy still attached, when a night fighter attacked NF923 over Holland. Three engines were knocked out, and a fire took hold in the bomb bay, forcing the crew to bale out. Five did so, F/Os Rupert and Petch and F/S Whitaker, bomb aimer, rear gunner and mid-upper gunner respectively, ultimately evading capture, but F/L Stout and his navigator, F/O Graham, died in the ensuing crash, and the flight engineer, P/O Benting, succumbed to his injuries while in captivity on the 25th. It had been their misfortune to stumble across the BF110 G-4 of Hauptmann Heinz-Wolfgang Schnaufer, operating at the time out of Dortmund, who would end the war as Germany's most successful night fighter pilot with a total of 121 kills from 164 sorties. On this night alone Schnaufer claimed four RAF bombers over Holland in the space of thirty-two minutes in the Enschede, Winterswijk and Zutphen area, and it seems likely that Stout was the first. Schnaufer recorded his first victory at 22.53, and Stout's Lancaster crashed at 23.00, ten minutes before Schnaufer recorded his second kill. This remarkable young man would survive the war, only to lose his life in an automobile accident in France in 1950 at the still tender age of twenty-eight.

The game of musical chairs flared up again on the 26th, when F/O Flatman arrived on posting from 5 LFS, to be followed three days later by F/L Gumbley. Also that day, F/L Marshall was added to squadron strength from 1654CU.

October 1944

The squadron parted company with its Mustang on the 2nd as it departed for 38 Maintenance Unit. The new month's operations began for 617 Squadron with a trip to the sea wall at Westkapelle on the island of Walcheren in the Scheldt Estuary on the 3rd, in company with elements of the main force. Heavy gun emplacements here were barring the approaches to the much-needed port of Antwerp, some forty miles downriver, and operations to bomb them during September had failed to produce the desired results. As they were proving to be such difficult targets to bomb, it was decided to inundate them with seawater, and also thereby to create difficult terrain for the enemy to defend in the event of a land invasion. Eight waves of thirty bombers each attacked the target, and the fifth wave created a breach, which was widened by those following behind. The 617 Squadron element consisted of Tait and Fawke in Mosquitos NT205 and DZ415 respectively, and the crews of Cockshott in ME555, with the recent arrival Mark Flatman as a passenger, Goodman in LM489, Iveson in ME554, Wyness in NG180, a new Lancaster operating for the first time, Sayers in DV402, Joplin in DV393, Castagnola in DV385 and Martin in ME562. Tait arrived at the target at 14.55, while the main force assault was still in progress, and remained in the area for ten minutes to assess the situation. Fawke took photos from 3,500 feet at 15.05, by which time the sea wall had been breached over a length of 330 feet, and the floodwater had reached the town. It was clear to Tait that the job had already been accomplished, and he sent the squadron participants home with their valuable Tallboys.

On the 7th of October thirteen 617 Squadron crews were briefed for a daylight attack on the Kembs Barrage on the Rhine, deep in southern Germany and on the very outskirts of the Swiss city of Basle.

Kembs Barrage's proximity to Swiss territory meant that exceptionally accurate bombing was required.

F/O Bruce Hosie in 1941. The New Zealander flew 72 operations as Wireless Operator with 75(NZ) and 617 Squadrons, before he failed to return from Kembs Barrage (John Sanders).

Immediately north of the city the river divides into two branches in the shape of the letter Y running roughly northwest to southeast, and the dam-like objective, with its steelwork superstructure, stretched across the right-hand or eastern branch a matter of two hundred metres north of the point of divide. This was also the spot where three countries joined, one neutral, one occupied and the other the occupier and aggressor. The western or left-hand bank of the right branch marked Germany's border with France, while Germany, France and Switzerland all met at the separation of the Rhine as it formed the Y shape. The plan of attack called for the force to be split into two elements, the first consisting of seven Lancasters, which were to bomb from above six thousand feet with Tallboys fused to detonate on impact. The second section of six aircraft was to go in at six hundred feet, with their Tallboys fused for a thirty-minute delay, and the whole force was to be escorted by three squadrons of Mustangs, which would be picked up at 4,000 feet over Manston.

The high Lancaster section consisted of Fawke in NG181, with the station commander, G/C Philpott, on board, Joplin in DV393, Iveson in ME554, Sayers in DV402, Gingles in LM489 with Mark Flatman as a passenger, Watts in LM485 and Castagnola probably in DV385, the last two also carrying an extra man. Tait was to lead the low section in EE146, with Cockshott in LM492, Sanders in ME562, Martin in DV391, Wyness in NG180 and Howard in LM482, the last mentioned carrying an extra gunner in the person of F/O Watkins, who had last flown with Oram. Wyness had not had an entirely settled crew since joining the squadron, and had flown with a succession of flight engineers and wireless operators. Those occupying these positions in his crew on the trip to Russia had died with Levy and crew on the way home. Wyness's wireless operator on this occasion, New Zealander F/O Bruce Hosie, was a veteran of seventy-two operations and still only twenty-one years of age. He had begun his first tour of operations in September 1942 as a member of 3 Group's 75(NZ) Squadron, which was equipped at the time with Wellingtons before converting to Stirlings. After completing thirty-one operations he was posted to 1665 Conversion Unit at Woolfox Lodge, from where he undertook five more sorties while instructing. He was posted to 617 Squadron in January 1944, and joined the crew of F/O Cooper. He flew operations with this crew until around the 22nd of April, when he presumably went on leave or fell sick, because he was not on board Cooper's Lancaster when it was shot down on the way home from Munich on the night of the 24/25th. Hosie then joined Bob Knights, and flew continually with him, up to and including the above-mentioned attack on the Tirpitz, which was his seventy-second operation. It is believed, that Hosie acquired his seat in the Lancaster of Drew Wyness on the toss of a coin. As events were to prove, it was an unfortunate toss to win. Navigator F/L Williams DFC had been in 5 Group since beginning his operational career in October 1942 with 106 Squadron, commanded at the

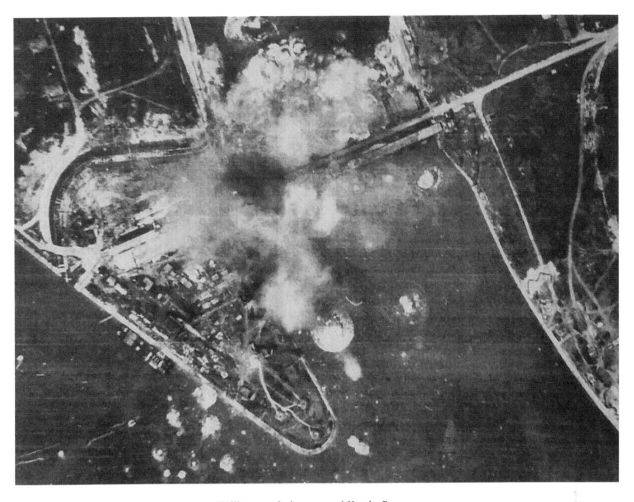

Tallboys exploding around Kembs Barrage

time by Gibson. Thereafter, he served with 61 Squadron before moving on to 57 Squadron, where he teamed up with "Duke" Wyness, and he had fifty-two operations to his credit.

The two sections took off between 13.07 and 13.38, the latter time being that of Watts, who was temporarily delayed through technical problems. With Watts lagging behind, the rest flew out together in formation, and crossed into enemy territory without incident, remaining at a low enough level for Martin's navigator, F/S Jackson, to be able to spot the bells round the necks of cows crossing a bridge as the target was approached. The high force climbed to run across the target from the west, while the low force began a triangular dogleg circuit to bring them in from the east, before arcing round to the north to pick up the aiming point, with the city of Basle behind them.

Tait described the weather as "touch and go" as they neared the target, but on arrival the area was found to be free of cloud and visibility was good. By the time that the low force was in position, some of the high force had already bombed. Watts was the first to do so, having caught up by cutting across the Swiss frontier. His Tallboy went down from 6,000 feet at 16.44½, and overshot by some fifty yards. Thirty seconds later, "Slapsie" Sayers opened his bomb doors at 7,300 feet, whereupon his Tallboy fell out, buckling the doors as it went. Three minutes later and six hundred feet higher Castagnola released his Tallboy, and watched it hit the barrage between the first and second piers. Within seconds Iveson bombed from 8,500 feet, but had to report his Tallboy falling onto the left riverbank some four hundred yards

F/O Bruce Hosie's log book for September 1944, including entries relating to the Tirpitz operation, routed via Archangel in the USSR. Note the overall total hours (bottom right) showing that he had accumulated nearly 750 hours by this time, a phenomenal total for bomber aircrew in 1943 – 44. His next operation, on 7th October, was to be his last (John Sanders).

southeast of the aiming point. A minute later Joplin bombed from 7,500 feet, and observed his Tallboy falling just beyond the barrage near the second pier from the left.

It was at this stage of the operation that the low section began to attack in staggered pairs, Tait first, with Wyness a few hundred yards behind. It is easy to imagine this attack as a daylight version of the run on the Möhne Dam, in which the Lancasters raced in low over the water and scraped over the parapet of the barrage to make their escape. This would be a false impression, however. At ultra-low level it is possible to merge into the background for part of the approach, and to flash across the field of fire of gun positions on the beam faster than they can traverse. Not so at five to six hundred feet, the minimum height considered necessary for the Tallboy to achieve the required trajectory for this operation. This was a kind of no-man's land altitude, at which the Lancasters would be in full view at all times, travelling relatively slowly across the sky, offering a large and inviting target for light flak. As had been tragically demonstrated at the Möhne, gunners learn quickly. After the first attack by Gibson had taken them by surprise, they knew exactly from where the next one was coming and where to aim, and that fact had cost the lives of Hopgood and four of his crew. Tait's run at the Kembs barrage also caught the gunners by surprise, and they were unable to fix their sights on him before he released his Tallboy accurately into the water ahead of the left hand sluice at 16.51. As he went in he noted that all trace of the detonations from the high level bombs had disappeared, and that the barrage displayed no signs of damage. Having swung their barrels round belatedly to meet the oncoming Tait, the flak gunners, in particular those on the power station were now ready to receive Wyness only seconds later. His Lancaster was raked unmercifully, and was apparently belching fire and smoke from both starboard engines before the release point was reached. Never the less, the Tallboy was discharged, and the flaming Lancaster roared over the steel superstructure of the barrage, weaving north along the right hand or eastern channel of the Rhine, its port wing brushing the French frontier

Now it was Howard's turn to run the gauntlet, with Martin about four hundred yards behind and a little to his left. In the nose of DV391, bomb-aimer Don Day was finding it impossible to get a fix on the aiming point as the Lancaster bucked in Howard's slipstream and was rocked by exploding flak shells. The low force aircraft had been fitted with bomb sights borrowed from Coastal Command, which had a sliding graticule, and had been designed for use against German E-Boats at low level. When the target appeared to keep pace with the graticule the bomb-aimer pressed the tit, but it wasn't happening for Don Day on this run, and he called for Martin to go round again. As he did so Howard also announced that he was pulling off for a second run after experiencing a hang-up. Martin called, "Hang on, we'll come round with you". As Howard and Martin banked in a tight turn to starboard, Cockshott and Sanders swept in to carry out their attacks. The turbulent air conspired with the flak shells to throw Cockshott's effort wide of the mark to the left and beyond the target at 16.54½, and Sanders's Tallboy also overshot a few seconds later, but at least both aircraft got through relatively unscathed.

By this time, Howard and Martin were back at their starting point about three miles from the target, and can have had no illusions about what awaited them. Before bending his head to his bombsight and the task ahead, Don Day watched Howard's Lancaster some four hundred yards directly ahead and a little higher. When about two miles from the target he saw Howard's starboard tanks erupt, and great sheets of flame shoot out behind. From above, the other crews could only observe the unfolding drama as eight of their colleagues experienced their last few moments on earth. The scene was a kaleidoscope of exploding flak shells, flames and oily smoke, with Mustangs darting to and fro firing at the flak positions, the sun glinting off their canopies as the picturesque, sparkling Rhine became the backdrop to tragedy. LM482 banked to starboard engulfed in fire, and fell away to crash into a wood at Effringen-Kirchen within sight of the barrage.

All of this had threatened to drag Don Day's eyes away from the moving graticule, but he resisted, shut his mind temporarily to the thought of an imminent violent death, noted that the shape of Howard's Lancaster was no longer in front, and sensed a Mustang, guns blazing, flash underneath at 45 degrees to his own line of approach. Another moment and he pressed the tit, feeling the floor of the Lancaster rise up to meet his prone body as the 12,000lbs of dead weight was shed. It was an overshoot by thirty to forty yards. In the rear turret Sgt Trebilcock had heard his pilot and bomb-aimer report that Howard had been hit, and was going down. It made him very angry. He opened up at the defences with his .303s, watching with satisfaction as his tracer scattered the gunners. He heard the call, "Bomb gone", and this was followed by a violent jolt and an explosion. He knew that they too had been hit, but his skipper calmly called each crewmember in turn to check on their status, even as he struggled with the controls to keep the aircraft straight and level. They rocketed over the target, banking round to starboard, and almost found themselves caught in balloons on the Swiss side of the frontier. As they pulled away with damaged controls to begin the long flight home, Paddy Gingles dropped his Tallboy from 8,300 feet at 17.04, and listened as members of his crew described it overshooting and hitting a railway line. Gerry Fawke delivered the final bomb a minute later from 8,100 feet, having experienced difficulty in persuading it to release. It was Fawke's third run, and even then the Tallboy hung up for five seconds before falling away to hit the west bank of the river. A 627 Squadron Mosquito remained overhead until the delayed action bombs detonated, and the crew was able to report a successful conclusion to the operation, with a breach clearly evident at the left hand end, where Tait's Tallboy had landed. An unconfirmed report suggests that a Tallboy was recovered intact from the dyke at the side of the barrage, and that it may have been Howard's, jettisoned as he pulled away to crash, but released at too low an altitude to achieve the correct trajectory.

Martin, meanwhile, had negotiated the barrage balloons, and with tracer still flying indiscriminately around the sky, he raced across the red rooftops, Don Day noting the upturned faces of the startled Swiss subjects below. Once clear, Martin confided in his flight engineer, Jack Blagbrough, that he was getting no response from the rudder controls. Blagbrough went back to investigate, and found one severed end of the control wire. He wrapped it round the handle of the fire axe, plugged into the intercom, and stood by to receive instructions from his pilot. In this way the Martin crew eventually got back to Woodhall Spa, where they inspected the damage around the rear end, marvelling as they did so at how rear turret occupant Tommy Trebilcock had managed to come through with all of his anatomical tackle intact. A total of 106 holes were counted in the Lancaster, but these were soon repaired by the ground crew. Martin was among those decorated for their exploits on this operation.

Wyness must have known that he and his crew would not be returning home. In a Lancaster threatening to blow itself apart at any moment, but too low for his crew to bale out, he had few options open to him. According to one unconfirmed report he headed northwest from the barrage following the course of the river, until he flew into the teeth of another flak position, which forced him to wheel back round to the south. A letter sent by the Air Ministry (New Zealand) to the parents of wireless operator Bruce Hosie in 1948 provides us with perhaps the most accurate sequence of events. It describes the Lancaster being hit by light flak and hitting a power line over or near the barrage, before coming down on the Rhine about five hundred yards further on. The aircraft must have been close to becoming uncontrollable, and Wyness opted for a ditching with the hope and intention of gaining the sanctuary of the Swiss bank. The Lancaster came to rest intact in shallow water near the village of Rheinweiler. Two members of the crew ran along the starboard wing, jumped onto the French bank, and disappeared into woodland, while the remaining five inflated the dinghy and paddled away, presumably in the direction of Switzerland to gain the sanctuary of the neutral bank. The Germans dispatched a boat to intercept them, and this persuaded one crewmember to abandon the dinghy and swim to the French shore. The three men now on French soil were the gunners, F/O Cansell and F/S Horrocks, and the flight engineer, F/S Hurdiss. They were never seen alive again, and their bodies have never been recovered. It is believed, that they were captured, perhaps by French gendarmerie, and handed over to the Nazi authorities, or simply by the German occupying forces, and following their murder, were buried in unmarked graves.

Wyness, navigator, F/L Williams, bomb-aimer, F/O Honig and wireless operator, F/O Hosie, were captured by the Wehrmacht, and taken to Rheinweiler to be met by the local Burgomeister, along with officials from the gendarmarie station at Schliengen, and the Kreisleiter of Mullheim, Hugo Grüner. They were put in pairs into two cars, one of them belonging to Grüner, and accompanied by a guard. One of the crewmen in Grüner's vehicle had an injured leg or foot. The car was driven in the direction of Schliengen, and at the village of Bellingen it turned off towards the river. It drew to a halt near the river bank at a place known as Steinplatz, and the guard, Rudolf Birlin, was ordered to take the prisoners to the water's edge, while a second guard, Hans Reimer, remained by the car. There is a strong suggestion, that Birlin was not a willing participant in what followed. Shots were fired, and the two airmen fell into the Rhine. Grüner, Birlin and Reimer returned to Rheinweiler to collect the two surviving airmen, and the bloody process was repeated. Grüner ordered the guards to remain silent about the incident, or at least to say that they had been ambushed, and that the prisoners had been taken from them. This kind of atrocity against RAF prisoners of war was a rarity, although there was a slight increase in 1945, as a desperate Germany's defeat loomed ever nearer. Even then, it was the civilian Nazi authorities, those individuals who owed everything to the party and knew their power was slipping from their grasp, that were most likely to commit war crimes.

The body of Wyness was recovered from the Rhine at Markolsheim, some fifty kilometres from where the ditching took place, and was initially buried there. The remains of F/L Williams were found nearby on the 24th of October, and interred at Salsbach, while F/Os Honig and Hosie were laid to rest at other locations. After the war all were re-interred in war cemeteries in Germany and France, and Wyness and Hosie now rest side-by-side in Choloy. After the war Rudolf Birlin was arrested and a trial convened by a French court in 1946. The case collapsed, however, because the crime had not taken place on French soil, and the victims were not French. The accused remained in custody at Neumunster pending a second trial by an American court. Hugo Grüner was arrested in May 1945, and indicted for the crime, remaining in custody until his trial in April 1946. In his defence he laid the blame on the Gestapo and Birlin, but escaped from custody at Recklinghausen in 1947, after being handed over to the Americans. He was never recaptured, but was tried in his absence at Hamburg in 1948, along with Birlin and Reimer. Reimer could not be found, and was assumed to be dead, and Birlin was found not guilty on the grounds that he had not actually committed the act, nor had he actively condoned or encouraged it. While he had not attempted to prevent the crime, it was accepted by the court, that any move on his part to do so would have resulted in his death also. Grüner was found guilty and was sentenced to death, but he remained at large to cheat the hangman. The writer of the poignant official letter mentioned above, sent to the parents of Bruce Hosie in a final confirmation of previous communications about his loss, spoke of the difficulty they would experience in learning of the manner of his death, but felt that they would, never the less, prefer to know the truth.

The loss of these two popular crews was a bitter blow to the squadron, but life and the war would go on, and Wyness was replaced as flight commander by F/L Iveson, who was promoted to Squadron Leader. Two more crews were posted in on the 14th, F/Ls Anning and Dobson arriving from 44 Squadron. This was the day when the Command launched Operation Hurricane, a series of operations against Ruhr cities to demonstrate the overwhelming superiority of the Allied bomber forces. The much bombed town of Duisburg was selected as the host for a raid by over a thousand aircraft at first light, which returned in similar numbers that night, to press home the point about superiority. 5 Group, however, did not participate, going instead to Brunswick, which after four previous failures, at last succumbed to a heavy and accurate assault. On the following day, the American Lt Knilans swapped his RAF blue for USAAF green on posting, following magnificent service with both 619 and 617 Squadrons. The citation for his DFC approved on the 9th of March 1945 reads; *"This officer has been operating with a special duties squadron and has participated in many sorties against small and precise targets, vital to the enemy's war effort. These attacks have been made in daylight and from low altitude in the face of intense enemy opposition from the ground. Lieutenant Knilans has participated in sorties against flying bomb and rocket installations and submarine pens at Brest, Lorient and Le Havre and by his imperturbability, courage and efficiency he has contributed largely to successes achieved."* Although volunteering for operational duties with the USAAF in the war against Japan, Knilans would fly no further operations before the end of hostilities.

Although 5 Group continued to operate, poor weather curtailed activity for 617 Squadron for much of the remainder of the month, but postings continued, with F/L Fearn going to 1661CU, F/L Williams to 1660CU, and F/L Gavin arriving from 51 Base, all during the last week. Operations waited until the 28th, when twenty aircraft flew to Lossiemouth and Milltown to join 9 Squadron for Operation Obviate, the second assault on Tirpitz, which, having been moved to Tromsö, was now close enough to reach from Scotland.

The crews were those of Tait in PD371, Fawke in DV405, Iveson in ME554, Knights in PB415, Hamilton in PD233, Pryor in LM492, Sayers in DV402, Oram in ED763, Marshall in DV391, Gumbley in DV380, Goodman in EE131, Gingles in LM489, Castagnola in DV385, Martin in PD238, Sanders in ME562, Joplin in ME561, Watts in LM695, Leavitt in NG181, Carey in NF920, and Dobson as a reserve.

Take-off from the advanced bases began shortly after 01.00 hours on the 29th, and it was not completed until an hour later. The route to the target took the aircraft from their forward bases to North Uist (position A), then A to 63.00N 02.00E (position B), B to 65.00N 06.47E (position C), C to 65.34N 15.00E (position D), D to 69.00N 19.50E (position E), E to 69.39N 18.50E (target). The return route was target to 69.20N 14.30E (position F), F to B, B to A, A to Lossiemouth. Although the weather was reported as fine in the target area, by the time the force of thirty-seven aircraft began final approach at between 12,000 and 16,000 feet, a layer of cloud was sliding across the aiming point, and completely concealing the ship from most crews just before the Tallboys went down. Oram was the first to bomb at 07.49 from 15,500 feet, closely followed by Iveson. After delivering his Tallboy at 07.51½ Sayers observed a big flash from the ship, believed to be a bomb burst, and Marshall actually saw a bomb enter the water just off the beam on the starboard side. Knights confirmed this, adding, that the ship rocked considerably, and thick brown smoke billowed from the midships area, while black smoke followed an explosion in the starboard bow. Castagnola watched a bomb fall towards the Tirpitz, and shortly afterwards there was a flash and a column of smoke. Joplin was another witness to a bomb burst on the forward end of the ship, and Martin thought he saw one at the stern, but for the others it proved impossible to assess the results.

Some crews made repeated runs to try to catch a glimpse of their quarry through the bombsight, but Pryor, Leavitt and Gumbley retained their bombs in the absence of a firm aiming point. Carey's NF920 was severely damaged by fire from Tirpitz immediately after bombing, after five previous runs across the target. Hits in a fuel tank caused excessive fuel loss, and this necessitated a forced landing in Sweden, which was safely accomplished, although Carey's knee struck the P4 compass as the Lancaster came to a sudden halt, and he sustained an extremely painful dislocated knee-cap. He and his crew were, of course, interned, and enjoyed the legendary hospitality of their hosts for a number of weeks while Carey's injury was being tended. The remaining crews returned safely to their advanced bases, after more than twelve hours in the air, although Joplin initially was forced to put down at Scatsta on the Shetlands because of fuel shortage, before continuing on to Milltown, and thence to Woodhall Spa on the following day. This proved to be "Mac Hamilton's final operation with the squadron, but he would remain at Woodhall Spa until being posted out in December. Though Tirpitz was still on an even keel and above water, she had indeed received a mortal blow during this attack. A Tallboy had exploded less than twenty yards from the rudders on the port side, opening plating and allowing the sea in, and the port propeller shaft was bent. The latter could only be repaired in a dockyard, and henceforth German authorities referred to the Tirpitz as the "floating battery". However, as this was still not apparent to British authorities from photographic reconnaissance, a third operation was deemed necessary.

November 1944

The decisive blow against the Tirpitz, Operation Catechism, was launched on the 12th, with F/O Kell first away, at 02.59 in NG181, and Jimmy Castagnola bringing up the rear twenty-six minutes later. The other aircraft and pilots on this momentous occasion were; Tait in EE146, Iveson in ME554, Sayers in LM492, Marshall in DV391, Dobson in PD371, Anning in ED763, Knights in PB415, Gumbley in DV405, Gingles in LM489, Flatman in PD233, Ross in ME555, Joplin in ME561, Castagnola in DV385, Watts in LM485, Sanders in ME562, Leavitt in DV393 and Lee in DV380. The operation proceeded as before, again in company with 9 Squadron, but on this occasion, there was no impediment to visibility, and the ship was presented to the approaching bomb aimers, in the opening stages at least, as a naked target. Tait could see steam issuing from Tirpitz's funnel as he arrived, and his Tallboy was the first to go down at 08.41 from 13,000 feet. He was unable to pick out its burst, but he did note that ensuing bombing was concentrated around the target. Over the next minute Tallboys went down from Iveson, Knights, Gingles, Joplin, Castagnola, Watts, Sanders and Lee. Knights watched the first four Tallboys fall and called their point of impact in order as; on or near the starboard quarter, starboard bow, port bow and near the funnel, and his own as ten yards off the port quarter. He remained over the target until the end of the attack, and saw a large explosion at 08.51, the timing of which was confirmed by Stuart Anning. A smaller explosion followed two minutes later.

By the time Knights left the scene he was able to report the Tirpitz listing heavily to port. He confirmed the accuracy and concentration of the 617 Squadron bombing, while noting bombs from 9 Squadron, who were using the Mk XIV bomb sight, falling 200 yards, 500 yards, ¾ of a mile and one mile away from the target. Gingles thought he scored a direct hit, but flak damage persuaded him not to hang around and he turned away. Castagnola reported his Tallboy falling towards the centre of the superstructure, and witnessed a direct hit followed by a cloud of smoke, which enveloped the ship. Joplin confirmed one direct hit and two near misses, while Watts saw a possible bulls eye, one overshoot, one undershoot and two wides. Sanders watched his bomb fall with someone else's, and both appeared to hit the edge of the ship near the centre. Lee's Tallboy disappeared into the smoke, by which time the Tirpitz seemed to have ceased firing. Kell made his approach along the length of the ship, turning to starboard and running in on the bows. His effort was a direct hit or very near miss, which was swallowed up by the reddish-brown smoke issuing forth from in front of the superstructure. A number of crews also reported a dull red glow from near the forward end. The squadron's last bomb, that of F/L Sayers, fell at 08.45. In all four direct hits were later confirmed by photographic reconnaissance, which showed the mighty ship to have turned turtle at her moorings.

Tirpitz had been brought to "action stations" at 09.00 German time, and the first visual rather than radar sighting of the approaching Lancasters took place at 09.27 when they were still twenty-five miles away to the south-east. There were no smoke generators operating on the ship itself, and those on the shore were ineffective. Tirpitz opened up with her main armament, her fifteen-inch A and B turrets, at 09.38 at a range of thirteen and a half miles, and the secondary armament of six and four-inch guns joined in when the attacking force had closed to nine and a half miles. The leading section of Lancasters led by Tait scored two direct hits, one Tallboy striking to the port of B turret and the other on the port side amidships, entering the ship through the catapult track and exploding as it passed through the armoured deck over the port boiler room. A gaping hole some forty-five feet in length was torn in the vessel's side from the bilge keel to the upper deck exposing its innards to the sea. This area flooded immediately, causing a list to port of between 15 and 20 degrees, a situation made worse by a near miss. Within the next two or

W/Cdr Willie Tait and his crew are understandably elated after potting the German battleship 'Tirpitz' (Crown).

three minutes a third direct hit on the port side and another near miss exposed the interior of the ship amidships along a length of more than two hundred feet.

By 09.45 the Tirpitz had heeled over to forty degrees to port, and Kapitän zur See Junge ordered the lower decks to be evacuated. The starboard armament had managed to maintain a gallant defence during this period of carnage above and below decks, but at 09.50, by which time the roll to port had reached seventy degrees, a fire reached the C turret magazine, and the ensuing explosion blew the turret out of its barbette. Just two minutes later mighty Tirpitz capsized having rolled through 135 degrees. The attack on the 29th of October had altered the profile of the seabed, which was in the process of being built up to provide a stable platform for Tirpitz to rest on. Those near misses increased the draught and allowed the battleship to turn turtle, when it would otherwise have been prevented from doing so by its superstructure. One can only imagine the horror of being on board Tirpitz during the engagement described above. In all 971 men lost their lives, many trapped inside the monster as it capsized, although eighty-five were pulled from this tomb when rescuers cut through the steel plates of the hull. Neither 617 nor 9 Squadrons incurred losses, and the crews landed back at Lossiemouth between 14.47 and 16.59. Ten of the triumphant crews returned to Woodhall Spa on the following day, and the remainder on the 14th, and W/C Tait went to London that day to take part in a radio broadcast about the raid.

There were no further operations to occupy the crews for the remainder of the month of November, but postings during this period involved S/L Calder arriving from 1652CU on the 9th, S/L Brookes from 22 OTU

Tirpitz lies capsized near Tromso following the successful operation by 9 and 617 Sqns. In fact, the battleship had been rendered almost unseaworthy in an earlier raid but the destruction of the ship was a major success for Bomber Command.

on the 21st, and F/Ls Horsley and Lancey from 5 LFS on the 25th. Calder was another graduate of the 4 Group academy of excellence, and had commanded the home echelon of 76 Squadron between July and August 1942, before handing over the reins to Cheshire.

Horsley's path to 617 Squadron was, perhaps, less exalted, but was an example of determination. A 5 Group man through and through, he had completed his first tour as a wireless operator/gunner with 50 Squadron on Hampdens and Manchesters in 1941/42. His final operation was the first one thousand-bomber raid against Cologne on the night of the 30/31st of May 1942 as a member of P/O Manser's crew. They were in a clapped-out Manchester borrowed for the occasion from 106 Squadron, which was hit by flak over the target and badly damaged. As the crippled aircraft lost height over the German/Belgian frontier, Manser ordered the crew to bale out, while he remained at the controls to give them a chance to do so. He was unable to save himself, however, and died in the ensuing crash. P/O Horsley and four others evaded capture, and their testimony was instrumental in sealing the posthumous award to Manser of the Victoria Cross. It took Horsley twelve weeks to get home via France, Spain and Gibraltar, and he was then sent to Canada as an instructor. While there he managed to get himself on a pilot's course, and was posted to 617 Squadron on his return home. Quite how this happened is unclear, in view of his inexperience as a bomber captain, and the fact that evaders were rarely returned to bomber operations in case they came down again in enemy territory, were captured, and revealed information about their helpers. Such men would normally continue their flying careers as instructors, or might transfer instead to another Command.

December 1944

December was another busy month for personnel movements at 617 Squadron, beginning on the 1st, with the departure of F/L Knights and F/O Gingles to RAF Hurn. S/L Powell arrived from 20 OTU on the 5th, F/L McLoughlin from 5 LFS on the 8th, and F/L Price also from there on the 9th. The first major operation of the month involved 1, 4, 6 and 8 Groups in a raid on Hagen in the Ruhr on the 2/3rd, and the town was left a shambles. With the Americans now in the Eifel region of western Germany, the town of Heimbach was attacked by a predominantly 1 Group force on the 3rd, and this was followed up on the 4th by a small scale 8 Group assault on the nearby Urft Dam, which failed to cause a breach. The Urft was built over a five-year period from 1900, and was a prototype for all future gravity dams in Germany, including the Möhne. At the time of its construction it was the largest dam in Europe. It stands fifty-five meters above the valley floor, is 226 meters in length and six meters wide at the top, holding back something like 45 million cubic meters of water.

On the 8th a second attempt was made on the Urft Dam, this time by over two hundred Lancasters of 5 Group, a force which included nineteen aircraft from 617 Squadron led by Tait in EE146. The others were Calder in NG181, Cockshott in PD238, Iveson in ME554, Brooks in DV385, Hamilton in DV380, Oram in ED763, Pryor in LM485, Sayers in DV402, Marshall in DV391, Goodman in NF992, Gavin in LM489, Dobson in PD371, Gumbley in DV405, Sanders in PB415, Leavitt in LM695, Martin in DV393, Flatman in ME555 and Joplin in ME561. Ten-tenths cloud greeted the force, and Tait assessed that there was no chance of the conditions changing. In the absence of any serious anti-aircraft fire the force remained in the target area for some time, orbiting and approaching from various directions, and the dam was glimpsed and identified from time to time. However, there was no chance of the 617 Squadron crews establishing a bombing run, and at 11.40 Tait recalled them, terminating their part in the operation for this occasion. 128 aircraft of the main force did bomb, however, but the effort was scattered, and no breach occurred. Oram, it seems, was able to deliver his Tallboy, which was seen to overshoot, and Joplin's Lancaster was hit by the single flak battery operating to the north of the target. He landed safely at Manston, as did most of the other squadron aircraft, and returned to Woodhall Spa in veteran DV405 on the following day, while his Lancaster underwent repair. Hamilton and Brookes also sustained flak damage, and the latter put down at the American base at Sudbury.

On the afternoon of the 11th seventeen of the squadron's aircraft again found themselves over the beautiful countryside of the Urftsee, which now lies within the Eifel National Park. The 617 Squadron element was in the company of over two hundred others from the Group to try again to hit the dam. The crews involved were those of Tait in EE146, Brookes in ME555, Iveson in ME554, Calder in NG181, Cockshott in PD238, Oram in ED763, Marshall in DV391, Pryor in LM485, Goodman in NF992, Dobson in PD371, Gavin in LM489, Martin in DV393, Joplin in DV402, Leavitt in LM695, Gumbley in DV405, Sanders in PB415 and Flatman in PD233. The crews' determination not to waste their Tallboys was made manifest by the spread of time elapsing between the first and last bombs to go down. Oram bombed first at 15.19 and Marshall last at 16.05, and a variety of altitudes was chosen between 6,000 and 10,000 feet. Tait found it difficult to assess the results, but saw his own bomb hit the apron, and another overshoot to the right. Iveson reported the first explosion to be on the dam itself, while his own bomb fell just to the left of the overflow. He saw two others fall into the water, one exploding, the other not, and as he pulled away from the target he witnessed a direct hit. Cockshott made five runs over a thirty-five minute period, each one hampered by cloud, and then his bombsight packed up and he brought his bomb back. Gavin completed eight runs, and eventually carried out a manual release after a partial hang-up, but his bomb overshot. Sanders was thwarted by smoke from the main force bombing, and in the end Tait ordered him to take his bomb home. It was later assessed that about thirteen feet had been blasted off the top of the dam. In fact, the overflow, which forms the right-hand third of the structure and is designed as a stepped cascade, was totally destroyed, and a giant V-shaped fissure was left in the main dam wall. However, the wall was not breached, and the Germans were able to release water whenever the mood took them to hamper the advance of American ground forces.

December's operations continued for 617 Squadron the 15th, when seventeen aircraft were dispatched to the older E-Boat pens at Ijmuiden, those designated AY by the Germans. This was in response to a SHAEF meeting on the 5th of December, in which the senior commanders recommended that the RAF's special squadrons should attack the giant installation. The crews were those of Tait in EE146, Brookes in DV391, Cockshott in PD238, Iveson in ME554, Calder in PB415, Goodman in NF992, Gumbley in DV380, Pryor in LM485, Oram in ED763, Marshall in DV402, Castagnola in PD371, Flatman in PD233, Ross in ME555, Joplin in LM489, Martin in DV393, Kell in NG181 and Watts in LM695. The force encountered heavy flak, which damaged a number of the Lancasters including PB415 of S/L Calder, who subsequently made an emergency landing at Woodbridge. Flatman had a hang up on his first two runs, and while opening his bomb doors in preparation for a third, the Tallboy fell out over the sea. A similar occurrence afflicted S/L Brookes, whose gyro toppled, requiring him to circle for fifteen minutes southwest of the target while he waited for it to settle down. This it refused to do, and while the bomb-aimer was attempting to re-cock the bomb, it fell out about four miles west of Ijmuiden. Tait claimed a direct hit on the southern end of the pens from a modest 9,300 feet at 15.11, some minutes after Goodman and Gumbley had delivered their Tallboys within fifteen seconds of each other. Both claimed a direct hit on the northwestern corner of the roof, although Gumbley assessed the other bomb as a near miss. In actual fact, ten bombs went down within seconds of each other between 15.03 and 15.04. In addition to those of Goodman and Gumbley mentioned above, they were those dropped by Cockshott, Iveson, Oram, Castagnola, Ross, Joplin, Martin and Kell. Inevitably, smoke began to obscure the aiming point very quickly, and it became increasingly difficult to interpret the scene below. Oram estimated six direct hits, but was unable to plot the fall of his own bomb. All of the crews returned safely, but the Lancasters of Watts and Marshall were hit by flak, and they brought their bombs home. The former sustained damage to the front turret, which reduced visibility, probably as the result of leaking hydraulic fluid, and the latter lost his starboard-inner engine, as well as having numbers 1 and 2 tanks holed on the port side. Photo-reconnaissance revealed two Tallboys to have penetrated the shelter destroying one S-Boot (Schnellboot, an alternative term for E-Boot) and damaging six others. Six pens were rendered unusable, and another boat was trapped inside by debris. Despite this, the scale of renewed E-Boot operations on the 22/23rd and 24/25th of December caused a top secret priority dispatch to be rushed to the Admiralty on Christmas Day calling for further operations against both Ijmuiden and Waalhaven (Rotterdam).

On the 21st sixteen 617 Squadron aircraft took off in the late afternoon for the distant destination of Pölitz, near Stettin, to attack a synthetic oil plant as part of a 5 Group effort involving over two hundred aircraft. The various Bergius synthetic oil refineries dotted around Germany were producing the bulk of the country's aviation fuel, and like the others, this one at Pölitz had been attacked earlier in the year by the American 8th Air Force. This night's effort was to be the first of a number of attacks on this target by Bomber Command over the ensuing weeks, until it was certain that no further production was possible. The operation came as something of a surprise to the 617 Squadron crews, who, in the face of generally unpleasant weather conditions, had been stood down after lunch. The information provided at briefing was not received with enthusiasm by the crews, who learned, that they were to carry Tallboys, but would be reliant on the accuracy of 83 and 97 Squadron marking. It was not, necessarily, that they lacked faith in the ability of the marker crews, but rather, that the system employed by them was insufficiently pinpoint for the accurate delivery of Tallboys. An additional bind was the expectation of a diversion to Scottish airfields on return, because of forecast foggy conditions in Lincolnshire throughout the night.

Engines were run up and the pre-take-off checks were about complete when a delay was called and engines were shut down. At the restart Jimmy Castagnola was first away at 16.44, and Brooks and Flatman brought up the rear, both timing their take-offs at 17.02. The squadron was ultimately led by S/L Cockshott in PD238, in the absence of S/L Calder, who was forced to abandon his sortie about ninety-five miles out from Bridlington, when EE146 suffered a port-inner engine failure. He would eventually put down at Milltown, his briefed Scottish diversionary airfield, some three hours later, having jettisoned his Tallboy. The other crews were those of Iveson in ME554, Brookes in LM489, Marshall in PD371, Pryor in DV380, Oram in ED763, Goodman in NF992, Gumbley in DV405, Kell in NG181, Watts in LM695, Flatman in PD233, Ross in ME555, Castagnola in LM492, Martin in DV393 and Joplin in ME561. The outward flight was relatively uneventful, but Watts discovered he had an unserviceable bombsight, and was within half an hour of Pölitz when efforts to repair it were finally abandoned. Never the less, he continued on to make a pass over the oil refinery with the rest of the squadron.

Once in the target area the force encountered poor visibility, and this difficulty was compounded by heavy defensive fire. The anticipated confusion over the accuracy of the markers also materialized, but a Master Bomber was on hand to recommend a group of markers as the correct aiming point, and the 617 Squadron crews began their bombing runs across the target. They were not accustomed to dropping Tallboys in the "approximate" area of a target, and made repeated runs in the pursuit of accuracy. Both Cockshott and Iveson had their bombsight gyro topple, but the former released his bomb on his fourth run. The latter was unable to identify the target after three runs, and decided to bring his Tallboy home, Marshall doing likewise. Brooks dropped his Tallboy at 22.08, but didn't see it burst, and was then hit by flak. Pryor was happy with his run and did see his bomb impact, but was not able to assess its accuracy. Oram plotted his bomb to have fallen a hundred yards north of the aiming point, which, under the circumstances, was a good effort. Perhaps Kell summed up the general situation best, when he described his experience as follows. "1 X Tallboy. 22.04. 16,350'. Impossible to assess bombing. T.I.s were very scattered. Target area very smokey from flares. We made two runs. The flares were too far east. We could not pick out the actual target. The yellow T.I.s were on the edge of the forest to the south, and the reds and greens to the north. So we chose a point in between the two. We bombed on the third run." Later photographic reconnaissance did show some damage to the installation, including the collapse of a power station chimney, which broke a section of pipeline.

There was now a long return journey to negotiate, which would take the crews over Denmark, and this was undertaken by most without incident. During the course of the homeward leg, conditions at the Lincolnshire airfields proved to be better than forecast, and the diversion to Scottish airfields was subsequently cancelled. However, the conditions took a turn for the worse at the last minute, and instructions were received from 54 Base for aircraft to land at the first available airfield. The murky conditions greeting the returning crews over Lincolnshire precluded landings at airfields not equipped with FIDO, and this meant that the circuits at Metheringham and Ludford Magna would soon become crowded. The Joplin crew could see the diffused glow from the FIDO installation at Ludford Magna, and began to circle it, while attempting to obtain landing instructions and keeping a sharp eye out for other aircraft. Joplin tried a number of channels, but heard nothing from the ground, while the dwindling fuel state reduced his options in terms of diverting elsewhere. He knew the minimum safety height for the area, and remained above it according to his altimeter, but suddenly, there was an impact, and the outer section of the port wing folded upwards.

Contemporary photograph of Group Captain Johnny Fauquier RCAF.

Joplin called for full power in an attempt to keep the damaged Lancaster airborne, but it continued to sink with engines roaring. In the few seconds remaining the crew scrambled to crash positions and braced themselves for the inevitable. There was an initial bounce, and then the main impact, and by the time that all forward motion had ceased, the front section had become detached and was some distance ahead of the main fuselage. A fierce fire took hold, but those crewmembers who were able, took control of the situation, and all of the survivors, including a badly injured Joplin, were removed from immediate danger. In the face of fire and exploding ammunition this required great courage, particularly on the part of navigator Basil Fish, who had initially been knocked unconscious, and was now the only member of the crew sufficiently mobile to seek help. He tried to get into the burning section of fuselage to rescue his two unaccounted-for crew mates, F/O Yates, the mid-upper gunner, and F/O Walker, the bomb-aimer, but was driven back by the searing heat after gaining an impression of one or perhaps two charred bodies.

Having settled his surviving comrades and ensured that Joplin was as comfortable as possible with his shattered legs, Fish set off into the bitter cold conditions to find help. His nightmare trek across fields and through hedges eventually brought him to a farmhouse without a telephone, but the kindly farmer escorted him to a public phone in the next village. Finally, almost three hours after the crash, help arrived at the scene. The death of F/O Walker was particularly tragic. He had initially joined the squadron with

Williams's crew, and completed twenty-eight operations before Williams was screened in August. He had then become Bob Knights's bomb-aimer for three more trips, leaving him on thirty-one when Knights was screened in December. Tait arranged for Walker to be declared tour expired, but Walker reckoned that his conscience would not be satisfied with anything less than the requisite number expected of everyone else. When Joplin's Bomb-aimer became unavailable for the Pölitz raid through sickness, Walker had fatefully jumped at the chance to fill in. Joplin believed at first, that all had survived the crash, and was devastated to learn of the two fatalities. He took the blame upon himself, and became seriously depressed. His injuries were such that he would take no further part in squadron operations, but one further blow awaited him at the hands of senior officers, who spent their winter nights in conditions of comfort and safety. An enquiry into the crash concluded, that Joplin had been disobedient in not adhering to standard approach regulations. These regulations were generally ignored by all even in decent weather conditions. His logbook was endorsed accordingly, as was that of Basil Fish.

On the 28th W/C Tait bade farewell to 617 Squadron, as did G/C Philpott, the station commander, to Woodhall Spa, and a joint party was held in their honour, at which was announced the award of a record third Bar to Tait's DSO. His replacement, the grizzled, tough and highly experienced Canadian, Group Captain Johnny Fauquier, was also introduced to the squadron during this occasion. Fauquier was a legend in 4, 6 and 8 Groups, and would end the war as Canada's most decorated airman. He was born in Ottawa in 1909 as the son of a construction tycoon who built the Ontario leg of the transcontinental railway. He excelled at all forms of sport, and academically he was particularly accomplished in mathematics. His family connections opened up a whole world of opportunity to him, and he initially became a stockbroker. This, however, was anathema to a man with a taste for fast cars, motorcycles and brawling. He learned to fly, proving to be a natural pilot, and started a bush-pilot operation during the mining boom in Quebec. He joined the RCAF at the outbreak of war, and was frustratingly put to basic instructing duties for the first eighteen months. By the time he got into the war with 405 (Vancouver) Squadron RCAF in 4 Group Bomber Command in 1942 he was already 32 years of age, and 10-12 years older than most of his contemporaries. He eventually gained command of 405 Squadron while it was a 4 Group unit in 1942, and returned again in 1943, when it became the only RCAF squadron to become a member of the Pathfinder Force. He acted as Master Bomber or deputy on a number of major operations, and like his predecessors at 617 Squadron, he was accustomed to leading from the front. G/C Philpott's successor as "station master" at Woodhall Spa was the newly promoted Air Commodore "Mouse" Fielden, who had distinguished himself back in 1942 as the first commanding officer of 161 Squadron, one of 3 Group's two clandestine units operating on behalf of SOE and SIS.

On the following afternoon, Calder led a force of sixteen aircraft to bomb the Waalhaven E-Boat pens at Rotterdam. He and his crew were in ME554, and the other crews involved were those of Brookes in NG228, Cockshott in PD238, Hamilton in DV380, Pryor in LM485, Gumbley in DV405, Dobson in PD371, Gavin in LM489, Goodman in NF992, Oram in ED763, Flatman in PD233, Ross in ME555, Kell in NG181, Leavitt in DV393, Watts in LM695 and Castagnola in LM492. They arrived at the target shortly before 15.00 hours, and Gavin and Flatman sent their Tallboys hurtling earthwards at 14.56. Within two minutes all but Dobson's had been delivered, and his was the last at 15.05. Brookes claimed a direct hit on the northern end of the pens from 18,000 feet, and the consensus was, that three Tallboys found the mark, with many others falling as near misses. Cockshott reported a hole in the centre of the structure as he made a second run right over the target. Reconnaissance revealed a great deal of damage to the shelters, but the Germans had learned from their past experience, and dispersed the vessels around the port, thus sparing them from destruction. On the following early evening, Calder again took the lead in ME554, for an operation by thirteen aircraft to a similar target at Ijmuiden. When they arrived, they encountered low cloud, and Calder went beneath it to 4,000 feet to assess the situation. As the cloud was moving in rather than out, he decided there was no point in hanging around, and sent the force home with their bombs.

On the 31st, Fauquier took the squadron into battle for the first time, when flying in Tait's favourite EE146. He was at the head of a twelve-strong force briefed to attack shipping in Oslo Fjord, where the principal targets were the German warships Köln and Emden. Each Lancaster carried a Tallboy fused to explode one hundred feet below the water. The accompanying crews were those of Calder in ME554, Brookes in NG228, Cockshott in PD238, Pryor in DV391, Gumbley in DV405, Goodman in NF992, Flatman in PD233, Oram in ED763, Ross in ME555, Leavitt in DV393 and Kell in LM695. Flying in Cockshott's front turret was the previously mentioned F/L Horsley, who although now a pilot, was reverting to his former trade to gain experience of the squadron's unique operating techniques. They arrived in the target area a fraction before midnight, and observed both vessels making for open water. The bombing began shortly afterwards, Fauquier's Tallboy falling around a hundred yards to port of one of them. He ordered the force to orbit to the north dropping flares, and activity continued in the target area for the next fifty minutes, as some crews made repeated runs in an attempt to draw a bead on the elusive quarry, but no hits were scored. A near miss off the port side of the Emden swung her to starboard and brought her to a standstill, but this was scant reward for the effort expended. The year's final personnel movements involved F/O Lee departing for 26 OTU and S/L Fawke going to Merryfield, while F/O Speirs arrived from 467 Squadron RAAF.

It had been a year of spectacular successes for the squadron, and extremely low losses after the disappointments and high casualty rate following the Dams operation in the previous Year. Some of the Lancasters entering the New Year had been on squadron charge since 1943, and this would have been almost unheard-of in a main force squadron. A succession of outstanding commanding officers had maintained the squadron at the absolute peak of efficiency and performance, and this was to be continued to the end of the bombing war. The Command, for its part, had emerged from the ashes of the winter campaign, and helped magnificently to ensure the success of the invasion. Bomber Command was now a juggernaut, capable of dispensing annihilation wherever it went, and some of the heaviest raids at its hands still lay in the future. The unmistakable scent of victory was wafting across from the Continent, but much still remained to be done before the proud, resourceful and tenacious enemy finally laid down his arms.

January 1945

Although the main force remained active, the weather at the beginning of 1945 was too inhospitable to accommodate the exacting operational flying requirements of 617 Squadron. Operations planned for the 5th, 6th and 7th were cancelled, and the runways were cleared of snow for another on the 11th, which too was called off because of the weather conditions. Matters had improved sufficiently by the 12th for the operation to go ahead, however, and it was to be a long trip to Norway to bomb the U-Boot pens and floating dock at Bergen, and shipping in the harbour. Fauquier was in Mosquito NT205, with Canadian S/L Glen Ellwood in the right hand seat, the latter not to be confused with the F/O M Ellwood flying as wireless operator to Ian Ross. Glen Ellwood had served with Fauquier at 405 Squadron, the only Canadian Pathfinder unit, and was at the 6 Group station at Skipton-on-Swale at the end of December, when the call came through from his former boss to join him at Woodhall Spa. The sixteen Lancaster crews were assigned to one of the specific objectives as follows; the U-Boot pens, Brookes in NG228, Powell in LM695, Leavitt in DV380, Iveson in NG181, Hamilton in Tait's old EE146, Dobson in LM485, Marshall in DV391, Goodman in DV402, Price in PD238 and Gavin in ME562; the floating dock, Martin in DV393, Sanders in LM489 and Pryor in PD233; shipping, Ross in NF992, Watts in DV405, and Castagnola in LM492. 9 Squadron also contributed sixteen Tallboy carrying Lancasters, and take-off took place between 08.25 and 09.15.

The target area was reached shortly before 13.00 hours, by which time the Mustang fighter support had been observed to sweep in from higher up. It was immediately clear that visibility was going to be compromised by ground haze, and the gaggle began to break up as the crews assigned to the floating dock and shipping searched for an approach offering a clearer view. The visibility problem was soon to be exacerbated by the smoke from the exploding Tallboys, the first of which, according to the ORB, was delivered onto the southern corner of the pens from 16,000 feet by S/L Brookes at 12.58. Goodman followed up two minutes later, only to find the bombsight unserviceable, and frustratingly, this would be the only time the target was clearly visible to his bomb-aimer. They made five more runs across the target over the ensuing thirty-eight minutes, as the bomb-aimer, F/L Hayward, tried to use his SABS as a fixed sight, but he never again obtained a fix through the smoke, and they turned for home with the Tallboy still aboard. Dobson, Price and Gavin also made up to five runs each with a functioning SABS but were forced to give up and likewise bring their Tallboys home. Leavitt dropped his bomb into the smoke at 13.04½, but was unable to pinpoint its burst, and Marshall's went down some three minutes later. The members of Marshall's crew were unable to determine the fall of their bomb, but did see what they thought was the first one to go down, possibly that dropped by Brookes, overshooting to the left by 150 yards. Hamilton's bomb-aimer identified the pens on the first run, but called for a second one, at the end of which the Tallboy hung up. By the time a third circuit was completed, the aiming point was obscured by smoke, and theirs became yet another Tallboy to be returned to store.

Powell gave up trying to find the aiming point at 13.41, but during the course of his runs across the target, he or his crew observed two detonations, one around three hundred yards to the south of the target, and the other on a hillside six miles due west. One of the former may have belonged to Tony Iveson, whose Lancaster found itself in heavy flak, and was attacked by an enemy fighter. The port-inner engine caught fire, and the tail plane and rudder on that side sustained damage. Iveson ordered the Tallboy to be jettisoned fused over an uninhabited area, and warned his crew to prepare to abandon the aircraft, which was wallowing along in a nose up attitude and losing height. Rear gunner, Ted Wass, plugged into the intercom to report that he and two others were now ready to bale out, and on hearing the confirmation "OK", assumed this was the order to go. He, the wireless operator, F/O Tittle, and mid-upper gunner, Sgt

Smith, departed the aircraft by parachute, and the fighter broke off the engagement. The Lancaster was hit again by flak as it turned away from the target area, and it looked as if a safe return across the sea was going to be out of the question. Directional control was proving difficult because of the damage to cables, and Iveson was forced to maintain pressure on the port rudder pedal to prevent the aircraft from turning to starboard.

Determined not to spend the last few months of the war in captivity, though, Iveson and the remaining crewmembers set about the task of getting home. Bomb-aimer Frank Chance lashed a rope around the port rudder pedal and secured it to the camera mount to enable Iveson to relieve the pressure on his leg. Flight engineer "Taff" Phillips went aft and found the severed cables, and through a process of trial and error he and his pilot worked out a system to get them back to Sumburgh in the Shetlands. They arrived in one piece, justly proud of their achievement, but devastated by the loss of three of their number, whom, they hoped had landed safely. In fact, wireless operator Les Smith had damaged a leg on landing, and came to on a stretcher being borne by four German soldiers. Both gunners were also ultimately taken into captivity. Arthur Kell flew up to Sumburgh on the following day to collect Iveson and the others, but they would fly no further operations with the squadron, and it would be July before the Lancaster came home.

The three crews assigned to the floating dock were experiencing great difficulty in picking out their target. Runs were made from various directions, but it was only visible from directly above, and with smoke drifting towards this aiming point from the pens, the prospects were poor. After ten runs Don Day spotted a merchantman heading for the town, and Martin, his pilot, called up Fauquier for permission to attack it. Fauquier, realising the floating dock was a lost cause, gave the go-ahead, and Day had the target smack in his sight just seconds from release, when a flak shell exploded beneath the Lancaster and peppered the underside with shrapnel. The Tallboy took most of it, and fell away minus part of its tail assembly. The arming wire had been cut, and this meant, that the bomb fell harmlessly into the sea without detonating. The bomb doors were riddled with holes, but, luckily, no vital parts of the aircraft had been hit. Sanders was also unable to identify the floating dock after making five runs, and followed Fauquier's orders to attack shipping instead. His bomb was dropped from 15,000 feet at 13.32, and was described as a near miss. The third member of the floating dock trio was Pryor, whose PD233 became another victim of fighters. They had already made six runs across their target, and were in the process of a seventh, when a fighter appeared on the starboard beam. Pryor turned towards the enemy in the standard evasive manoeuvre, and as he did so, a second fighter closed the trap by attacking from the port side. The port-outer engine was damaged and had to be feathered, and at least one other engine lost power. Pryor threw the Lancaster around the sky like a fighter, and the Tallboy was jettisoned. This was most likely the explosion on the hillside witnessed by Powell. The damage was sufficiently serious to persuade Pryor that there was almost no chance of negotiating the sea crossing to Scotland. He considered a crash-landing, but the hilly terrain precluded that option, and when a FW190 drew alongside, its pilot gesticulating to the crew to get out, the game was effectively up.

Pryor dragged the crippled aircraft up to around fifteen hundred feet over an island, and was the last to leave, having pointed the nose of his Lancaster out to sea. All but one of the crew landed safely, the exception being F/O Kendrick, who, it will be recalled, had been severely injured almost exactly a year earlier, when O'Shaughnessy crashed on Snettisham beach during training. He was the first to leave the aircraft through the front hatch, and was observed from the ground to fail to deploy his parachute. Only recently returned to operations, it seems he hit his chin on his way through the hatch, and was knocked unconscious. He was found in deep snow with severe head and back injuries, and despite being tended by local people, he succumbed three days later without regaining consciousness.

Witnesses on the ground also reported the empty Lancaster being chased out to sea by the FW190s, which belonged to either the 9th or 12th Staffel of III/JG5 operating out of Herdla. One of the fighters appears to have collided with the Lancaster, and following an explosion, both aircraft went into the sea. The German pilot, Unteroffizier Kirchner, was killed. It was later reported, that the second FW190 ran out of fuel on the way back to its base, and although Feldwebel Lieber was observed to carry out a ditching, he also failed to survive.

Castagnola was able to watch the opening of the raid as he stalked a ship, upon which he intended to drop his Tallboy, and he confirmed Marshall's observation, that the first bomb to go down on the submarine pens was an overshoot. He unloaded his 12,000 pound monster weapon at 13.09 from 14,850 feet, and his bomb-aimer, P/O Hoyland, watched it all the way down to the stern of the vessel, a minesweeper, which it penetrated like a hot knife through butter. The effect was immediate, and the ship could be seen to settle in the water. After about three minutes it was rent by an explosion, possibly from its boiler, and then rolled over onto its side and sank with twenty of its crew killed or missing. As it disappeared beneath the waves Watts was aiming his Tallboy at another vessel, a tramp steamer, which turned out to be the Olga Siemens, but he missed by around seventy-five yards. Never the less, the explosion caused a serious leak in the hull of the 3,300 ton vessel, and it had to be beached. As he pulled away Watts's attention was attracted by the sight of Ross's Lancaster trailing smoke, and being chased out to sea by two FW190 fighters. He was clearly losing the fight with gravity, and his crippled Lancaster sank lower and lower over the cold ocean. Watts instinctively dived in pursuit of the pursuers, at the same time seeking and obtaining permission from Fauquier to do so. Both of Ross's port engines were by now feathered, but at least they had stopped smoking. The front turret of Watts's Lancaster opened up at around 250 yards, and the two fighters broke away and disappeared. Ross was seen to ditch off the Norwegian coast, and he and his crew were then observed to climb out onto the wing and inflate their Mae Wests. The Lancaster showed no signs of sinking, but, worryingly, there was no evidence of a dinghy. Watts climbed up to five thousand feet to get off an air sea rescue call, and saw the rest of the squadron heading homewards high above. Remarkably, Castagnola had also raced to help Ross, and was circling the area, but neither crew was aware of the other's presence until they compared notes back home.

Watts remained at the scene until his fuel situation forced him to leave, by which time he knew, that an Air Sea Rescue Warwick was on its way from Sumburgh. The Warwick took off at 14.43, and arrived a little over an hour later to find the Lancaster still afloat, but only just. By the time it had circled and dropped a lifeboat at 16.05, the Lancaster had disappeared beneath the waves, and the crew was in the water. In the fading light, one man was seen to be swimming towards the lifeboat, but the approach of an enemy fighter forced the Warwick crew to turn for home. Watts, meanwhile, had landed at Sumburgh, having completed the final approach on fumes, and as he taxied off the runway, the engines cut. Throughout the night Coastal Command Catalinas searched the sea right up to the Norwegian coast, one of them with a Leigh Light, but no trace was found of the Ross crew or the lifeboat. Three Warwicks and three Ansons continued the search on the following day with a fighter escort, but they also found nothing, and the search was called off as darkness fell. It is believed by some, that the enemy fighter seen earlier by the Warwick crew strafed and killed the unfortunate crewmembers. The month saw four aircrew officer arrivals on posting, those of F/L Beaumont from 5 LFS, F/L Hill from 61 Squadron, Lt Adams from 630 Squadron and F/L Warburton from 57 Squadron.

February 1945

It was the 3rd before 617 Squadron operated again, this time with a visit to the midget submarine pens at Poortershaven, from where "Biber" operations were launched. The Biber was an ill-conceived and desperate attempt by Germany to interfere with Allied naval supply and support operations at a time when the war was essentially lost. The one-man craft was hastily developed and put into service. It carried a torpedo on each side, was powered on the surface by a petrol engine and when submerged by batteries. Once its power was exhausted it was at the mercy of the current, and many drifted into oblivion with their pilots. Other unfortunate pilots died of carbon monoxide poisoning as exhaust fumes infiltrated the tiny cockpit compartment. Sadly, life in Germany was cheap at this stage of the war, and few Biber pilots survived to tell their sorry tale.

Fauquier led the squadron into battle in NG445, and the others involved in this operation were Cockshott in PD238, Goodman in PB415, Horsley in ME554, Flatman in EE146, Gavin in LM489, Gumbley in DV405, Price in DV380, Watts in LM695, Martin in DV393, Brookes in NG228, Powell in PD371, Oram in ED763, Marshall in DV391, Lancey in LM485, Castagnola in DV385, Calder in NG489 and Sanders in ME562. Fauquier was first away at 14.00 hours, and it was an hour and fifty-one minutes later that the Tallboys began to fall. Fauquier reported a good gaggle formation, and all of the Tallboys went down on the first run with good concentration. As always, smoke made it difficult to accurately assess the outcome, but Flatman reported three bombs in the water close to and outside of the breakwater, three to four more close to the entrance to the pens, one on a nearby railway and another about two hundred yards north of the aiming point. Price and Powell claimed direct hits, and others watched their bombs fall into the smoke directly over the aiming point. All aircraft returned safely to Woodhall Spa either side of 17.00 hours, after barely three hours in the air. Post-raid photographs of craters revealed that five to six Tallboys had inflicted heavy damage on the pens and quays. The entrance to the southern dam of the basin had been cut, military installations south-east and north-west of the pens were seriously afflicted, the floating crane used for lifting the vessels in and out of the water had been hit, and the railway line north of the target area serving the pens had been cut in three places. None of the submarines themselves appeared to be damaged, but they were unable to carry out any operations for a month, and this allowed vital Allied supply convoys unmolested access to the River Scheldt.

This successful operation was followed by an intended assault by seventeen aircraft on the important viaduct at Bielefeld on the 6th. Fauquier led the squadron away in NG445 at 08.14, but by the time the target was reached some two hours or so later bad weather had intervened, and the attack was abandoned. All of the Tallboys were brought home. This day's failure became the start of what was effectively a campaign against the viaduct until its eventual destruction some weeks later, while the structure's stubborn refusal to fall was almost a symbolic reflection of Germany's dogged commitment to continuing the fight despite the war having already been lost. What we know as the Bielefeld Viaduct actually stands on the outskirts of the small town of Schildesche, one of a number of similar communities making up the Bielefeld urban area, and it is known in Germany as the Schildesche rather than the Bielefeld Viaduct. Construction of the impressive twenty-eight arch edifice began in 1845, and was completed two years later. It was built to carry the new Cöln-Minden railway line across the Johannisbach Valley, and would eventually become a vital link in the east-west communications network. Between 1914 and 1917 a second viaduct was built alongside as a mirror image to cope with the increasing amount of traffic, and it was this imposing twin structure that now faced 617 Squadron. As ground forces moved towards the German frontier during the autumn of 1944, American bombers began to target the Bielefeld area, pitting the landscape around the viaduct with bomb craters, and inflicting casualties upon the local populations.

While 617 Squadron had been attending to the submarine pens at Poortershaven on the 3rd, 9 Squadron had visited the new and, as it turned out, abandoned E-Boot pens at Ijmuiden. Now 617 Squadron returned alone to the latter on the 8th to finish the job. Fauquier was again in NG445, and the others were Calder in NG489, Castagnola in DV385, Sanders in ME562, Martin in PB415, Watts in LM695, Flatman in NG339, Lancey in LM485, Gumbley in DV405, Oram in LM492, Cockshott in PD238, Brookes in NG228, Goodman in NG340, Dobson in ED763 and Price in DV380. Taking off either side of 08.00 the squadron reached the target area at 09.30, and ran in at heights ranging from 14,200 to 16,000 feet. Twelve Tallboys went down at 09.33, a minute after Castagnola's, and two minutes before the remaining two, and at least two direct hits were observed by Fauquier and one near miss. The Germans had again dispersed the vessels around the port, however, and none of them was damaged. A vertical reconnaissance photograph taken by a 542 Squadron pilot and an oblique one provided by 541 Squadron produced an interpretation report describing a hit at the north end of the pens where the final concrete roof had not yet been laid. This portion of the roof was declared to be destroyed over three pens with additional damage to the north wall. It further described a near miss and five other craters, one of which was within a hundred feet of the west side of the shelter. In fact, no hits were scored, but a very near miss had knocked a section of wall out of alignment. This was the only operation by 617 Squadron against the new bunker, but the Americans made a number of attacks employing Disney bombs.

The night of the 13/14th brought the Churchill-inspired attack on Dresden, which caused a firestorm and cost the lives of around twenty-five thousand civilians. Later that morning 617 Squadron sent nineteen Lancasters back to Bielefeld, but cloud prevented the attack from taking place, and all the Tallboys were returned to the dump. On the afternoon of the 22nd, while 9 Squadron took a dogleg southerly route to another architecturally impressive viaduct at Altenbeken, 617 Squadron adopted an almost due easterly track from Cromer straight across the Ijsselmeer and Holland and into Germany to return to Bielefeld with eighteen Lancasters armed with Tallboys. Fauquier led in NG445, and he was accompanied by Carey, fresh from his sojourn in Sweden, in NG494, Castagnola in DV385, Gavin in LM489, Powell in NG228, Anning in LM492, Sayers in DV402, Dobson in PD371, Sanders in ME562, Goodman in ME554, Gumbley in DV405, Marshall in DV391, Calder in NG489, Watts in LM695, Leavitt in PB415, Price in PD238, Martin in NG340 and Hill in NG339. The first Tallboys went down shortly before 16.00 hours during the initial run, but some crews went round for a second or third run. Fauquier bombed on his second run, and saw his bomb overshoot by fifty yards. Carey undershot by around forty yards, but noted a possible direct hit on the northern end. Castagnola thought his bomb may have been a direct hit on the northern end, but it was at least a near miss, while Calder claimed a direct hit. The structure was peppered with near misses of around forty to fifty yards, and although some crews believed it had been damaged, photo-reconnaissance revealed it to be still intact.

On the 24th cloud prevented 617 Squadron from delivering an attack on the Dortmund-Ems Canal at Ladbergen, for which eighteen aircraft had taken off, led again by Fauquier. Marshall suffered a coolant leak in his starboard outer immediately after take-off, and did not proceed beyond local airspace. Among his crew were original "Dambusters" Len Sumpter, formerly Shannon's bomb-aimer, and Doug Webb, Townsend's rear gunner. This abortive trip proved to be the squadron's last operational activity of the month. Pilot postings during the month were as follows; F/Ls Quinton and Rawes came in from 5 LFS, S/L Gordon from 189 Squadron, and F/L Trent from 1 Group's 625 Squadron, while P/O Huckerby went to 1660CU and S/L Iveson to 6 LFS.

March 1945

The clean aerodynamic lines of W/Cdr Johnnie Fauquier's B1 Special PD119, YZ-J make the Lancaster look very different from the aircraft on the Main Force squadrons. The removal of mid-upper and front turrets also saved weight, enabling the aircraft to carry the 'Grand Slam' bomb. The Allies' air superiority by this time would have made the crews feel so much better about their own lack of defensive armaments.

A further attempt to take out the Bielefeld viaduct was launched on the 9th with Fauquier this time in Mosquito NT205, accompanied in the right-hand seat by F/L Bayne. Nineteen Lancasters were also involved, take-off beginning with Castagnola at 14.25 and ending with the squadron commander at 14.56. Some three and a half hours later they were back with their bombs still attached, having been thwarted by cloud. The 11th brought an all-time record for the Command, when 1,079 aircraft, the largest force ever dispatched to a single target, took off in the late morning to raid Essen for the last time. The record lasted for a little over twenty-four hours, and was surpassed on the following afternoon, when 1,108 aircraft departed their stations for Dortmund. This was a record, which would stand to the end of hostilities.

Like the scent of a fox to a pack of hounds the lure of the Bielefeld viaduct drew 617 Squadron on yet again on the 13th, when Fauquier reverted to a Lancaster, this time PB119. A further nineteen Lancasters were involved in the early afternoon departure from Woodhall Spa, captained by Cockshott, Calder, Brookes, Powell, McLoughlin, Goodman, Hill, Gumbley, Warburton, Sayers, Lancey, Anning, Rawes,

Adams, Flatman, Martin, Speirs, Castagnola and Carey. Once again the weather intervened, however, and around four hours later they came home to return their valuable stores to the dump. Although the ORB describes the bombs carried by Fauquier and Calder as Tallboys, they were both flying in Lancaster BI Specials. PD119 and PD112 respectively were among a batch of aircraft belonging to C Flight, which had front and dorsal turrets removed, no bomb doors, a modified bomb bay faired fore and aft, strengthened undercarriage, uprated engines, and two less crew members, specifically to carry Wallis's scaled up Tallboy, the 22,000lb Grand Slam. They also bore a YZ code, while A and B Flights retained KC. The Grand Slam earthquake bombs had been going to war for the first time, but Fauquier and Calder were now forced to make a landing with the war's heaviest bomb still on board. For extra insurance they put down on the very long emergency strip at Carnaby.

The operation was rescheduled for the following afternoon, and the target's charmed life was soon to be brought to an abrupt end. Sixteen Lancasters were prepared on this occasion, but Fauquier's PD119 became unserviceable immediately before take-off. Calder, not wishing to be the victim of a hijack by his commanding officer, turned a Nelsonian blind eye to the gesticulations of his superior, gunned the engines, and took off to become the first to drop a Grand Slam in anger. Anger was the emotion felt by Fauquier as he watched the graceful upward arc of PD112's wings bearing the ten-ton monster weapon aloft. The other crew captains and Lancasters were; Brookes in NG228, Powell in PD371, Goodman in NG494, Hill in LM489, Gumbley in DV405, Warburton in DV380, Sayers in DV402, Lancey in LM485, Anning in LM492, Rawes in DV391, Flatman in NG339, Martin in PB415, Speirs in LM695 and Carey in NG489. There was no cloud on this occasion to protect the viaduct, and Calder's Grand Slam went down from 11,965 feet at 16.28¼ on the squadron's second pass over the target, and at precisely the same moment that Martin released his Tallboy. Other Tallboys dropped within seconds either side came from the Lancasters of Gumbley, Brookes, Hill, Lancey and Flatman. Sayers's Tallboy had actually been the first to go, but this fell out as the bomb doors were opened during the initial approach at 16.12. The bomb seemed to be undamaged as it fell away, and was seen to rotate in the prescribed manner, but whether or not it detonated is not recorded. Rawes was unable to pick up the aiming point along with the others, so went round again, trying to follow the road from Bielefeld to the south of the viaduct. The Tallboy was released at 16.37, and only then did the crew realise, that they were off track. The bomb fell onto a crossroads some 750 yards southwest of the target.

On return to Woodhall Spa Calder reported a thirty-yard undershoot of his Grand Slam on the southern end of the viaduct on the Schildesche side, and this was confirmed by photographic reconnaissance. He also saw a direct hit, which was one of a number claimed by other crews, among them Hill and Gumbley, and Brookes thought his might have been. Goodman saw his Tallboy explode on the railway line by a road crossing, while Flatman believed his impacted on the road running beneath the viaduct. The result was the collapse of this formerly illusive structure over a hundred yards, and all aircraft had returned safely to base. On the 15th Calder and Cockshott took Grand Slams to the Arnsberg viaduct in PB996 and PD114 respectively in company with fourteen Lancasters of 9 Squadron. Cockshott bombed on his fourth run from 13,600 feet, but haze obscured its point of impact, and Calder brought his bomb home from what was an unsuccessful operation.

On the 19th the operation to the Arnsberg viaduct was repeated by nineteen aircraft, and this provided Fauquier with the opportunity to deliver his first Grand Slam. The crews involved were those of Fauquier in PD119, Cockshott in PD238, Powell in PD121, Calder in NG445, Gumbley in PD117, Warburton in LM489, Sayers in PB997, Anning in PB998, Rawes in PD113, Dobson in PD116, Trent in LM485, Gavin in PD131, Goodman in PD130, Hill in PD118, Flatman in PD129, Carey in PD132, Martin in PB996, Speirs in

Australian Phil Martin in PB996, YZ-C, drops a 22,000 lb 'Grand Slam' bomb (Crown).

PB415 and Adams in ME562. Fauquier, Gumbley, Gavin, Goodman, Flatman and Martin were all armed with Grand Slams, and the commanding officer released his at 10.54 from 13,000 feet, noticing that the bombing generally was tending to overshoot the mark. Never the less, Dobson claimed a direct hit with his Tallboy, and Hill reported seeing this and a second one, and when the smoke had cleared sufficiently, at least two arches of the viaduct were seen to be down. The second direct hit observed by Hill may have come from either Cockshott or Speirs, the former claiming to have nailed the aiming point, while the latter saw his effort hit near the right hand or tunnel end. Sayers experienced a hang-up on his first run and went round again with the same result.

The Arbergen railway bridge in the southeastern suburbs of Bremen in northern Germany was the target for an attack by twenty 617 Squadron aircraft on the 21st. The crews were those of Fauquier in PD119, Calder in PB996, both carrying a Grand Slam, Gordon in PD115, Cockshott in PD114, Gavin in PD116, Goodman in PD130, Hill in NG494, Gumbley in PD117, Price in PD118, Warburton in PD128, Powell in PD133, Dobson in PD130, Rawes in PD113, Sayers in NG445, Anning in LM695, Trent in PD238, Lancey in NG489, Flatman in NG339, Carey in PB997 and Speirs in PD129. Calder released his Grand Slam from 13,690 feet at 10.05½, but was unable to determine its point of impact. Fauquier's fell away ten seconds later from 14,000 feet, and he plotted its impact as 200 yards north of the target. The Price crew was the only one to report seeing a direct hit, but the structure succumbed anyway under the weight of numerous near misses. PD117 was hit by heavy flak, and was seen to fall in flames a dozen or so miles south of the centre of Bremen, before exploding on impact. As a BI Special it contained a five-man crew, and sadly, Barney Gumbley and his colleagues were all killed. No remains were recovered, and the names of the crew are perpetuated on the Runnymede Memorial. Five other aircraft also sustained damage, but all returned safely.

A bridge over the River Weser at Nienburg, northwest of Hanover, was the target for twenty 617 Squadron aircraft on the afternoon of the 22nd, six of them carrying Grand Slams. These were Gordon in PB996, Cockshott in PD114, Powell in PD121, Gavin in PD134, Rawes in PB997 and Anning in PD133. Those with Tallboys were Fauquier in NG445, Calder in PD115 or PD113, Price in PD135, Goodman in PB415, Hill in NG494, Warburton in PD128, Sayers in PD132, Trent in LM485, Lancey in NG489, Horsley in PD238, Flatman in LM695, Carey in PD131, Speirs in PD112 and Brookes in NG228. Fauquier observed three direct hits, one of which was Cockshott's Grand Slam, and Rawes also believed his to have found the mark. In order not to waste the precious bombs the 4th and 8th rows of the gaggle had been instructed not to bomb on the first two runs, and in the event, the bridge was destroyed without them. This enabled Powell to bring his Grand Slam home, along with the Tallboys carried by Brookes and Speirs.

On the following day a similar number of aircraft returned to the Bremen area to attack another railway bridge. Fauquier led the operation in PD119, with Powell in PB996, Calder in PD112, Cockshott in PD114, Gavin in PD134 and Flatman in PB997, all armed with Grand Slams, and Brookes in PD133, Gordon in PB998, Price in PD113, Goodman in PB415, Hill in NG494, Warburton in LM695, Sayers in PD132, Anning in PD118, Trent in PD115, Lancey in NG489, Horsley in PD238, Carey in PD131, Speirs in PD130 and Leavitt in LM492, each with a Tallboy. Powell was forced to abort his sortie while still over the airfield twenty minutes after take-off. A problem with his starboard outer would have prevented him from maintaining gaggle speed, and it seems he jettisoned his Grand Slam over a designated area. Sayers managed to gain a little more distance before he too suffered a starboard-outer engine failure, and he returned his Tallboy to store. A few minutes after Sayers landed, Trent came back with a complete failure of the oxygen system, and his Tallboy was also saved for a future occasion. It was a rare occasion indeed, if not a unique one, for three 617 Squadron aircraft to return early from the same operation with technical failures.

A little over three hours after take-off, at 10.04, Fauquier released his Grand Slam from 16,500 feet. According to Brookes, the first three bombs to fall were direct hits, but in the space of a minute from 10.03.47 Warburton, Gordon, Gavin, Anning and Carey all claimed hits, as did Cockshott and Horsley shortly afterwards. Opposition in the form of flak and jet fighters was fierce, and a number of aircraft sustained damage. Lancey's was hit by flak just ten seconds before bomb release, and the air pressure to the bombsight was cut. The bomb was dropped as soon as the bomb-aimer regained composure, but it would have undershot the aiming point. Goodman's, on the other hand, overshot after hanging up for fifteen seconds. Calder's Grand Slam was released as planned, but his bomb-aimer was unable to observe its fall through a shattered clear vision panel. By the time Hill came in to bomb, the aiming point was obscured by smoke, and it was decided to abort. For the same reason an immediate assessment of the damage to the bridge was impossible, but the number of direct hits suggested a successful outcome.

The month's final operation took place on the 27th, when twenty aircraft were sent to the U-Boot pens at Farge, a small port on the eastern bank of the Weser northwest of Bremen. In his classic book, The Dambusters, Paul Brickhill describes the target as the largest concrete structure in the world, measuring some 1,450 by 300 yards, with a reinforced concrete roof twenty-three feet thick. The massive structure contained a tank large enough for completed U-Boots to be tested under water. At the time of the attack it was still under construction and was not operational. In fact, the concrete for the roof had only recently been poured, and had not had time to set before the attack took place. This time fourteen 617 Squadron aircraft carried Grand Slams, and they were Fauquier in PD119, Calder in PD118, Brookes in PD131, Cockshott in PD114, Powell in PD121, Price in PD128, Sayers in PD113, Anning in PD139, Trent in PD116, Leavitt in PD129, Marshall in PD115, Flatman in PB996, Carey in PB997 and Lancey in PD130, while Tallboys were transported by Goodman in NG228, Hill in LM485, Warburton in LM695, McLoughlin in PD371, Beaumont in PD238 and Speirs in NG339. Goodman aborted his sortie almost immediately after take-off when an engine failed, and he landed back twenty minutes later. Lancey was, likewise, still over the airfield gaining altitude when he too was forced to call a halt, but he remained airborne for a little over two hours, probably to burn off fuel before landing with his monster bomb.

The seventeen remaining aircraft pressed on, arriving in the target area shortly before 13.00 hours, and Warburton's Tallboy was the first to go down, just thirty-three seconds after the hour. Eleven seconds later Fauquier's Grand Slam arrowed towards the aiming point, followed by those of Leavitt and Flatman almost simultaneously six seconds later. Fauquier recorded his effort as an overshoot by ten yards, and he observed a second bomb undershoot by a similar margin, but was unable to confirm anything beyond this. Calder saw one direct hit on the roof about a hundred yards east of the aiming point, and Brookes claimed a direct hit right on it. Other direct hits were claimed by Warburton, Anning, Marshall and Speirs, while Beaumont had to abort when another aircraft slid in directly beneath his just as the point of release approached. It was another masterly display of precision bombing, though, and photo reconnaissance confirmed two direct hits by Grand Slams, which had penetrated the partially completed roof and caused a great deal of it to collapse. The structure was still incomplete at the end of hostilities. Crew postings during the month brought F/L Wilson from 227 Squadron, F/O West from 463 Squadron, and S/L Ward from 57 Squadron, while out went F/O Stanford to 11 PDRC, and F/O Sanders and F/L Oram to 54 Base, all at the conclusion of their tours.

April 1945

April would see the final operations by 617 Squadron before the end of hostilities, but the month's first effort by fourteen aircraft on the 6th, to attack shipping at Ijmuiden, fell foul of the weather conditions. 617 Squadron joined forces with 463 and 467 Squadrons RAAF for this operation, the two latter carrying 1,000 pounders. The process of attaining operational altitude with a full bomb load was a protracted affair, and it took almost an hour and three quarters to reach the Dutch coast. On arrival nine-tenths cloud was visible to the north, while over the target itself there were no breaks. Calder, who was in temporary command of the squadron while Fauquier took three days leave, assessed the situation as hopeless, and the operation was aborted. The time was 09.43, and Calder touched down at Woodhall Spa sixty-three minutes later. The operation was rescheduled for 617 Squadron alone on the early evening of the following day, and was led this time by Cockshott in PD114. He had been detailed to act as controller for the previous day's effort, but had been forced to pull out with intercom trouble. Also operating were Calder in PD132, Powell in PD131, Goodman in PB998, McLoughlin in PB996, Horsley in PB997, Price in PD133, Leavitt in PD129, Marshall in PD134, Lancey in PD130, Anning in PD135, Castagnola in PD113, Adams in PD128, Gordon in LM485 and Beaumont in PD238. All were carrying Tallboys, and Leavitt, Beaumont and Gordon claimed direct hits on the target ship, the 4,500 ton Van Riemsdijk, a merchantman, which had been built in Amsterdam and launched in April 1941, but never completed. She was seized by the Germans in October 1941, and was eventually towed to Ijmuiden in September 1944 to be sunk between the two jetties to block the harbour entrance. Probably because of the effectiveness of German E-Boot operations from Ijmuiden, which required the port to remain accessible, the sinking was not carried out.

The rest of 617's hardware fell onto the quayside or close by into the water, and as the force withdrew the ship seemed to be down by the stern, and was later reported to have sunk. The interpretation report confirmed this, stating: "the block ship is down by the stern and listing to starboard with the after well-deck awash on the starboard side. The vessel is probably resting on the bottom. Six large craters are to be seen around the Berghafen, five on the southern side and one on the northern." In fact, the Van Riemsdijk had not been hit, but a number of very near misses had opened up her bottom and allowed the water in. Remarkably, she was raised in October 1946, completed and put to work, remaining in service with Dutch operators until 1967, when she became Panamanian registered until being sold for scrap in 1979. That night 5 Group attacked a benzol plant at Molbis near Leipzig, and put an end to all further production. On the following night the oil refinery at Lützkendorf was dealt a similarly fatal blow, and it would not be necessary for the Command to return.

On the 9th heavy flak greeted the squadron's seventeen aircraft over the U-Boot pens at Hamburg, and six aircraft were hit. The force, which took off around 14.30, consisted of Fauquier in PD119, Calder in PD112, Gordon in PD115, Powell in PD131, Goodman in PB998, Beaumont in NG339, McLoughlin in PB996, Horsley in PB997, Price in PD133, Leavitt in LM695, Warburton in PD127, Marshall in PD134, Anning in PD135, Sayers in PD130, Speirs in PD118, Castagnola in PD113 and Adams in PD139. Fauquier and Calder carried Grand Slams, which were released from 17,000 feet within seconds of each other at 17.36. The former struck the north-eastern corner of the roof and the latter the west side, while Beaumont, McLoughlin, Horsley, Price, Leavitt, Anning and Castagnola all claimed direct hits with their Tallboys. Some of the others were unable to assess the accuracy of their delivery because of smoke, but members of Anning's crew reported all but two bombs falling on the target. A heavy escort of Spitfires and Mustangs engaged the enemy fighters, and the operation was a complete success.

An attempt to take out the warships Prinz Eugen and Lützow at Swinemünde on the Baltic coast on the 13th was frustrated by cloud and was abandoned. It was a long round-trip of six and a half to seven hours, made even longer by the fact, that there was nothing to show for it. The Lützow had actually begun life as the Deutschland, and was completed on the 1st of April 1939 as one of three "pocket" battleships. The others were the Admiral Scheer and the Admiral Graf Spee of Battle of the River Plate fame. Not wishing to risk the loss in battle of a ship bearing the name of the fatherland, Hitler ordered the renaming in February 1940, after the sale of the original Lützow to the Russians. The 15th brought a similar disappointment, when cloud was encountered during the outward flight and persisted all the way. The force continued on to within eighteen miles of the target, but the operation was then abandoned and the Lancasters landed back at Woodhall Spa within four hours. Relaunched on the 16th in excellent weather conditions, eighteen Lancasters converged on the aiming point shortly before 18.00 hours. The crews were those of Fauquier in PD119, Gordon in PD115, Brookes in PD130, Powell in NG228, Gavin in PD116, Hill in PB997, Horsley in PB998, Quinton in NG494, Price in PD133, Leavitt in PD114, Warburton in PD128, Anning in PD132, Rawes in PD371, Trent in NG340, Flatman in PB996, Speirs in PD118, Castagnola in PD113 and Adams in PD139. Most had Tallboys in their bomb bays, but Powell, Quinton, Rawes and Trent were each carrying twelve 1,000lb bombs.

Fauquier misidentified the target, and his bomb was aimed at a vessel on a canal closer to the town of Swinemünde, missing it by ten yards. The force encountered murderous flak, and the Lancasters captained by Gordon and Gavin sustained damage. Gordon was forced to abandon his first run after flak severed his throttle controls, causing a loss of power in his port-outer engine. A second run was found to be inaccurate and was scrubbed, and as the squadron made its second run, Gordon found himself about ten miles behind and unable to catch up. He tried again to go it alone, but found the target enveloped in smoke, and bombed a village instead on the way home. Gavin jettisoned his live Tallboy short of the target after being hit, and he estimated it undershot by a quarter of a mile. S/L Powell's NG228 was another victim, and was seen to go down in flames having lost a wing, before ultimately crashing into woods. One parachute was observed at around 2,000 feet, but there were no survivors, and this was the last operational casualty to be suffered by the squadron. A number of crews reported seeing a possible direct hit on the stern of the Lützow, and there were many near misses. Hill thought his Tallboy may have found the mark, and the Lützow had, in fact, been mortally wounded, although it seems did not sink. In the context of the war, though, it was scant consolation for the loss of the Powell crew so close to the end. In the event, Lützow was blown up and scuttled by her own people on the 4th of May. As for Prinz Eugen, it is uncertain whether she was at Swinemünde at the time, but she was one of only two major German surface vessels to survive the war and was surrendered on the 8th of May to eventually be commissioned into the US Navy.

On the 18th over nine hundred aircraft bombed the town and naval base on the island of Heligoland, leaving it with the appearance of a cratered moonscape, and this was followed up on the late afternoon of the 19th by twenty Lancasters of 617 Squadron and a contingent from 9 Squadron. The purpose of the operation was to knock out the heavy gun emplacements, which barred Allied access to the north-western German ports. The 617 Squadron crews were those of Fauquier in NG445, Calder, now shown in the ORB as a Wing Commander, in PD118, Gordon in PD115, Brookes in PD121, Gavin in PD116, Horsley in PB998, Quinton in PD238, Beaumont in NG339, Hill in NG494, Leavitt in PD129, Adams in PD139, Warburton in PD128, Trent in PD132, Lancey in NG340 or PD130, Anning in PD135, Rawes in PD130, Marshall in PD133, Flatman in PD114, Speirs in LM695 and Castagnola in PD134. Calder, Gordon, Brookes, Anning, Flatman and Castagnola each carried a Grand Slam on its final employment, while the others dropped Tallboys. Under the umbrella of a strong fighter escort the force came in from the north at an average height of 10,000 feet, and according to the spread of bombing times in the ORB, the crews took their time to ensure as far as possible an accurate delivery. Brookes appears to have bombed on the first run at 16.39, but as this is more than twenty minutes before the next bomb went down, it is possibly a typographical error, and should perhaps read 17.39. In the event he reported his Grand Slam undershooting by about thirty yards and hitting the base of the cliffs, but observed another bomb hit the centre of the battery. This could have been Gavin's, which was the next to fall at 17.01, and he did claim a direct hit. Fauquier bombed on his second run at 17.08, and his Tallboy struck ground about twenty yards east of the aiming point. Nine bombs went down more or less together at 17.32, and Calder's Grand Slam accompanied Marshall's Tallboy at 17.33 to bring the raid to an end. Rawes was the only one not to bomb, having been unable to achieve a correct heading in time to set up the SABS, and he brought his Tallboy home. Any lingering threat from the batteries on Heligoland was now removed. Later that evening a force of over a hundred 5 Group Lancasters returned to Czechoslovakia, and dealt effectively with the railway yards at Komotau.

On the 25th, 359 Lancasters and sixteen Mosquitos of 1, 5 and 8 Groups, including sixteen from 617 Squadron, carried out, what was for most squadrons the final bombing operation of the war, an attack on the SS barracks at Hitler's Eaglesnest retreat at Berchtesgaden in the Bavarian mountains. Taking off between 04.15 and 04.40 the 617 Squadron aircraft and crews for this fitting and almost symbolic operation were; PD131 S/L Brookes, PD121 S/L Ward, PD116 F/L Gavin, PB998 F/L Goodman, PB997 F/L Hill, PD127 F/L Horsley, NG494 F/L Quinton, NG339 F/L Beaumont, PB129 F/L Leavitt, PD139 Lt Adams, PD134 F/L Marshall, PD130 F/L Lancey, PD135 F/L Trent, PD114 F/O Flatman, PD132 F/O Speirs, and NG340 F/O Frost, a new arrival, and operating with the squadron for the first time. Brookes, Ward and Gavin were unable to identify the aiming point in time, and did not bomb. Leavitt was dissatisfied with his first run and asked permission to carry out a second. He was unable to raise S/L Brookes, however, because of confusion over the radio frequency, and by this time was alone in the target area. This was not a healthy position to be in, so he turned for home, and to give himself a chance to catch up with the others, the bomb-aimer, F/S Oldman, aimed the Tallboy at a viaduct over a road on the track home. It missed. Marshall was unable to identify the aiming point, and he dropped his bomb on a railway and road junction. New boy Frost picked up the aiming point only when directly over it, and bombed the town of Berchtesgaden as an alternative. Trent and Speirs, meanwhile, had suffered the frustration of hang-ups. At 12.59 that afternoon, F/O Mark Flatman landed PD114 at Woodhall Spa, and in so doing brought to a conclusion the operational wartime career of a squadron, which, in two short years, had become an indelible part of RAF folklore and a byword for excellence. During the afternoon almost five hundred Halifaxes and Lancasters of 4, 6 and 8 Groups attacked heavy gun positions on the German Frisian island of Wangerooge, which stood between the Allies and the north German ports. That night, 5 Group bombed an oil refinery at Tonsberg in Norway, and then, except for the Mosquitos of 8 Group and elements of 100 Group, it was all over.

On the 28th G/C Fauquier relinquished command of the squadron on a posting to the Air Ministry. He had completed three tours and almost a hundred operations, and was the proud bearer of the DSO and two Bars and a DFC. He died in April 1981. He was replaced at 617 Squadron by W/C John Grindon, who had been in command of 630 Squadron at East Kirkby since October. Grindon was a native of Newquay in Cornwall, where he was born in 1917, just a few weeks before his father was killed at Ypres. He was educated at Dulwich College and the RAF's University of the Air at Cranwell. After passing out in 1937 he joined 98 Squadron, before moving on to 150 Squadron in 1939. Equipped with the Fairey Battle 150 Squadron became part of the Advanced Air Striking Force, which moved to France as the Second World War began. Grindon was absent from the squadron on a navigation course during May 1940, when 150 Squadron and the others equipped with Battles suffered massive casualties during the German advance across the Low Countries and France.

He spent the next four years as an instructor in Canada and as a staff officer at Bomber Command, before re-entering the operational scene as a flight commander with 106 Squadron at Metheringham in July 1944. He completed sixteen sorties with 106 Squadron, beginning at Kiel on the night of the 23/24th of July, and ending at Bremen on the 6/7th of October. The posting of Grindon to 617 Squadron was testimony to his calibre as 630 Squadron's commanding officer, and later in the year he would be awarded the DSO in recognition of his wartime service. His citation read; *"In the course of numerous operational sorties, W/C Grindon has established an excellent reputation for leadership, energy and courage. The worst weather or the heaviest opposition have never deterred him from the accurate completion of his allotted tasks. Over such heavily defended targets as Königsberg, Bremen and Bergen he has braved intense anti-aircraft fire, and despite damage to his aircraft on more than one occasion, has always fulfilled his mission. On one occasion, during a daylight attack on Homberg, severe damage was sustained and his aircraft became difficult to control, but, in spite of the danger, W/C Grindon continued to lead his formation with skill and determination. He has at all times set an outstanding example."* W/C Grindon died on Remembrance Day 2001 at the age of 84.

On VE Day five aircraft took part in operation Exodus, the repatriation of Allied prisoners of war. Crew postings had continued through the month, as some of those who had helped drive the final nails into the Nazi coffin completed their tours. F/Os Watts and Carey went to 54 Base on the 9th and 20th respectively, and F/L Dobson to 6 LFS on the 23rd. In their place came F/Ls Bullock and Sheridan from 467 Squadron, F/L Langley, F/O Adams and the already mentioned F/O Frost from 5 LFS, F/L Brian from 189 Squadron, and finally, F/L Barker from 630 Squadron

It is perhaps true to say that 617 Squadron was the most effective small force employed by the Allies in any theatre of operations, but it is unfair to use the squadron as a yardstick by which to judge the performance of others. 617 Squadron was never part of the nightly grind of operations during the area offensives, and always enjoyed the very best in equipment, personnel and leadership. From the start it was a special unit, entrusted with special tasks which it rarely failed to accomplish, and although it occasionally operated as part of a larger force, or in concert with 9 Squadron, it always assumed the leading role.

Key Facts about 617 Squadron

STATIONS

SCAMPTON	21.03.43. to 30.08.43.
CONINGSBY	30.08.43. to 10.01.44.
WOODHALL SPA	10.01.44. to 17.06.45.

COMMANDING OFFICERS

WING COMMANDER G P GIBSON	21.03.43. to 03.08.43.
WING COMMANDER G W HOLDEN	03.08.43. to 16.09.43.
SQUADRON LEADER H B MARTIN (Temp)	16.09.43. to 10.11.43.
WING COMMANDER G L CHESHIRE	10.11.43. to 12.07.44.
WING COMMANDER J B TAIT	12.07.44. to 29.12.44.
GROUP CAPTAIN J E FAUQUIER	29.12.44. to 28.04.45.
WING COMMANDER J E GRINDON	28.04.45. to 09.08.45.

AIRCRAFT

LANCASTER 1/111	03.43. to	06.45.
MOSQUITO	03.44. to	05.45.
MUSTANG	06.44. to	10.44.

AIRCREW KILLED

190
(includes some on detachment for specific operations)

Operational Record

Operations	Sorties	Aircraft Losses	Loss Rate
101	1599	32	2.10%

CATEGORY OF OPERATIONS

Bombing	Leaflet	Other	Total
99	1	1 (D-Day Spoof)	101

LANCASTER

Operations	Sorties	Aircraft Losses	Loss Rate
101	1478	32	2.20%

MOSQUITO

Operations	Sorties	Aircraft Losses	% Losses
36 (included in above)	75	0	0.00%

MUSTANG

Operations	Sorties	Aircraft Losses	% Losses
6 (included in above)	6	0	0.00%

Aircraft Histories

LANCASTER   (from March 1943)

W4358	DX-L	From 57 Sqn on loan. Returned to 57 Sqn.
W4822	DX-P	From 57 Sqn on loan. Returned to 57 Sqn.
W4921		From 106 Sqn. No operations. To 619 Sqn.
W4926		From 97 Sqn. No operations. To 1654 CU.
W4929		From 61 Sqn. No operations. To 619 Sqn.
W4940		From 57 Sqn. No operations. To 1660 CU.
W5008	DX-B	From 57 Sqn on loan. Returned to 57 Sqn.
DV155		To 44 Sqn.
DV156		To 50 Sqn.
DV178	EA-N	From 49 Sqn on loan. Returned to 49 Sqn.
DV246	KC-U	To 1661 CU.
DV380	KC-N/X/P	To EAAS.
DV382	KC-J	Crashed in the South Downs while in transit to Woodhall Spa after the Antheor Viaduct raid 13.2.44. Pulford of Gibson's Dams crew killed.
DV385	KC-A/V/T	Flew on 2 Tirpitz operations. To 46 MU.
DV391	KC-W/O/Y	Flew on all 3 Tirpitz operations. To 46 MU.
DV393	KC-T/R/E	To 9 Sqn.
DV394	KC-M	FTR München 24/25.4.44.
DV398	KC-Z	FTR Liege 20/21.12.43. Rice and crew, survivors of the Dams operation.
DV402	KC-P/X	Landed in Sardinia following operation to the Antheor Viaduct 12.2.44. Martin's aircraft. Dams survivor, F/L Hay killed.
DV403	KC-L/G/X	FTR Wizernes 24.6.44.
DV405	KC-J	Flew on all 3 Tirpitz operations. To 44 MU.
ED305	KM-S	From 44 Sqn on loan. Returned to 44 Sqn.
ED329	EM-T	From 207 Sqn. Training only. To 57 Sqn.
ED437		From 50 Sqn. Training only. To 622 Sqn via 1661 CU
ED631	KC-E	From 622 Sqn. To 115 Sqn.
ED735	KC-R	From 44 Sqn. Lost without trace in the Bay of Biscay area during transit from Rabat 17/18.11.43.
ED756		From 49 Sqn. Training only. To 619 Sqn.
ED763	KC-D/Z	From 467 Sqn. Flew all 3 Tirpitz operations. SOC 14.5.44.
ED765/G	AJ-M	Crashed on Ashley Walk Range while training 5.8.43.
ED817/G	AJ-C/X-	Type 464 2nd prototype. To 46 MU.
ED825/G	AJ-T/E	Type 464 3rd prototype. Dams operation McCarthy. FTR from SOE sortie for 138 Sqn (617 Sqn crew) 9/10.12.43.
ED864/G	AJ-B	Type 464. Astell. FTR Dams operation 16/17.5.43.
ED865/G	AJ-S	Type 464. Burpee. FTR Dams operation 16/17.5.43.
ED886/G	AJ-O	Type 464. Townsend, Dams operation. FTR from SOE sortie for 138 Sqn (617 Sqn crew) 10.12.43.
ED887/G	AJ-A	Type 464. Young. FTR Dams operation 16/17.5.43.

ED906/G	AJ-J	Type 464. Maltby. Dams operation.
ED909/G	AJ-P/P	Type 464. Martin. Dams operation.
ED910/G	AJ-C	Type 464. Ottley. FTR Dams operation 16/17.5.43.
ED912/G	AJ-N/S	Type 464. Knight. Dams operation. To 46 MU.
ED915/G	AJ-Q	Type 464. To 46 MU.
ED918/G	AJ-F	Type 464. Brown. Dams operation. Crashed on Snettisham beach during training 20.1.44.
ED921/G	AJ-W	Type 464. Munro. Dams operation. To 46 MU.
ED924/G	AJ-Y	Type 464. Anderson. Dams operation. To 44 MU.
ED925/G	AJ-M	Type 464. Hopgood. FTR Dams operation 16/17.5.43.
ED927/G	AJ-E	Type 464. Barlow. FTR Dams operation 16/17.5.43.
ED929/G	AJ-L	Type 464. Shannon. Dams operation. To 46 MU
ED931	DX-C	From 57 Sqn on loan. Returned to 57 Sqn.
ED932/G	AJ-G/V	Type 464. Gibson. Dams operation. To 61 Sqn.
ED933/G	KC-N	Type 464. To 46 MU 2.45.
ED934/G	AJ-K	Type 464. Byers. FTR Dams operation 16/17.5.43.
ED936/G	AJ-H	Type 464. Rice, Dams operation. SOC 28.7.44.
ED937/G	AJ-Z	Type 464. Maudslay. FTR Dams operation 16/17.5.43.
ED999	EA-A	From 49 Sqn on loan. Returned to 49 Sqn.
EE130	AJ-A	FTR Dort Mund-Ems Canal 15/16.9.43.
EE131	KC-B/L	Crash-landed in Russia during the first Tirpitz operation 11.9.44.
EE144	AJ-S	FTR Dort Mund-Ems Canal 15/16.9.43. Deering, Spafford, Taerum, Hutchison of Gibson's Dams crew, and Powell of Townsend's, all
EE145	KC-T	Crashed on landing at Scampton while training 6.6.43.
EE146	AJ-K/D	Flew 2 Tirpitz operations (Tait). SOC 24.4.45.
EE147	AJ-L	To 619 Sqn.
EE148	AJ-U	To 626 Sqn.
EE149		To 619 Sqn.
EE150	AJ-Z	To 619 Sqn.
EE170		Training only. To 619 Sqn.
EE185	KM-K	From 44 Sqn on loan. Returned to 44 Sqn.
EE197	DX-Y	From 57 Sqn on loan. Returned to 57 Sqn.
JA703	KM-W	From 44 Sqn on loan. Returned to 44 Sqn.
JA705	OL-M	From 83 Sqn. Training only.
JA874	AJ-E	From 61 Sqn. FTR Dort Mund-Ems Canal 15/16.9.43. Allatson of Brown's Dams crew killed.
JA894	AJ-C/T	From 49 Sqn. To A&AEE.
JA898	KC-X	From 619 Sqn. FTR Dort Mund-Ems Canal 15/16.9.43.
JA981	KC-T	Crashed in North Sea after recall from the Dort Mund-Ems Canal operation of 14/15.9.43. Maltby & crew, Dams survivors all killed.
JB139	KC-X/V	From 49 Sqn. FTR Brest 5.8.44.
JB144	KC-N	FTR Dort Mund-Ems Canal 15/16.9.43. Knight, Dams survivor, killed.
JB370	KC-U	From 57 Sqn. Returned to 57 Sqn.
LM309		From 9 Sqn. Training only. To 619 Sqn.
LM482	KC-W/Q	FTR Kembs Barrage 7.10.44.

LM485	KC-N/U/H	Flew on first and last Tirpitz operations.
LM489	KC-L/A/N	Flew on all 3 Tirpitz operations.
LM492	KC-Q/W	Flew on all 3 Tirpitz operations.
LM695	KC-N	From 463 Sqn.
ME554	KC-F	Flew on all 3 Tirpitz operations.
ME555	KC-C	To 9 Sqn.
ME557	KC-O/S	FTR Rilly-La-Montagne (Reid VC) 31.7.44.
ME559	KC-Q/Y	Crash-landed on arrival in Russia for the first Tirpitz operation 11/12.9.44.
ME560	KC-H	Crashed while landing at Woodhall Spa during training 14.7.44.
ME561	KC-R/T	Flew on all 3 Tirpitz operations. Crashed in Lincolnshire on return from Politz 22.12.44.
ME562	KC-Z/K	Flew on all 3 Tirpitz operations.
ND339	KC-Z	On detachment from 106 Sqn. Returned to 106 Sqn.
ND472	KC-O	On detachment from 57 Sqn. Returned to 57 Sqn.
ND554	KC-N	No operations. To 630 Sqn.
ND631	KC-B/Z	From 44 Sqn. Returned to 44 Sqn.
ND683	KC-P	Detached from 49 Sqn. Returned to 49 Sqn.
NF920	KC-E	FTR Tirpitz (force-landed in Sweden) 29.10.44.
NF923	KC-M	FTR Dort Mund-Ems Canal 23/24.9.44.
NF992	KC-B	FTR Bergen 12.1.45.
NG180	KC-S	FTR Kembs Barrage 7.10.44.
NG181	KC-M	To 195 Sqn and back. Flew 2 Tirpitz operations.
NG228	KC-V	FTR Schwinemünde 16.4.45.
NG339	KC-G	
NG340	KC-L/U	
NG445	KC-E	
NG489	KC-M	
NG494	KC-B	
NN702		From 630 Sqn.
PB342		From 61 Sqn. To 1653 CU.
PB415	KC-S/O	Flew on all 3 Tirpitz operations. SOC 4.45.
PB416	KC-V	Missing on return from Russia (First Tirpitz operation) 17.9.44.
PB996	YZ-C/K	B1 Special.
PB997	YZ-E	B1 Special.
PB998	YZ-N/D	B1 Special.
PD112	YZ-S/Z	B1 Special.
PD113	YZ-B/T	B1 Special.
PD114	YZ-B	B1 Special.
PD115	YZ-C/K	B1 Special.
PD116	YZ-W/A	B1 Special.
PD117	YZ-L	B1 Special. FTR Arbergen Rail Bridge 21.3.45.
PD118	YZ-B/M	B1 Special.
PD119	YZ-J	B1 Special.
PD121	YZ-S/Z	B1 Special.
PD126	YZ-L	B1 Special.
PD127	YZ-F	B1 Special.
PD128	YZ-N	B1 Special.

PD129	YZ-O	B1 Special.
PD130	YZ-D/W/U	B1 Special.
PD131	YZ-A/V	B1 Special.
PD132	YZ-X	B1 Special.
PD133	YZ-P	B1 Special.
PD134	YZ-Y/U	B1 Special.
PD135	YZ-W	B1 Special.
PD136	YZ-N	B1 Special.
PD139	YZ-W/L	B1 Special.
PD233	KC-G	FTR Bergen 12.1.45.
PD238	KC-B/H	
PD371	KC-S/W	
PD418		To 467 Sqn.

MOSQUITO (from March 1944)

DZ415	AZ-Q/A	From 627 Sqn on loan as required.
DZ418	AZ-L	From 627 Sqn on loan as required.
DZ421	AZ-C	From 627 Sqn on loan as required.
DZ484	AZ-G	From 627 Sqn on loan as required.
DZ521	AZ-M	From 627 Sqn on loan as required.
DZ525	AZ-S	From 627 Sqn on loan as required.
DZ547	AZ-E	From 627 Sqn on loan as required.
DZ637	AZ-O	From 627 Sqn on loan as required.
DZ641	AZ-C2	From 627 Sqn on loan as required.
KB215	AZ-H	From 627 Sqn on loan as required.
ML975	HS-M	From 109 Sqn on loan as required.
ML976	HS-N/L	From 109 Sqn on loan as required.
NS992	AJ-S	To 515 Sqn.
NS993	AJ-N	To 515 Sqn.
NT202	AJ-N	To 417 Sqn and back. Crashed at Wainfleet Sands while training 7.8.44.
NT205	AJ-L	

MUSTANG (from June 1944)

HB837	AJ-N	To 541 Sqn.

HEAVIEST SINGLE LOSS. 16/17.05.43. Operation Chastise. 8 Lancasters FTR.

Some of the aircraft coded KC will have carried AJ markings earlier, and the precise date of the code change is not apparent. For the purpose of this profile, the move to Coningsby is used as a convenient date of changeover, although it is known that AJ adorned some aircraft after this time.

Key to Abbreviations

A&AEE	Aeroplane and Armaments Experimental Establishment.
AA	Anti-Aircraft fire.
AACU	Anti-Aircraft Cooperation Unit.
AAS	Air Armament School.
AASF	Advance Air Striking Force.
AAU	Aircraft Assembly Unit.
ACM	Air Chief Marshal.
ACSEA	Air Command South-East Asia.
AFDU	Air Fighting Development Unit.
AFEE	Airborne Forces Experimental Unit.
AFTDU	Airborne Forces Tactical Development Unit.
AGS	Air Gunners School.
AMDP	Air Members for Development and Production.
AOC	Air Officer Commanding.
AOS	Air Observers School.
ASRTU	Air-Sea Rescue Training Unit.
ATTDU	Air Transport Tactical Development Unit.
AVM	Air Vice-Marshal.
BAT	Beam Approach Training.
BCBS	Bomber Command Bombing School.
BCDU	Bomber Command Development Unit.
BCFU	Bomber Command Film Unit.
BCIS	Bomber Command Instructors School.
BDU	Bombing Development Unit.
BSTU	Bomber Support Training Unit.
CF	Conversion Flight.
CFS	Central Flying School.
CGS	Central Gunnery School.
C-in-C	Commander in Chief.
CNS	Central Navigation School.
CO	Commanding Officer.
CRD	Controller of Research and Development.
CU	Conversion Unit.
DGRD	Director General for Research and Development.
EAAS	Empire Air Armament School.
EANS	Empire Air Navigation School.
ECDU	Electronic Countermeasures Development Unit.

ECFS	Empire Central Flying School.
ETPS	Empire Test Pilots School.
F/L	Flight Lieutenant.
Flt	Flight.
F/O	Flying Officer.
FPP	Ferry Pilots School.
F/S	Flight Sergeant.
FTR	Failed to Return.
FTU	Ferry Training Unit.
G/C	Group Captain.
Gp	Group.
HCU	Heavy Conversion Unit.
HGCU	Heavy Glider Conversion Unit.
LFS	Lancaster Finishing School.
MAC	Mediterranean Air Command.
MTU	Mosquito Training Unit.
MU	Maintenance Unit.
NTU	Navigation Training Unit.
OADU	Overseas Aircraft Delivery Unit.
OAPU	Overseas Aircraft Preparation Unit.
OTU	Operational Training Unit.
P/O	Pilot Officer.
PTS	Parachute Training School.
RAE	Royal Aircraft Establishment.
SGR	School of General Reconnaissance.
Sgt	Sergeant.
SHAEF	Supreme Headquarters Allied Expeditionary Force.
SIU	Signals Intelligence Unit.
S/L	Squadron Leader.
SOC	Struck off Charge.
SOE	Special Operations Executive.
Sqn	Squadron.
TF	Training Flight.
TFU	Telecommunications Flying Unit.
W/C	Wing Commander.
Wg	Wing.
WIDU	Wireless Intelligence Development Unit.
W/O	Warrant Officer.

Other Bomber Command books from Mention the War

Striking Through Clouds – The War Diary of 514 Squadron RAF
(Simon Hepworth and Andrew Porrelli)

Nothing Can Stop Us – The Definitive History of 514 Squadron RAF
(Simon Hepworth, Andrew Porrelli and Harry Dison)

A Short War – The History of 623 Squadron RAF
(Steve Smith)

Some of the Story of 514 Squadron – Lancasters at Waterbeach
(Harry Dison)

A Special Duty (Autumn 2015)
(Jennifer Elkin)

DFC and Bar (Autumn 2015)
(Ed Greenburgh)

Beach Boys and Bombers – The Aircrew of 514 Squadron (June 2016)
(Simon Hepworth, Andrew Porrelli and Roger Guernon)

The above books are available through Amazon, book shops or direct from the Publisher. For further details or to purchase a signed and dedicated copy, please contact *bombercommandbooks@gmail.com*

13354344R00092

Printed in Great Britain
by Amazon.co.uk, Ltd.,
Marston Gate.